THAILAND

Books by the same author

THE UPANISHADS (with Peter Russell)
(*Harper & Row (USA), 1978; Wildwood House (UK), 1978*)

EFFORTLESS BEING
(*Wildwood House (UK), 1982*)

THE TRAVELLER'S KEY TO NORTHERN INDIA
(*Alfred Knopf (USA), 1983; Harrap Columbus (UK), 1987*)

THAILAND

The Lotus Kingdom

Alistair Shearer

JOHN MURRAY

For my father,
with love and gratitude

© Alistair Shearer

First published 1989
by John Murray (Publishers) Ltd
50 Albemarle Street, London WIX 4BD

Typeset at The Spartan Press Ltd,
Lymington, Hants
Printed and bound in Great Britain by
Mackays of Chatham

British Library Cataloguing in Publication Data

Shearer, Alistair
    Thailand: the lotus kingdom.
    1. Thailand to 1980
    I. Title
    959.3
    ISBN 0-7195-4572-2

Contents

Contents

Illustrations

All photographs by the author

Acknowledgements

My thanks are due first of all to Thai Airways International Ltd, and especially to the late Lerson Nopvichai, for two complimentary return tickets to Thailand, without which much of the research for this book would have been greatly hindered. Within the country, the Tourist Authority of Thailand was often helpful, especially in those places less frequented by visitors.

The people of Thailand are generally surprised and delighted to find a foreigner who has a genuine desire to understand their country, and I have received considerable kindness during my travels there. Among those who helped directly in the gestation of the book, I am particularly grateful to: the Venerable Mettananda, for an enlightening meeting one spring afternoon in Oriel College, Oxford; Kumnon Sutabutr and 'Papa Bill' Preecha, for their profound knowledge of Thai culture and their willingness to share it; Rangsan Darawan for his kind assistance in Khon Kaen; Mrs Sureeporn Ariyanuntaka for many useful contacts; and Chairat and Nittaya Kantawong who extended me so much gentle hospitality in the south. Doug Wholey and Glynn Baker contributed some valuable *farang* perspectives on life in Isaan, while Russ Wingfield and Nigel Hosking facilitated several of my lecture tours to the country which yielded much useful information and experience.

In the production of the book, I must thank Margaret, Jack and Ruth Trevenna who read the manuscript and made helpful comments, and to Val Trevenna for her speedy and painstaking typing. I am also grateful to Duncan McAra, my editor, who not only suggested improvements in the text but showed patience worthy of a Thai with my tardiness in delivering it.

A.S.

Prologue

'Can you get these photos enlarged by Tuesday?'

The pretty oriental head behind the counter of my local chemist's shakes. 'No, not till Thursday at the earliest.'

'Oh, that's too late,' I reply, 'I'll be in Bangkok by then.'

'Bangkok? That's where my family are. Going on holiday?'

'No, I wish I were. I'm going to research for a book. I'm a writer.'

'Write something nice, won't you? Don't write anything, you know, like they normally do.'

'What do you mean?' Now it's my turn to show some interest.

'You know, that disgusting stuff they usually write.'

'You mean about the massage parlours and all that?'

'Yes. Write something nice. Go to the south, to Phuket, and write something nice about my country.'

'Well, I'll do my best,' I promise, 'but it rather depends on what happens to me.'

I

BANGKOK

1

Welcome to Americasia

Bangkok: the Queen Srisuriyothai touches down at 6.15 on a March morning. The landing, as the advertisements promise, is 'as smooth as silk'. Well, raw silk anyway. The sun is rising and outside it is already 83°F. This is nothing unusual, the average annual temperature here shifts only from a sweltering 86°F to a marginally less sweltering 79°F, and it is always oppressively humid. The doors open to admit a solid wall of heat that pins the breath at the back of the throat and makes the head spin. You can smell this heat as it shimmers up off the tarmac like a vast, amorphous creature, sluggishly alive, a musty hothouse odour that moves with reptilian, implacable slowness. Descending the steps is like entering a sauna. After the thirty yards to the transfer bus I have broken out into a sudden sweat, feverish and acrid, that trickles between my shoulder blades and down the back of my legs. The whole affair seems unreal.

After the brief bus journey to the terminal the air conditioning is already a relief. Inside all is cool, orderly and imbued with a particular fragrance that is one of my strongest olfactory cues for Thailand. It is a fresh smell, clean and slightly soapy, that is probably nothing more romantic than the after-scent of the washing powder that everyone seems to use. But it is a distinctive smell, to be found in hotels, offices, and public buildings alike, and it is rich in associations and memories for me, telling me more surely than any of the other intruding sensory information that I am back in Thailand. I love that smell; one day I must track down its source precisely, but perhaps that would destroy its magic.

We move rapidly through the olive-uniformed checks and controls, manned by efficient personnel and ringed by heavily armed soldiers, insectile with their shiny helmets and dark glasses. The presence of the military is immediately evident; a fact no visitor to Thailand will be allowed to forget. These officials exude a silent yet unequivocal authority. Here there is a smartness of manner not readily found in this part of the world, a crispness that could, if necessary, turn very hard indeed.

Even my suitcase is sweating; a few minutes on the luggage truck outside has it weeping. At first I think something has been spilt on it, but on closer inspection the fibre glass around the locks is oozing beads of condensation that run together to trickle in a thin stream along the grooved lid. After all, it is the hot season, everybody knows that Thailand is like a furnace in March and April, so I have only my own bad timing to blame.

I run a mild and polite gauntlet of characters offering trips and sightseeing deals – again very orderly and muted by Asian standards – to find a car. Freelance taxis (known as 'black-plated' as opposed to the 'green-plated' hotel fleets) are banned at Don Muang. They lurk just beyond the *cordon sanitaire* of monopoly enjoyed by the government-owned fleet of Thai International limousines. Time is money nowhere more obviously than in a taxi and, with the ride to the city centre twenty kilometres and at least forty minutes, the cost of a cab with pre-paid taxi coupons bought from the official counter is 350 *baht* (£8.50). By Thai standards this is exorbitant, but it is shared between three of us, and for an air-conditioned Mercedes complete with stereo, NO SMOKING sign and driver embellished with livid tattoos to ward off the evil eye, I for one am not complaining.

The drive south along the superhighway reveals the emerging city as a hybrid of East and West, the twentieth century coming up for air from the ancient swamp of Asia. To eyes accustomed to the temperate neatness of northern Europe, the East always appears untidy, inchoate, half-finished, and Bangkok is no exception. The roadside clutter of shacks and street markets – already in operation though it is barely seven o'clock – is a familiar Third World scene, but here they are shambled together under huge Marlboro hoardings and winking neon signs that proclaim bars, clubs and cocktail lounges. The concrete apartment blocks, mercifully only four or five storeys high, are probably no more than thirty years old despite their tattiness, as they rise steaming above palm trees, rubbery jungle foliage and the prehensile embrace of sinuous creepers. Overhead stretch wires, wires, and more wires, too expensive to lay underground and too numerous to count, meeting every so often in great untidy nodes of intertwined cable supported raggedly on poles.

The names that flash past betray Bangkok's growth from the Vietnam days when it was a 'Rest and Relaxation' haven for American troops: Hollywood Hotel, Golden Gate Massage Parlor, Lucky Strike Bowling Alley. Beneath them, blurring the pavement life, flash the ambassadors of a fresh wave of foreign influence – Toyotas, Mazdas, Daihatsus – glinting metallic in the rising sun as they hurl themselves into the accelerating rush hour. This is the new Asia, Asia on the move, the transformation of a country that has gone from the ox-cart to the automobile in barely forty years. Yet it is Asia nonetheless: new buildings already peeling at the edges, trucks overflowing with labourers in from the country for the day's work, thin limbs and dark faces under wide-brimmed straw hats, some still asleep amidst rattan panniers and cloth bundles; lorries piled precariously with bamboo poles or spiky baskets of pineapples, watermelons stacked up like mounds of dull green cannon balls, those already sampled split with a pink and fleshy grin. To be sure, a closer acquaintance with this extraordinary city will reveal layers of cultural influence deeper and more rewarding than the Japanese or American – but to the visitor unprepared, or one brought up on a milksop diet of travel brochure sunsets, exotic temple dancers and Yul Brynner cavorting around in sequinned pantaloons, the first taste of Bangkok is something of a smack in the mouth.

The somewhat chaotic vista that greets the visitor is the result of the energetic but desultory building boom that gripped the city in the 1950s, a confused and turbulent epoch writ large in concrete. For while the Western world was regrouping itself in the shell-shocked aftermath of the Second World War, the Kingdom of Thailand was undergoing changes that in their own way were no less momentous. The supreme symbol of these changes is its capital city, the rather confused child of several marriages of convenience.

It was during the 1950s that Thailand was ushered, more or less forcibly, into the twentieth century, by one of the key figures of her history: Field Marshal Pibul. Pibul had risen to power in the 1930s with the People's Party, the military and civilian group which engineered the 1932 coup ending the absolute supremacy of the monarchy. The ideological leader of this group was Pridi Panomyaong, a lawyer trained in France. The next twenty-five years were dominated by the struggle between these two, with Pibul, the more consistently successful, backed by the army, and Pridi commanding the support of the intelligentsia. At the end of 1932, King Rama 7 signed the Parliament Constitution, which promised universal suffrage and general elections every four years. But the abrupt transplanting of Western-style democracy into the traditional monarchist soil of the country was too sudden, and resulted in a series of governmental crises, as the country staggered between democratic experiments and military take-overs. Nevertheless, Pibul was able to pursue what he called a 'civilising campaign' to educate, or if necessary drag, his compatriots into modernity: Western dress and mores were forced on the people and foreign influence courted. This campaign was backed up by measures which were intended to make Thailand appear more Western: betelnut chewing and traditional dress were discouraged, hats and coats were declared *de rigueur* in public, women were encouraged to abandon the custom of cropping their hair short. Even the country's name was changed to reflect its new hybrid identity: the old Siam became Thailand, 'thai' being the indigenous word for 'free'. During the war Pibul's government collaborated with the Japanese, hoping that the reformed Thailand would emerge from the conflict on the back of the victors, her position in the new Asia assured. But after the Japanese defeat, the Pibul regime collapsed and Pridi, who had actively supported an underground resistance move-ment during the war, returned to power. His rule was short-lived. The King, who had officially abdicated three years after the 1932 coup, had been living in England. In 1941 he died, leaving as the heir his ten-year-old nephew Ananda Mahidol, then at school in Switzerland. A Regency Council of three members was appointed to act during his minority. Ananda stayed in Europe until 1945 when, at the age of twenty, he returned to a rapturous welcome from his people. But one morning only a year later, the young King was found shot in his bedroom in the Grand Palace. His death was never explained satisfactorily, and Thai diplomacy has drawn an impenetrable veil of silence over the affair.

Ananda's death had two crucial consequences for modern Thailand. One was the succession of his younger brother, the extraordinary man who is today King: His Majesty Bhumipol Adulyadej the Great (Rama 9). The other was the political exit of Pridi and the return of Pibul and his policy of Westernisation. These events were soon to be overshadowed on the world stage by the changes taking place in China, where the Imperial dragon had sloughed its hoary skin to become the newly awakened leviathan of Communism. Fearful of Chinese aggression, Thailand joined SEATO and Pibul embarked on a rigorous and disciplinarian anti-Communist, pro-American policy. American aid began in 1950, and developed as Thailand's strategic importance in the anti-Communist crusade became ever clearer. By the time the United States became embroiled in the bloody quagmire of Vietnam, this aid was Thailand's major source of income. Most of it was intended for military purposes and the establishment of a communications network to service the US war effort. However, a fair proportion, legitimately or otherwise, ended up in Bangkok, materialising as the office blocks, department stores, cinemas and hotels of the new city inadvertently thrust into the international arena.

Pibul was eventually toppled from power in 1957, replaced by a triumvirate of generals who held onto power until the early 1970s. By then the power of the military was beginning to weaken in the face of democratic demands, but the policy of rapid urban growth supported by foreign aid and free market exports was here to stay. It received fresh impetus in 1965, when the Americans built six air bases to support their deepening involvement across the border in Vietnam. These bases brought with them not only money for roads but a dizzying overnight change in expectations for millions of Thais. The story that Bangkok tells is the story of these changes. It is a fable for our times: the story of a Buddhist kingdom about the size of Texas, where half a century earlier the people crawled on all fours in the presence of their king, and how it entered the brave new world.

If Bangkok has a reputation as a city of excesses, it is only living up to its name, which runs in Thai to no less than forty-one letters: *Krungthep Mahanakhon Bovorn Ratanakosin Mahintharayutthaya Mahadilokpop Noparatratchathani Burirom Udom Ratchaniveymahasathan Amornpiman Avatarnsathit Sakkathattiya- avisnukarmprasit.* This staggering mouthful – according to the *Guinness Book of Records* the longest place name in the world – is roughly translated as follows: *The Great City of Angels, the Supreme Repository of Divine Jewels, the Great Unconquerable Land, the Grand and Illustrious Realm, the Royal and Delightful Capital City, Home of the Nine Noble Gems, the Highest Royal Dwelling and Grand Palace, the Divine Shelter and Dwelling Place of the Reincarnated Spirits.* To the Thais it is known for short as Krungthep, City of Angels; only foreigners call it Bangkok. Angelic it may once have been; but the essential spirit of the place eludes many whose stay is limited. Most of these probably leave with a sigh of relief, agreeing with Somerset Maugham who found the Bangkok of the 1930s 'strange, flat, confused'. Relentless traffic, pollution and noise combine to make Bangkok more like its namesake Los Angeles than the anticipated oriental city of gilded spires and fairytale palaces.

The city appears at first to be devoid of a clear-cut centre, coherent plan or discernible personality. In fact, there are centres and personalities, but they are multiple and localised. Apart from the Grand Palace and Dusit areas, Bangkok was not planned; its growth from an area of 8 square miles in 1900 to over 200 by 1980, took place with uncoordinated energy. Compared to the average European city, Bangkok is unwalkable. An outing has to be planned like a minor military exercise to negotiate the heat, traffic and ineluctable one-way system, and one's time on the streets is plotted from one air-conditioned oasis to another – hotel lobby, bookshop, coffee shop. (But be warned: the pick-me-ups in such home bases are not always that effective. Bangkok caters with almost embarrassing solicitude for most human frailties, but it pays scant regard to the caffeine addict. The Thais are not coffee drinkers, though they grow a little in the south; and tea, especially the Chinese variety, is usually a better bet.) Never colonised, this capital has none of the Raj Victoriana that dominates the milling crowds of Bombay or Calcutta, or adds nostalgic charm to Rangoon. However, there are some very pleasant streets, such as Wireless Road, the home of the British Embassy and Hilton Hotel, and its near neighbour Henri Dunant Road, lined with rain trees and containing the dignified campus of Chulalongkorn University. Although the five public parks seem swamped amidst the surrounding activity, hardly able to perform their function as the lungs of a city in danger of choking on its own fumes, the royal areas of Dusit and the Sanam Luang, in front of the Grand Palace, provide some relief to the pedestrian. Lumpini Park, originally considered vast, is now becoming cluttered by kiosks and restaurants and the one newly created park, Chatuchat, is to the north of the city and too far out to relieve its congested centre. The Bangkok Metropolitan Administration has said the city needs five more parks to cope with its growing population, and is thinking of siting the first over the river in Thonburi. With a 50-acre plot of land costing almost £20 million the project is a daunting one.

Devoid of memorable vistas, Bangkok also lacks good contemporary buildings, and seems particularly bereft in this respect when compared to the futuristic beauty of its Asian sister, Hong Kong. Nevertheless, the capital is not entirely devoid of architectural interest. It was originally conceived, after all, as a city of palaces and is dotted with buildings erected to house the enormously diffused royal family and its entourage. The Dusit area remains an island virtually unaffected by the building boom of the last three decades. Here there are tree-lined boulevards and imposing structures in an elegant, if formalised, setting. The

Suan Dusit ('Celestial Garden') was laid by King Chulalong-korn (Rama 5) in 1899, two years after his European tour. While abroad he had been impressed with the habit of setting royal residences at a distance from city centres, and on his return had these gardens built, linked to the Grand Palace by the Siamese version of the Champs-Elysées, Rajadamnoen Avenue. This dignified boulevard provided an escape route from the stuffy and crowded Grand Palace, and was enjoyed by the royal family and the court, sometimes in motorcades, sometimes on bicycle or foot, whenever the official duties allowed. Two years later a new royal residence was built, the Vimanmek Palace. This fine teak building was opened to the public in 1985, and contains no less than thirty-one suites of rooms in turn-of-the-century décor and set off by Siamese, Chinese and Russian *objets d'art*. The huge neo-classical building at the end of Rajadamnoen Avenue is the Marble Throne Hall, built as a conscious symbol of the international awareness Rama 5 brought to his country. The inside cupola and ceiling is decorated with scenes from Thai history, in particular episodes from the fortunes of the Chakri dynasty. To set such a heavy structure on the soft soil of Bangkok must have given a headache to the Italian architects, but despite their achievement the Throne Hall was used as such only for a few years before it became the first seat of the National Assembly after the 1932 coup. It was Rama 6 who built the villa in the Dusit area that was to become the Chitralada Palace (1910–25), residence of the present King. He was an enthusiastic builder, and sprinkled his capital with grand houses, a fine example of which is the elaborate Venetian baroque Phitsanulok Mansion, the official residence of the Prime Minister. Many other former palaces or courtly houses now do duty for the government; the buildings that accommo-date the Ministry of Education and the Ministry of Foreign Affairs are both noteworthy, as is the Army Headquarters on Rajadamnoen Avenue. The French and Portuguese Embassies, not far from the General Post Office just south of the mouth of Klong Krung Kasem, are both charming buildings that date from the nineteenth century.

Perhaps the best-known building of the Dusit area is the Royal Chapel, Wat Benchamabophit, popularly called the Marble Temple. Started by Rama 5 in 1901 and completed ten years later shortly after his death, it is the most recent of the royal temples in Bangkok. The architect was the King's half-brother, the accomplished Prince Naris, and he chose for his design a traditional plan of a cruciform assembly hall (*vihan*) topped by a series of overlapping roofs. What was unconventional was the choice of white Carrara marble to face the buildings and courtyard. This gives the complex an austerity that is well set off by the brilliant gilding of the eaves and brackets, and the curved yellow-orange roof tiles. Another unique feature of the Marble Temple is its cloisters around the courtyard behind the *vihan*. Here a gallery set up by Rama 5 presents a display of the evolution of the Buddha image in Thailand. The fifty-one figures exemplifying not only Thai art but some Indian, Burmese and Japanese schools as well, gaze down calmly on the world of suffering. Most are original, but even the reproductions are impressive, such as the skeletal Fasting Buddha from the Museum in Lahore where Rudyard Kipling played when his father was curator there. The Walking Buddha from the Sukhothai period, the most distinctive of all Thai images, is the highlight. The gallery is a good place to get an idea of the schools of Thai art; it is worth a visit for the Walking Buddha alone.

There is one day each year when these images, as if in some fairy-tale, seem to come alive, stepping down to walk among the multitude. This is Visakha Puja, the festival held in the first week of May to commemorate three of the holiest occasions in the Buddhist story: the birth, Enlightenment and death of the Master. My visit coincides with the celebrations, and everybody says that the Marble Temple is the place to see them.

When I arrive at a little after four o'clock I am greeted by an extraordinary spectacle. The front courtyard, normally a well-kept area sprinkled with lawns and flower beds, is crammed with soldiers. They stand in serried ranks, a dark green heavy-booted mass, but the several hundred crew-cut heads are bowed reverently, and the hands hold not guns but a bunched offering of

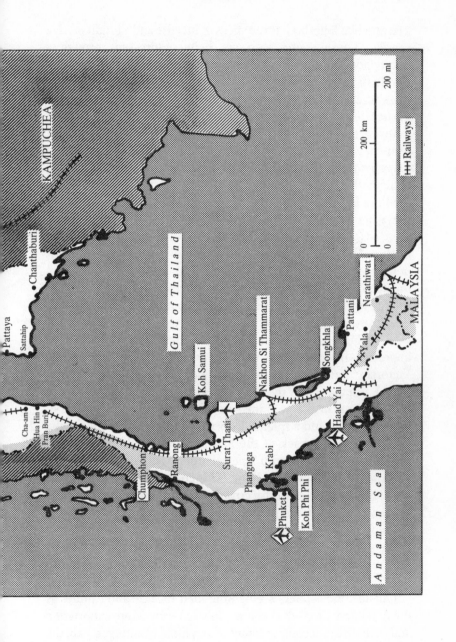

a large white lotus bud, three sticks of incense and a bright orange candle. These young men are being addressed through a microphone by a senior-looking monk, perhaps the abbot, who stands in the main doorway of the temple, flanked by a pair of massive marble lions under the richly decorated gable of the portico. Their concentration is intense.

Inside the temple there is an air of expectancy. People, mainly women, come and go with baskets of flowers and other offerings to lay before the Buddha. This particular image is doubly sacred, being both a replica of one of Thailand's most revered Buddhas, the Phra Buddha Chinnaraj in Phitsanulok, and the repository of the ashes of Rama 5. Each worshipper prostrates three times, then sits back, legs tucked to one side to shield the ritually unclean feet from the image, and contemplates the scene or chats quietly to her neighbour. Several Chinese teapots sit on trays on the deep red carpet, the worshippers sip tea in a leisurely fashion, refreshing their devotions. The decoration of the temple's interior is in keeping with its Europeanised exterior: a subdued gold wallpaper over a marble dado, pastel murals of various important Buddhist relic mounds (*chedis*) and, incongruously, Victorian stained glass windows portraying celestial beings (*theps*). But thankfully there are unrepentant Thai touches too, in the brilliance of the gold image against its plain background of midnight blue, and a splendidly ornate and gilded throne for the chief abbot. The back of the hall looks more like a recording studio than a temple, with tape recorders, amplifiers, wires and cassettes lying all over the floor. This equipment is used to relay chants and speeches to the crowd, and the young monks are as fascinated with it as any of their secular contemporaries would be. A group of women is busy in the back courtyard, hanging little baskets of flowers from the low eaves of the cloisters. The baskets are suspended from garlands of white jasmine intertwined with purple orchids, and each bears a tag with the name of the donor.

Outside, the soldiers are lighting their incense and candles as the first heavy drops of evening rain slap down. More exhortation and then, to the accompaniment of amplified chanting in Pali, the sacred tongue of Buddhism, they set off in silent circumambulation of the building. Even the boots seem muffled. Three abreast they move through the cloisters and back again three times, trailing wraiths of sandalwood smoke. I catch sight of a lone foreigner among the uniformed ranks, a tall man in his fifties, head and shoulders above most of the Thais, perhaps a military adviser or a diplomat. Their rounds finished, the soldiers reassemble and after more words from the senior monk, are dismissed, laying what is left of their smoking, scented flowers on altar tables set up in the courtyard. Once they have left, a trickle of individuals begins to wind its way round the temple. This is to continue for the next five hours, increasing all the time, and always accompanied by the hypnotic drone of chanting. Next comes a group of women. In the front, white robed and barefoot, are lay sisters from some organisation; behind them stand others in everyday dress, and behind them men and women together. More sermons, chants, and then, led by a particularly peaceful looking monk they set off on their three rounds, silent except for the pad of hundreds of bare feet on the marble flagstones. This body of women projects a tangible aura of the feminine, power concentrated through softness. The procession is set off by dramatic colour contrasts: orange against the white of robes, white against the black of skirts and hair, black against the green of foliage. And every so often the cerise blush of a half-opened lotus bloom, as the evening sun caresses the gilded eaves of the temple. Looking up at the sky I see a magnificent rainbow has formed over the complex. The signs are there for those who wish to read them.

By the time darkness falls, the trickle of people has become a flood: young and old, families and sweethearts, even a sprinkling of foreigners who come not only to photograph but to participate. Buying their lotuses, candles and incense at the gates, they join the flickering tide of lights as it washes around the building, now itself sparkling from the hundreds of candles that have been set up on its low walls and parapets. Some have brought their own lamps, larger and more ornate than the simple orange candles; others, the wise virgins, have a special shade attached to their candle to shield it from the evening breeze. I am hopelessly inept at keeping my candle alight and have to relight it several times from neighbours, but I'm relieved to see that many Thais are having the same problem. Suddenly a stream of orange washes into the courtyard from the wooden buildings of the residential compound adjacent to the temple, the compound that housed Rama 5 while he served his time in the robe. Perhaps 200 young monks, some mere children, filter wordlessly through the crowds and slip into the temple to take their places in the packed interior for an hour's chanting and prayers, all relayed over the public address system. The raised platform on which the temple sits is now aglow from a couple of bonfires, as mounds of discarded flowers catch light from the candles ringed around them, each new wave of worshippers adding more flowers, more candles. At times it seems as if the whole compound is to be offered up in flames. Finally the monks emerge to move in a group around the temple, cutting a glowing saffron swathe through the people, all of whom are performing the Thai bow of respect (*wai*), hands folded together under the chin. Even this *pièce de résistance* is carried out in silence, yet there is a palpable feeling of festivity bubbling just below the surface. In Thailand the sacred may be serious, but it is never too solemn.

Tired but elated, I return to my hotel.

The receptionist flashes me a big smile. 'Been to temple?' she asks.

'Yes! It was marvellous.' Then, wondering if an air of sanctity is somehow clinging to me, I ask, 'But how did you know?'

She giggles, and I follow her gaze down to my trousers, whose whiteness is spattered with globules of bright orange wax.

Although Bangkok is renowned for its profusion of temples, there is another category of buildings that should be mentioned in its architectural defence: the private residences. Most of these traditional Thai homes are not open to the public, but there are a few which can be visited and provide charming reminders of the gracious living of a bygone age. The most celebrated of these is the Suan Pakkard Palace ('Lettuce Garden Palace') on Sri Ayutthaya Road, formerly the residence of Princess Chumbot, a member of the royal family, and one of Thailand's leading art collectors. The five traditional wooden houses here form a domestic museum decorated with Thai furniture and antiques, and the admission fee goes to a fund to support promising young artists. The showpiece of the Palace is the famous Lacquer Pavilion, a superb example of decorative art from the eighteenth century. The Pavilion is a romantic structure in a romantic setting, and there is a romantic story behind it. A European friend told the Princess that there was a disused library mouldering away in a temple near Ayutthaya, the former capital. She visited the place, fell in love with the building, and her husband had it dismantled, transported and reassembled here as a present for her fiftieth birthday.

The Pavilion comprises two interlocked buildings: a library (*ho trai*) which contained manuscripts, and a surrounding writing room (*ho khien*), and is raised on stilts. Libraries were usually elevated and often set in ponds to discourage the attentions of hungry termites. The interior is an Aladdin's cave of ebony and gold, the best sustained example of gilded lacquer work in the world. This essentially Thai art form first appeared in the seventeenth century, and was employed mainly in the decoration of manuscript cabinets. Gold, the most precious metal, was already used for covering and worshipping Buddha images. It was only fitting that it should also be applied to decorate and magically protect chests containing the words of the Master and the doors and windows of the temple which housed them. Favourite subjects for gilded lacquer were the *Ramakien* (the Thai version of the Indian epic *Ramayana*), the *Life of the Buddha*, and scenes from the *Three Worlds* (a major Thai epic, which dates from the fourteenth century). Early examples of the art show gilded figures laid on a large, flat and distanced 'blackground', but by the time of the Suan Pakkard panels the composition was an integrated whole – balanced, delicate and glowing with its own ethereal light. Many of the hallmarks of Tai mural art are recognisable: the graceful treatment of bodies that sway like flowers in the breeze, the smiling faces with lotus eyes under arched brows, the stylised restraint of the divine or noble fixtures juxtaposed with the earthy,

humorous and naturalistic representatives of the common people. Two features of the late eighteenth-century style can also be
seen here: the Chinese influence in rocks and trees, and the
portrayals of contemporary Europeans – merchants or ambassadors – mounted on horseback and wearing tall feathered hats.
They look a rather dour bunch in the midst of this oriental
dreamworld.

Modern visitors descend by the busload on what was another of
Bangkok's fine residences: Jim Thompson's house. Thompson, a
former OSS officer who disappeared mysteriously in the Malaysian jungle in 1967, is famous for creating the Thai silk industry
after the Second World War, turning what had been a cottage
industry into an international business. Despite the enthusiastic
backing of *Vogue* magazine, it took Thompson eight years to weld
the scattered and independently minded weaving families into a
coherent outfit. Ironically, one of the biggest boosts to what was to
become a source of national pride was *The King and I*, itself more a
source of national shame. The Rodgers & Hammerstein musical
and, later, film were based on Margaret Landon's book *Anna and
the King of Siam* about Anna Leonowens, a Victorian governess
who had tutored the children of King Mongkut (Rama 4) in
English. A large part of the success of the original Broadway
production starring Yul Brynner and Gertrude Lawrence was the
magnificence of the costumes. Thompson had worked closely
with the designer, suggesting styles from old Siamese books of
the period and even producing special weights and colours of silk
to her specifications. The public was overwhelmed. Orders
started pouring in, and they continue to this day.

The King and I represented Mongkut as a frivolous despot,
forever embroiled in harem intrigue – an image passionately
resented by the Thais. They believe that a King is beyond
reproach and any open criticism of the monarchy is strictly taboo.
Today many Thais are in prison for crimes of *lèse-majesté* – and
this sensitivity is something the visitor should be well aware of.
Thai sources make virtually no reference to Miss Leonowens's
five years at the court and the film is still officially banned in the
kingdom, though Chinese entrepreneurs peddle black-market

videos of it. Nevertheless, even the most loyal subject cannot deny that Mongkut's sexual appetite was considerable. Taking over the throne from his elder brother Rama 3 in 1851, after twenty-nine years in a monastery, he soon made up for lost time by fathering no less than eighty-three children by thirty-five wives, many of whom he inherited from the former ruler. But Mongkut's achievement was more profound than this, for it was his reign that linked the old and the new Thai history. As the first king to recognise that Siam could not stay aloof indefinitely from foreign influence, he pursued a policy of careful co-operation with the great colonial nations, granting favourable trade treaties, for example, to Britain in 1855 and later to France and the United States. He was, moreover, a man with a passion for knowledge. Much of his time as a monk had been spent studying; he knew English, Latin and Pali, and read voraciously in history, geography, and the sciences. His chief love was astronomy, but it proved to be a fatal attraction. From the observatories he had himself designed, Mongkut calculated a total eclipse of the sun on 18 August 1868. Despite the scepticism that greeted his prediction, the King journeyed with a large party, including some Europeans, to the marshy south-east coast of the Gulf of Siam to observe the phenomenon. It duly occurred as forecast, but Mongkut's triumph was short-lived. During the expedition he contracted malaria; two months later he was dead.

Thompson's house is in Soi Kasemsong 2, a side road opposite the monumentally ugly National Stadium on Rama 1 Road. His house was an assemblage of seven traditional Thai houses brought down from up country, in much the same way as the Suan Pakkard Palace. (Mobility was an essential feature of the traditional Thai house, a prefabricated structure consisting of five parts: floor, posts, roof, walls and decorative elements. Such a move can still be made today using skilled craftsmen from the area in which the old house was originally built, though these elegant and fragile wooden buildings do not take kindly to such new-fangled devices as air-conditioners and modern plumbing. Nowadays new prefabricated houses are quite common. They are built, displayed, sold, dismantled and transported 'completely knocked down' like automobile parts or furniture, to be reassembled on the purchaser's land – a system which also serves to circumvent laws prohibiting the transport of unworked timber.) The site was chosen partly because nearby on Klong Saensaep was a collection of silk weavers, whose houses can still be seen across the canal from the veranda. Again like Suan Pakkard, the house has the high, slightly curved roof typical of central Thailand, a luxuriant garden in the Thai style, and a fine collection of antiques; these are presented *in situ* and create a charming and relaxed atmosphere that no museum, with a better or more extensive display, could match.

The fruit of Thompson's commercial labours, the most famous silk emporium in the world, is the Thompson Silk Company on Suriwongse Road. Although silk of the same quality can be bought more cheaply elsewhere, especially in the northeast where most of it is made, the selection here is dazzling, enough to excuse even the most lurid of governesses' fantasies.

One other private house that is well worth a visit is not in fact typical of Bangkok but of the north. This is Kamthieng House, in the grounds of the Siam Society located just off Sukhumvit Road, in Soi ('minor road') Asoke. This area is a pleasant part of the city, with large houses and gardens, set back from the buzz of the tourist ghetto that has crept along Sukhumvit Road and just the right side of the girlie-bar area that begins with Soi 22. Sponsored by the royal family, the Society valiantly supports all aspects of traditional Thai culture. It publishes books, pamphlets and a magazine (*Journal of the Siam Society*). It also runs a reference library, and arranges lectures, cultural tours and events. The Kamthieng House was the ancestral home of an old family near Chiang Mai which donated it to the society in 1963. It was dismantled and reassembled here in a typical Thai garden a couple of years later, and now serves as an ethnological museum. Two animistic aspects of the house remained with it on its journey south. One is the beautifully carved teak lintels over the entrance to the main room of the house. These are known as the *ham yon* ('sacred testicles') which protect vital but invisible qualities contained in the room: the ancestral spirits of the family and the virility of the present occupiers. It is the tradition in the north that when a new owner moves into a house the old *ham yon* are symbolically castrated by being beaten, thus destroying the power that has been stored in them by the spirit of the previous owner. The other familiar is the Kamthieng ghost. She is a fierce old woman, bare breasted and wearing the traditional *phaasin* sarong, who returns to play some of the musical instruments in the house when the place is empty. She has also been seen by a number of reliable witnesses, each of whom she has berated because she no longer receives her due respect. Her anger has scared off more than one employee, and the reconstruction of the house was considerably delayed because of the fear her appearance generated among the hapless workmen.

In a sense, the obvious modernism of Bangkok is a façade that obscures the true nature of what is one of the last great oriental cities. This private, more diffident nature can be glimpsed in the elegance and charm that are there if you know where to look behind the veneer of sophisticated streets and busy flyovers. The intimate Bangkok takes time to discover, but time is unfortunately what most visitors do not have, and so they must settle for the surface. On the Thai side, there seems at last to be a growing awareness of the harm done by unchecked development, and, in the face of modern urban problems, a nostalgic hankering for what is truly Thai. In 1982, extensive restoration of many of the older monuments was undertaken to celebrate the city's bicentennial, and the programme was continued to mark the sixtieth birthday of the King in 1987. These are hopeful signs, part of a reappraisal of national identity and an antidote to the counsels of despair so often heard about the quality of life in Bangkok. The City of Angels has its problems, but to many Thais it still remains the city of dreams, the place that draws thousands each year in the search for fortune, or glamour, or just a decent living. As the repository of so many hopes, Bangkok has an extraordinarily vibrant atmosphere, and is by turns racy and refined, full of both poise and intrigue. The sheer intensity of life here is enough to empower the city with its own myth, its own destiny.

2

Traffic and Temples

No visitor to Bangkok can fail to remark on the appalling traffic. The widely travelled say it isn't the worst in the developing world – Lagos seems to merit that dubious distinction – but it must be near the top of the list. I have seen it relent only on two occasions. One is regular: those blessedly cool hours between three and six in the morning, when a breeze stirs the streets and walking is comfortable. The other is occasional: when some army or government 'big frog' is expected to pass by. Then a sudden and sinister quiet descends while police roadblocks clear a path for a motorcade invariably announced by flashing lights and wailing sirens, in conformity with the Thai preference for power and status to be visibly displayed. Otherwise, the traffic just never lets up and a good (or rather, bad) proportion of any day seems to be spent in one jam or another, relieved only by the distractions of illegal vendors, the kids who patrol the queues selling flowers, food and cassettes or cleaning the windscreens for a *baht*. Bangkok traffic lights are a phenomenon unto themselves. They can hold one up for an eternity. I recently timed a wait of no less than thirteen minutes at the junction of Ratchadamri Road and Rama 4, surely a record, even for this notorious spot. And then, at the first flicker of green the front row of waiting traffic, a cluster of motor bikes revving and spitting, roars off like a batch of Grand Prix drivers coming out of their grid, front wheels bucking off the ground, back wheels screaming, to leave behind them the stink of burnt rubber and acrid smoke.

On the bright side, these long waits can afford unexpected glimpses into Thai life that might otherwise slip by unnoticed. While drumming my fingers at the Rama 4/Ratchadamri junction the morning after my visit to the Marble Temple, I glance over at the statue of Rama 6 that stands guarding the entrance to

1 Looking across the Chao Phya river to Thonburi, the site of Taksin's original settlement, from the haven of the Oriental Hotel, Bangkok

2 Wat Phra Keo, Temple of the Emerald Buddha, is the repository of Thailand's most revered Buddha image; the temple is adjacent to the Grand Palace at the heart of old Bangkok

3 The floating market at Damnern Saduak in the Chao Phya delta, south-west of Bangkok; it is one of the few remaining markets where local people buy their daily food from boats in the traditional way

4 A typical juxtaposition of East and West on the streets of Bangkok – a shrine to the Hindu deity Brahma sits next to a fast-food outlet

Lumpini Park. A small group of people is watching a line of seven or eight men, a couple of whom are in tracksuits, solemnly *wai*-ing the statue. No one seems to know what it could be, so I assume it is a personal rather than an official ceremony. The next morning, however, a photo of the scene in the *Bangkok Post* informs me that I had witnessed the committee of the Football Association of Thailand, led by a Major-General Chalor, swearing an oath 'in front of the sacred statue of Rama 6 that they will do their duty honestly and sincerely and will help to raise the standard of soccer in the country during their term of office'. Thus is ritual woven into the fabric of everyday life.

One indomitable feature of the Bangkok traffic is the three-wheeled scooter-taxi (*samlor*, literally: 'three wheels') popularly known as the *tuk-tuk* after the ear-splitting din of its two-stroke engine. These machines buzz through the streets like angry hornets, garishly decorated in various combination of red, yellow, blue and green with lashings of chrome and the word Daihatsu emblazoned across the back. To the unwary tourist, it could as well be kamikaze, as he is transported in a series of swerves and lunges reminiscent of the dodgem rides of childhood fair-grounds. Mostly driven by refugees from the poverty-stricken north-east, *tuk-tuks* can be very convenient (taking officially three, but unofficially up to eight, passengers) and they are cheap, providing you bargain and don't take them for long distances, which are usually more economical by taxi. Photographers like them too, as they provide an open and elevated vantage point for street snaps. Vulnerability to exhaust fumes notwithstanding these boneshakers have a life of three to five years and are exported to over a dozen countries.

Sitting in a *tuk-tuk* you may well be blasted by a tremendous surge of heat from behind. This will be a bus of the long-suffering Bangkok Mass Transport Authority breathing fire down your neck, like some metallic dragon. The smoke of this dragon, however, actually comes from its rear, as all Bangkok buses, even the new Mercedes and Mitsubishi models, tend to announce their presence by belching out a vast cloud of sooty blackness. This at least acts as an early-warning system to alert would-be

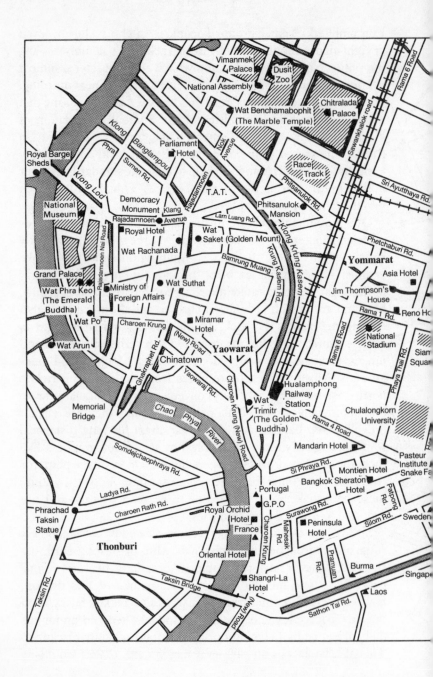

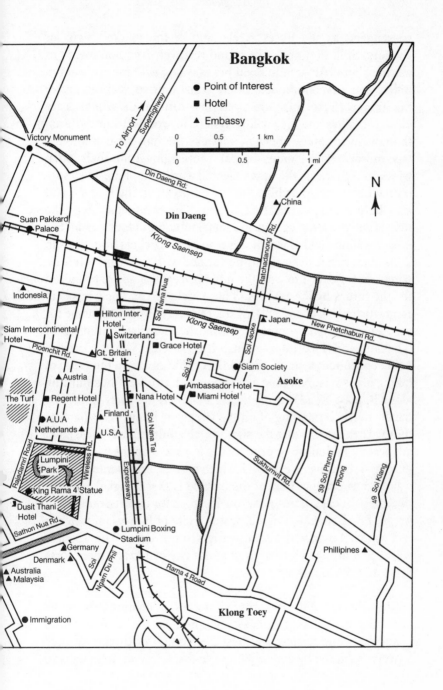

Bangkok

- ● Point of Interest
- ■ Hotel
- ▲ Embassy

| 0 | 0.5 | 1 km |
| 0 | 0.5 | 1 ml |

N

To Airport

Superhighway

Victory Monument

Din Daeng Rd.

Din Daeng

▲ China

Klong Saensep

Ratchadanong Rd.

Suan Pakkard
● Palace

▲ Indonesia

Soi Nana Nua

Klong Saensep

▲ Japan

New Phetchaburi Rd.

Soi Asoke

■ Hilton Inter. Hotel

Siam Intercontinental Hotel

Ploenchit Rd.

▲ Switzerland

▲ Gt. Britain

■ Grace Hotel

Soi 13

● Siam Society

Asoke

▲ Austria

The Turf

■ Regent Hotel

■ Nana Hotel

■ Ambassador Hotel

■ Miami Hotel

● A.U.A

Netherlands ▲

Finland ▲

▲ U.S.A.

Soi Nana Tai

Rajdamri Road

Wireless Rd.

Expressway

Sukhumvit Rd.

39 Soi Phrom Phong

49 Soi Klang

Lumpini Park

● King Rama 4 Statue

■ Dusit Thani Hotel

Sathon Nua Rd.

● Lumpini Boxing Stadium

▲ Germany

Denmark ▲

▲ Australia
▲ Malaysia

Soi Ngam Du Phii

Rama 4 Road

Phillipines ▲

Klong Toey

● Immigration

passengers, as the buses rarely stop at the marked signs or shelters. Still, they are a cheap and relatively frequent means of getting about. Air-conditioned buses cost 5 *baht* for up to seven miles, non air-conditioned 2 *baht*. Most tourists seem to prefer the former. In fact these are often very stuffy, as the windows are closed to allow the air cooling system to work effectively (even though it very often doesn't), whereas the non air-conditioned type always have some natural ventilation from their open windows. Off-peak, the buses are well worth sampling. They save on the hefty transport bills the city enforces on the visitors, and they have a unique ticketing system. The conductor keeps the tickets and the loose change in a metal tube about fourteen inches long, the hinged lid of which serves to clip off tickets from the roll. This operation is dexterously performed with one hand, while he hangs on for dear life with the other. Great things are promised for the future by the BMTA. These include 1200 new buses to renovate their fleet and a 'Bangkok Discovery by Bus' scheme for the tourists, in co-operation with the Tourist Authority of Thailand and Thai International. It is not clear why the latter is being consulted; some of the BMTA vehicles are on the verge of taking off as it is. Not long ago I spotted a 'two *baht*' bus hurtling along Rama 1 Road bearing the sign *You only live once* – a fact one hardly needs reminding of on the streets of Bangkok. What was more alarming was that the sign, which could equally have been advocating hedonism or prudence, was pasted on the windscreen exactly at the driver's eye level, which may have accounted for the way he was driving. Part of the trouble is that Bangkok was not designed for cars. It was not even designed for oxcarts, but for the barge. For Bangkok, originally, was a city of houses on water, a fact which fascinated all the early visitors here. The English traveller John Crawford arrived in the city in 1822, a mere forty years after its founding:

> On each side of the river there was a row of floating habitations resting on rafts of bamboo, moored to the shore. These appeared the neatest and best description of dwellings: they were occupied by good Chinese shops. Close to these aquatic

habitations were anchored the largest description of native vessels, among which were many junks of great size, just arrived from China. The face of the river presented a busy scene, from the number of boats and canoes of every size and description that were passing to and fro. The number struck us as very great at the time, for we were not aware that there are few or no roads at Bang Kok, and that the river and canals form the common highways, not only for goods but for passengers of every description.

Even thirty years ago the city was criss-crossed by these canals, which the Thais call *klongs*, serving as both the major and minor thoroughfares. Residents who can remember living on a *klong* are full of nostalgic memories of languid days punctuated only by the endless variety of small craft that glided past and the varied cries of the vendors. Lovely I'm sure it was, though the experience of the smell of a Venetian summer leads me to suspect that Bangkok must have suffered greatly from the rotting refuse and lack of sanitation. Nevertheless, the early travellers' accounts are all full of wonder at the water-borne city.

Ironically, it was not long after Crawford wrote his glowing report that the European consuls banded together to petition the King, Rama 4, to build some roads in his capital. They were used to riding and promenading, and found that their health was suffering from the lack of this accustomed exercise. He agreed to their request, and by his death in 1868 there was a network of streets along the south end of New Road (Charoen Krung), on the edge of Chinatown.

Things stayed much as they were until the late 1950s, when, to cope with the increase of traffic and the speed of Thailand's entry into the modern world, the *klongs* began to disappear, filled in and converted to roads. Though this may have temporarily eased the growing congestion, it deprived the city of its drainage channels and thus created another of the crosses that the citizens of Bangkok have learned to bear with notable cheerfulness: flooding. Every October, at the end of the four-month rainy season, Bangkok resembles a bowl within a bath; it is awash with not only its own rainfall, but the water draining down from the saturated paddy fields north of the city. South lie flood tides that have nowhere to go. Every three or four years the flooding is especially heavy and causes considerable hardship. The last serious flooding was in 1984. Much of the city was a lake, knee-high and deeper in some places. Traffic was stranded, especially the public transport buses and the *tuk-tuks*. Some vehicles were completely submerged, others peeped forlornly above the grey waters. People were paddling boats to work, thousands of homes had to be evacuated, some of the hotels were offering temporary accommodation at special flood-relief rates. Especially hard hit were the street vendors – a sizeable proportion of the city's workforce – unable to set up their stalls. Even the religious were not spared: Buddhist monks were unable to go out on their early morning alms round to collect food, and those who wanted to pray for an end to the chaos were having a hard time as well, many of the temples being under water. Perhaps some prayers were heard, as, miraculously, not many died, though thirteen people were electrocuted in public telephones, such is Bangkok's wiring, and 20,000 were taken to hospital with watersnake bites. The financial damage was huge – an estimated £1500 million – and especially ruinous in a city where few people have insurance and many earn their living on a day-to-day basis. The water lingered in some parts until the following April, only two months before the next rainy season began, as the few existing *klongs* are largely silted up and natural evaporation is slowed to a minimum in Bangkok's oppressively humid air. Luckily the rains of 1985 were light.

In an attempt to forestall the problem in the future, officials are asking the government for almost 20,000 million *baht* (£500 million) over the next five years. But it is not only a question of money; the underlying problem, literally, is subsidence. The City of Angels is sinking much faster than Venice, the worst areas lose five inches a year. The highest parts of the city are barely six feet above sea-level, the lowest already below the nearby Gulf of Thailand. Two superficially impressive indicators of the capital's rise are also hastening its spectacular decline: the heavy traffic and the huge building projects, both of which are destabilising the already precarious ground. The problem is worsened by virtually unchecked use of artesian wells. About 9000 of these currently suck the water out from under the city (40 per cent of which goes to the municipal authority) and as the water-table drops, so does Bangkok. The future looks even soggier, and Bangkok may yet return to the waterbound metropolis the early travellers reported. One man who has been lobbying the authorities to do something before it is too late is Prinya Nuta Laya, a geological engineer at the prestigious Asian Institute of Technology. 'Ten years from now, if the government does not act, most of Bangkok will be under water for the entire year,' he warns. Either luckily or wisely, Mr Prinya's Institute is located some thirty miles out of the city.

Bangkok's design was the offspring of practicality and nostalgia. In 1767 the ancient capital of Ayutthaya, fifty-three miles upriver, was overrun by Thailand's old enemy, the Burmese. Remnants of the Thai army straggled down to Chantaburi on the south-east coast of the Gulf of Siam. Here a fresh force was raised under General Phya Tak Sin who, after seven months, returned to Ayutthaya and expelled the invaders. But the capital, a *klong*-dissected island at the junction of two rivers, had been virtually rased, and with it 400 years of Thai history. Taksin, as he was popularly known, decided that the new capital would be better situated near the sea, a position facilitating foreign trade – especially the shipment of arms – and generally safer from the Burmese threat from the west and north. So he moved down to a small fishing village known as Bang Kok ('village of wild olives') that, since the middle of the seventeenth century, had served Ayutthaya as a port. The settlement, with its fortifications built by the French, straddled both sides of Thailand's main artery, the Chao Phya River. Taksin settled his court on the west bank in what is now known as Thonburi, and proclaimed himself king. Here he stayed until 1782, struggling to unite a disintegrated country. That he managed to do so is a testimony to his considerable abilities, but the strain of ceaseless campaigning began to tell, and slowly but surely he lost his sanity. A just and able ruler turned into a capricious and cruel tyrant.

Taksin began to consider himself divine, increasingly seduced by that frequent bedfellow of power, paranoia. Suspicious of those closest to him, he systematically tortured not only his officials but his wife and children. In March 1782, a revolt broke out, and the first of many coups in Bangkok's 200 years of life took place. The mad king fled to the safety of a monastery, his vacant throne was offered to the commander-in-chief of the forces, General Chao Phya Chakri, recently returned from a successful campaign in Laos. On 6 April 1782 the new dynasty, the Chakri dynasty, was established. Taksin, still a threat to the kingdom's precarious stability, was executed in the manner reserved for royalty, whose blood should never touch the ground. After a performance of sacred dance and music had sanctified the scene, he was wrapped in a black velvet sack and his neck was broken with a club of scented sandalwood.

The new king, later to take the title Rama 1, moved his court across the river to the site of modern Bangkok and set about recreating the glories of the former capital. He had what remained of its buildings transported down from Ayutthaya and laid out the new city as a replica of the old. Thus Bangkok is built as a rather wiggly grid. The heart of the city is in its western end, nestling in the wide curve of the river, centred on the Grand Palace area. South of this lies the original commercial centre, the area now known as Chinatown. Though very few of the *klongs* remain today, those that do give a glimpse of what life was like here in an earlier and perhaps more agreeable age. Klong Saensaep, dug in the early nineteenth century to carry waterboats all the way from the original walled city to the Gulf of Siam and beyond, still runs east/west through the middle of the city. North, and roughly parallel to it, is Klong Samsen. On the north/south axis, three major arteries – Klong Lod, Klong Banglampou and Klong Krung Kasem – curve in an arc through the downtown area. In the Dusit district the Chitralada Palace is surrounded by small canals, as befits the descendant of the man who laid out Bangkok as a network of water courses.

Klong Lod, the earliest and best preserved *klong*, was dug in Rama 1's time to create an island on which his Grand Palace could sit in splendid isolation. It is still possible to walk along this, a rare treat in Bangkok, and one to be savoured. Here, well off the beaten tourist track, one can get a flavour of the city's past. The canalside walk passes behind several government buildings – the Ministries of Justice, Defence and Foreign Affairs – and continues past the diminutive Wat Rajapradit (founded in 1864) clad in white and grey Chinese marble with a Sri Lankan-style *stupa* and Khmer (Cambodian)-style monuments. It also has good, though recent, murals, depicting scenes from daily life in the mid-nineteenth century. On the opposite side is one of the most pleasing buildings in the city: the Ministry of the Interior, a gracious European-style structure, typical of the best late nineteenth-century architecture in Bangkok. The *klong* then skirts the picturesque cemetery of Wat Rajabopit, another small temple complex relatively unvisited by tourists and full of charm. Built in 1863 by Rama 5, the temple reflects its builder's interest in blending Thai and European styles, and serves as a forerunner to the famous Marble Temple (Wat Benchamabopit) built forty years later. Here it is the decoration that catches the eye – the sparkling coat of blue, green and yellow Chinese porcelain that covers the lower part of the *chedi*, the cloister around it and the monks' assembly hall (*bot*). Most surprising of all is the interior of the *bot*, which bears no resemblance to anything Thai, being more an oriental version of Italian Gothic, its brown vaulted ceiling picked out with gilded ribbing in an imitation of a European cathedral. Though the purist may find it alarming this little hybrid has considerable charm, and it is a good example of the stylistic accretions that characterise the Bangkok period and Siam's surrender of her cultural isolation.

The *klong* walk finishes in the Ban Mo area, the old goldsmiths' quarter, not far from the wholesale market of Pak Klong Talad, at the foot of the Memorial Bridge. Across this bridge, on the Thonburi side, the *klongs* continue to play more of their traditional role as waterways, streets, bathing areas, places to wash, swim and play. Here in Taksin's original capital one can appreciate at first hand the amphibious nature of the Thais. Straight after they are born babies are dipped in the *klong* as a natural immunisation against future disease, and they never lose

their love of water. They seem totally in their element here, the
black-headed children wriggling, shrieking and splashing like
happy tadpoles. Tucked away in this forgotten half of the city lie
some of its most interesting temples, havens for those who like to
wander a little adventurously and get a feel of the old Bangkok.
Several of them actually pre-date the founding of the capital. Wat
Kalayanimit has a courtyard decorated in the Chinese style, much
in vogue during Rama 3's reign, and dotted with Chinese statues,
which, like all such figures, came from China as ballast in returning
rice ships. The paintings inside the *bot* are traditionally Thai,
however, as is Wat Hong Rattanaram, a bit further along the *klong*.
This temple was already old in Taksin's time, when it was
extensively restored, and is worth visiting for its beautifully carved
doors and pediments, the impressive Buddha image from the
Sukhothai period (thirteenth to fifteenth centuries), and the library
set in tranquil grounds. A good example of the Bangkok eccentric
genre is Wat Raja Crot, located on Klong Dan, that runs off the
arterial Klong Yai. Begun by Rama 2 and completed by his successor, Rama 3, this folly again displays marked Chinese influence.
The dragon-bearing mother-of-pearl doors, one of the best
examples of the art in Thailand, are particularly noteworthy.

One of the most rewarding Thonburi temples is Wat Rakang,
directly across the river from the Grand Palace and just north of
Wat Arun, Temple of the Dawn. This was the last major *wat* rebuilt
by Rama 1. The highlight here is the group of three wooden houses
which lies behind the temple proper. These delicate examples of
traditional Thai domestic architecture were the residence of
Rama 1 while he was still a general in Taksin's army. When he
ascended the throne in 1782 they were given over as monks' living
quarters, and a few years later converted into a library, an
important part of any temple complex. The building succeeds just
where some of the more touted Bangkok sites, to the Western eye at
least, do not: in striking the balance between purity of line and
enthusiastic decoration.

It is in their paintings that the temples of Thonburi most excel.
Wat Dusit, Wat Daowadings and Wat Bangyikan are good
examples, and all can be reached by a pleasant ferry journey from

the landing just above the National Museum. The pride of Thonburi is Wat Suwannaram, near the mouth of Klong Bangkok Noi. The buildings, facing the *klong*, date from the beginning of the Bangkok period, the restoration by Rama 3 being completed in 1831. Even the visitor with little time should spend some of it here.

The theme of much of Thai painting is the Tosachat, the name given to the last ten *Jataka* tales, the stories of the previous incarnations of the Buddha. These popular tales which feature the future Enlightened One as a man or animal are found throughout the Buddhist world. Each one is a homily expounding a particular virtue on the long path to Enlightenment, or the inevitable consequences of leading a good or bad life. Compiled in the early days of the Buddhist religion, the *Jatakas*, numbering 547 in all, are a charming blend of traditional folklore, pre-Buddhist legend, down-to-earth wisdom and exalted spirituality. In Thailand, the last ten, almost to the exclusion of the others, have been preferred both for teaching and as the subject of artistic expression. The Tosachat is represented not only in murals, but on temple banners, sets of small paintings on cloth or wood, manuscripts and bookcases and in a variety of media: tempera, lacquer, gold leaf and carving.

The most popular is the Vessandan, a tale which teaches the virtue of generosity through the story of Prince Vessandan (the future Buddha) who is so generous he is prepared to give away everything, including his wife and children. Its thousand verses are usually chanted at temples over a three-day period in October, at the end of Phansa, the Buddhist Lent which coincides with the rainy season. In Wat Suwannaram the Vessandan covers the entire left-hand wall as well as a large portion of the front wall. The area above the windows is devoted to four bands of celestial beings paying homage to the Buddha image, a traditional arrangement ensuring the maximum visibility for the main story, which is placed in the panels between the windows. The colours are mercifully well preserved, in a far better state of repair than many of their Thonburi contemporaries, and radiate an imaginative vividness of their own, independent of the dim light of the hall. Thai temple painting is tempera, applied on a dry surface, and as a result has not adhered well. Rising damp, humidity, rain seepage, and fire have wrought havoc with most murals; only the paintings of the Ayutthaya and Bangkok periods have survived, and there are precious little of those.

Two general characteristics of Thai painting are clearly demonstrated here. One is the emotional range of the artist, who moves effortlessly from the stylised and formal gestures and poses of the Buddha, deities, monks and royalty to the naturalistic and humorous treatment of everyday life. Even in the most sacred scenes one can distinguish deftly realised vignettes of people working, relaxing, gossiping, flirting. This ritualised dichotomy between sacred and profane is common to all south-east Asian art and dance, but the irrepressible and earthy humour of the Thais allowed them to enjoy the irony of such juxtapositions to the full. The second characteristic is the lack of the Western convention of a vanishing point and consequent perspective. Here the figures were painted in blocks of colour without toning, so they act out their parts on a mystical stage that is simultaneously and miraculously present at all points. Different scenes are portrayed on the same panel separated only by zigzag lines, a fence or a line of trees. Such divisions are the only ruptures in a unified field in which the participants float, unbounded by the normal conventions of time and space, and radiating an unearthly bliss.

And what of modern art in Thailand? As in all traditional societies that are rapidly becoming more secular, the Thai artist faces a considerable challenge. Much of his heritage was the work of monks, and all of it was created within the framework of religion, subject to the decrees of ecclesiastical custom and royal patronage. Today, taste is dictated by the market-place, not the monastery. The immediate artistic past has not been spared the Western influence that has shaped so much of modern Thailand. In the fine arts the most influential figure was the Italian sculptor Corrado Feroci, who, invited to the court of Rama 6, created both the Democracy Monument (1939) and the Victory Monument (1941) in the style of Heroic Realism popular in Italy and

Germany at the time. Anything further from the subtle oneiric vision of the Thai aesthetic is difficult to imagine. This stress on muscular realism continued for almost twenty years, during a period in which the government dictated which artistic styles were permissible. Since the 1960s, Thai artists have experimented with the whole gamut of Western styles, ranging from figurative representation to abstract expressionism, but it must be admitted that these imported genres were too foreign to take root in the Thai psyche and emerge as something authentic. Significantly, those painters who rose above mere mimicry were all concerned with expressing traditional Buddhist subjects. The political turmoil and banning of all dissent in the mid-1970s caused many artists to re-think their position. Since that time, things appear to have come full circle, as the most successful artists working today, people such as Thawan Duchanee and Prateung Emjaroen, are reinterpreting their inherited Buddhist vision in a way relevant to contemporary life. For the first time, a modern art is being created that derives from the Thais' unparalleled graphic sensibility and which is truly Thai in spirit. This is an optimistic situation, but art will never return to play as vital a role in the mainstream of Thai life, as it did when the temple dispensed education and guidance.

3

People and Palaces

Mr Nut sits cross-legged on the pavement outside the Miami Hotel awaiting business. His taxi is parked up the street near the spirit house that protects the car park of the Ambassador City complex, in whose shadow the Miami nestles. The shrine was erected a few years ago when the complex was built, as a home for the displaced local spirit, as Thai custom demands. History does not relate whether it was the spirit, or something more tangible, that smoothed the passage of the building with the authorities, for the whole place is quite illegal, never having received planning permission. The enormous structure, with its hotel, conference centres, discothèques, restaurants and coffee houses is one of the biggest in Bangkok, yet it was presented to the municipal authorities as a *fait accompli*. Apparently such flagrant disregard for planning legislation is not uncommon; occasionally hotels or department stores are closed pending the overdue settlement of their planning permission. One wing of the complex contains the Ambassador Food Centre, one of the best inexpensive eating places in town. Self-service, it offers a huge range from Korean dishes to vegetarian Italian, and a good meal costs about £2. The Centre is much frequented, especially by refugees from the indifferent food of the nearby Miami.

Mr Nut whiles away his time by reading the black, white and green pages of *Thai Rath*, the heady cocktail of sex, scandal, violence and persecution campaigns which is the country's most popular paper. He gossips and plays cards with the other drivers, or sometimes he just watches the world go by. Every so often he gets up and strolls round the corner to one of a cluster of food stalls such as are to be found bursting the seams of many a Bangkok pavement, catering at any hour of the day or night to the city's insatiable stomach. His favourite is the stall outside the

Thermae Massage Parlor, whose dilapidated façade sports several classical maidens in swirling draperies, thrusting their incongruous way through the neon lights and tangled wires. The lady who owns the stall mixes up a particularly good *nam prik* ('pepper water'), the fiery garlic and chilli sauce that accompanies so many Thai dishes and has taken the roof off so many unsuspecting Western palates. Of the dozen or so types of chilli common to Thai cuisine she favours the little green torpedo *prik kee nu* ('mouse-shit peppers') over the hottest, the red-orange bombshell known as *prik ke nu lueng*, and her regular speciality is *nam prik kapi*, a sauce made from a paste of small shrimps that are pounded, mixed with salt and left to dry and ferment in the sun, achieving a pungent smell in the process. But sometimes, because she likes Mr Nut, the stall lady will bring in some of her *nam prik maeng dah*, the sauce made from the four-inch beetle which resembles a cricket. The male exudes a strong perfumed smell in the mating season and is therefore much prized, sometimes fetching as much as 10 *baht* a piece. Each night during the rainy season thousands of these creatures are swept from the air with long-poled nets as they circle lamp bulbs. Later in the year the male is weighed down by carrying his wife's eggs on his back, and more easily snared by the gourmets. You can see women in the markets carefully sniffing each beetle they buy, to make sure they have not been palmed off with the female of the species. Then they will go home to grind the roasted insect with garlic, onion, chilli, tomato, fermented fish and other ingredients of the maker's choice. After *nam prik* with some rice or noodles and a little chicken or pork, a dozen yards down the street will bring Mr Nut to where the fresh pineapples, water melons, and papayas are chopped into pieces, jazzed up with a sprinkling of salt mixed with paprika and sold in polythene bags for 2 *baht*, with a six-inch-long wooden spear that doubles as a toothpick. If he's still hungry there's always the little old lady squatting down beside her charcoal grill serving baked bananas and corn on the cob, while her grandchildren chase around among the feet of the passers-by. The whole lot goes down very nicely with a bottle of Singha beer, or some Mekhong Whisky, made from rice, a quarter the price of

Scotch, and hugely popular all over the country. He can get these
from the man from Laos, whose pavement pitch is a large tin ice-
bucket and a bamboo stool, next to where the deaf mutes spread
out their Burmese wall hangings and Hong Kong Rolexes to
catch the tourists coming and going from the Ambassador. In
fact, the Hong Kong watches are not selling so well these days;
the gold yellows after six months and word has got round that the
Taiwan ones are a better buy. Still, Hong Kong or Taiwan, they
cost about £8 – a mere £2500 cheaper than the genuine article.

These street stalls are an indispensable feature of Thai urban
life. Recently it was announced that the French clothing company
Lacoste is interested in doing a deal with a Thai manufacturer.
They are a little late. Every second stall here has mounds of fake
designer clothes for next to nothing, and you can even buy
handfuls of the little green crocodiles themselves. The *farangs* –
as the Thais call all white non-Thais – spend a lot of time at such
roadside stalls all over the city, their browsing set to music by
amplifiers that blare out the latest Western music at about
75 pence a cassette. At less than half the price of the genuine
article, nine out of every ten music cassettes sold in Thailand are
illegal, and this is for both foreign and Thai music. There is
massive piracy in films, videos, music, pharmaceuticals, books,
and even the computer software and service industries. A lot of
money is involved. In 1986, for example, nearly £526 million
worth of pirated goods was sold here in the pharmaceutical field
alone. This greatly upsets American companies who, together
with their government, have recently persuaded the Thai authorities to enforce copyright laws to protect what they call 'American
intellectual property'. Fiercely contested, this piece of legislation
very nearly caused the downfall of the coalition government. On a
humbler note, some of the goods on sale on the streets have taken
a devious route. Recently I watched someone buy a shoulder bag
embroidered with the word 'Tibet'. After she had gone, I chatted
to the stall owner. It transpired that the bag did not come from the
lofty Himalayas, but was made in Burma, smuggled across the
Thai border to some Gujerati middlemen and then sold on to the
Bangkok street vendors! Such is the global village.

If Mr Nut had some Chinese blood in him, as do over 65 per cent of the citizens of Bangkok, he might be more interested in such commercial matters. But he doesn't and he isn't. He is happy to drive his taxi, earn about 500 *baht* a day, and take life as it comes. Like half the cabbies here he does own his car, though he is in debt to his brother-in-law for its purchase. Like many Thais he doesn't care much for the Chinese, scorning their obsessive materialism and grasping, closed mentality. In neighbouring Malaysia, there is virtually a civil war between the Chinese and native Malays, but such dislike is very rarely expressed openly in Thailand, a country that abhors the open display of aggression. This reticence, together with a distaste for competitiveness, enables the Thais to live with their Chinese neighbours easily despite the obvious material discrepancy between the two communities taken as a whole, and frequent exploitation of Thais by Chinese businessmen and entrepreneurs.

Set between the great Asian civilisations of India and China, Thailand has derived much of her culture from these neighbours, but the character of her people is unique. Indian culture is serious about the spiritual: the meaning and conquest of suffering, the nature of God, the ultimate questions of life and death. Chinese culture is serious about the material: making money, family stability and continuity, being practical and ensuring food. What the Thais are serious about is having a good time. This quality is known as *sanuk* – which translates roughly as 'good fun'. At its best *sanuk* manifests as a natural and infectious sociability. The Thais have above all a capacity for spontaneous and wholehearted enjoyment; an ability to live life to the full that no visitor to the country can fail to observe. But at its worst *sanuk* can be a symptom of a refusal to confront situations that may be difficult or painful, a determination to keep things on an easy-going, superficial level, whatever the eventual consequence of such an evasion may be. The *farang*'s confrontation with *sanuk* can thus be his greatest source of pleasure, or a cause for very real frustration. Anyone who knows Thais will recognise how a conversation can tail off into evasion just when the nub of what appears to be an important or interesting subject is reached, because to continue the discussion might involve embarrassment, or loss of face or reputation for someone concerned. Or it may be that the talk has touched a raw social nerve – such as taboo subjects concerning authority figures such as the royal family or monkhood. Whatever the topic, the Westerner can come away from a discussion feeling that he has not really encountered what Thais think or feel, but only a polite, and often charming, façade. On more than one occasion, half-way through a conversation on the sort of things that any Westerner would consider important and worth discussing I have been told 'Oh, you think too much!' and the subject has slid sideways onto something less taxing or thought-provoking. Perhaps I do think too much; perhaps it is just that the Thais don't like to discuss sensitive or profound topics with foreigners. But, more than this, I suspect there is an unintellectual bias in the Thai personality, cultivated perhaps by the pervasive influence of a Buddhist outlook that undercuts the thinking mind so valued in the Cartesian West. Perhaps the Thais are so much happier than us because they don't waste their time thinking as much. I do not know of a truly great thinker or philosopher in Thai intellectual history, nor even a generally renowned commentator on their received Buddhist religion. Though there have been, and are, Thai saints, Thais seem to have preferred the heart to the mind, and chosen the practical or ritual aspects of their religion rather than the abstractions of its philosophy and esoteric practice.

A moon-faced man probably in his late forties Mr Nut is a living and somewhat corpulent embodiment of *sanuk*. Possessed of an irrepressible joviality, his reaction to most of life's vicissitudes is to laugh; a laugh that starts way down in his well-rounded belly and proceeds to shake his whole frame with a hilarity that feeds on itself and nourishes others.

Our friendship was forged in a rather hair-raising way. Some years ago, I was on my way out of Bangkok to Karachi for a lecture tour of Pakistan. Booked on a flight that went only twice a week, with the tour due to start the evening of my arrival, it was imperative I caught the plane. I took Mr Nut's cab for the forty-minute drive to the airport, and we arrived in good time, a little over an hour before departure. No sooner had we pulled up outside the terminal than I realised with horror that I had left my camera case and films behind the desk at my hotel. There was nothing for it but to go back. We turned round and drove back at breakneck speed; his ancient Toyota clanking in protest whenever the speedometer went above 100 km/h. I duly retrieved the camera, we turned round again and continued our mad dash. The drama of the return leg was both heightened and put into perspective when we were temporarily halted by strident police sirens. At first I thought we were to be booked for speeding, but it turned out they were bewailing the aftermath of a gruesome accident. The flashing blue lights revealed a decapitated body, sprawled at the edge of the road like a broken doll. The head was nowhere to be seen.

Somehow, we made it to the airport with five minutes to go to take-off. As we pulled up with the engine banging and smoking like a circus car I thanked Mr Nut profusely, thrust my remaining Thai money into his hands and sprinted to the check-in desk. My frantic and breathless arrival was greeted by a Thai International assistant, as cool as a cucumber. Her tolerant amusement at my very un-Thai display of panic made me feel not a little foolish, as she soothed away my agitation with the phrase that is the essence of applied *sanuk*: *'Mai pen rai'* ('don't worry, there's no problem; everything's OK'), *'mai pen rai*, sir' as if speaking to a child frightened by its own bad dreams, and I was on my way to Karachi. *'Mai pen rai'* is a phrase one hears a great deal in Thailand; it has become the country's motto, the Thai equivalent of the ubiquitous 'No worries!' in Australia, applied in all sorts of situations. It reassured me after my panic, and no doubt someone would offer it as a crumb of consolation to the mourners of the headless corpse. The dramatic nature of our drive, plus no doubt the size of my grateful tip, cemented a bond between Mr Nut and me. Ever since he has been my driver in Bangkok and, important for a traveller in a strange city, my ally.

Even the stoutest of allies can sometimes fail. I have an appointment with the Tourist Authority Office downtown, and Mr

Nut's new car, a violet Datsun with orange plastic seats, refuses to start. While he fiddles around under the bonnet I flick through a battered photograph album he keeps on the dashboard. It is full of faded shots of young GIs sitting at the formica-topped tables of the Miami coffee shop. They look so young, crew-cut faces blank and mindless, name tags pinned to their uniforms proclaiming them to be 'Robertson', 'Jeffries' or 'Skutch'. Each fresh-faced youth has a Thai girl with him. Some are perhaps the mothers of the girls at the very same tables right now, listening to the same juke-box that still takes only American quarters. Mr Nut emerges from under the bonnet grinning sheepishly. 'Batterly no good,' he confides. How much will a new one cost? A thousand *baht*. Maybe eight hundred if he's lucky. He doesn't have the money on him. It crosses my mind to lend him it before I realise that I don't have that much either. Anyway, such an offer would probably involve considerable loss of face for him. There is only one other taxi in sight, belonging to the grey-haired Muslim known as 'Old Man'. It has a flat tyre.

Deprived of a car, I turn to the group of motorbike youths, tattooed and coiffured like a gang of oriental James Deans, who congregate outside the hotel and provide yet another form of public transport in the city. In the heat of the day these drivers give a spectacular demonstration of the Thai ability to sleep anywhere, lying prone along the saddles of their Kawasaki 500s, arms thrown over their faces, stretched in sensuous abandon like cats in the sun. I haggle a price with one of the gang, who introduces himself as 'Number One Champion' and we set off into the blur of Sukhumvit Road. I should have paid attention to his name, as what follows turns out to be the most frightening journey of my life. I have had a few wild ones, involving Afghan trucks in the Khyber Pass, Bhutanese mountain mules, Pakistani jeeps threatening to slide off the Karakoram Highway and buffalo-skin rafts getting dragged towards angry rapids in Nepal – but this beats them all. It's not that 'Number One Champion' is a bad driver – far from it. In fact, it would be better if he were, as then he wouldn't be tempted to squeeze through the minutest of gaps between cars, buses, *tuk-tuks* and anything else on the road as he does so unfalteringly. His instinct is unerring as he roars full throttle towards what seems like total disaster, with never more than a couple of inches clearance. His judgement is impeccable; my nerves are in shreds. After a hundred yards I close my eyes, cast a prayer towards the Emerald Buddha and resign myself to my fate. The problem is compounded by the fact that Sukhumvit has six lanes running one way from east to west into the maelstrom that is the heart of the city, and one bus lane running the other way. 'Number One Champion' resolutely insists on using this bus lane against the oncoming traffic, a policy that has the obvious advantages of speed but equally obvious disadvantages. Every so often the bulk of a BMTA bus looms ahead of us; our last-minute swerves are straight out of the Keystone Cops. In the brief respites of traffic lights, when I can open my eyes without fear, I am ashamed to notice that all the other pillion passengers, including some ladies sitting demurely side-saddle, have their hands resting nonchalantly on their knees or laps. I, however, am clinging ashen faced and white knuckled to the pillion bar, thankful only that the nearby Thais are too polite to laugh at my obvious terror. After what seems an eternity of weaving, screeching brakes, clouds of sooty exhaust and sudden, vicious potholes, we finally arrive at the TAT office on Wisukasat Road, not far from the Democracy Monument and the spire of Wat Saket, rising gilded and lofty above the shacks and corrugated iron roofs that line Klong Banglampou. Inside, ordered, internal Bangkok takes over from its frenetic external counterpart. The cool atmosphere is a balm to my jangled nerves. In an office on the third floor I ask for my contact in a state of anticipation, as I am never quite sure what gender to expect on the other end of a Thai name. She turns out to be a diminutive and very efficient young lady, and while she is typing a valuable letter of introduction for hotel managers, museum officials and the like, I have a chance to study my surroundings. What strikes me at once is the air of relaxation that pervades the place. A couple of children wander from desk to desk and are indulgently received by men and women alike. A rather glamorous young lady with a lemon silk blouse and the pale skin and high cheekbones of a

Chinese is eating a plate of noodles at her desk; an old friend of one of the staff turns up, is greeted effusively and stays to chat; a secretary comes in, sits down on her desk and does her make-up with unselfconscious care. The only person who seems to be taking things seriously is a splendid old girl in a *phaasin* (the traditional long skirt) and flip-flops who moves from desk to desk making minute adjustments to the alignment of various piles of paper, or altering the position of a pencil by an inch or two, stopping every so often to hitch up her ample bosom with a loud sniff and an air of intense concentration. To be fair, it is now after twelve and getting into lunchtime, but I have witnessed this easy-going atmosphere before in Thai workplaces. I do not mean to suggest that no one does any work. Far from it, even now typewriters are clacking, phone calls being made, decisions no doubt being taken left and right. It is just that this work is not allowed to cast a pall of solemnity over the intrinsically pleasurable business of being alive. Someone once said that the Thais work at play and play at work. In the office, as in free time, *sanuk* is the essential ingredient of anything worth doing, and perhaps it is no coincidence that the same word – *ngan* – means both 'work' and 'party'.

Much calmed and business completed I return downstairs to find 'Number One Champion' cross-legged on his bike eating a mango, its soft yellow flesh paler than its Indian cousin and incomparably more delicate than the Mexican or Caribbean varieties. I envy his skill and climb aboard for the return journey, with a tight grin. Forty-five scorching minutes later we slew to a halt outside the hotel. There sitting on the pavement with a film magazine spread out before him is Mr Nut. He waves to us. 'No batterly! No batterly!' he guffaws. 'No work for two days!' Too dazed to commiserate, with nostrils clogged by burnt diesel fumes and nervous system humming like a telephone exchange, I totter past him for the haven of my room and my third shower of the day.

There is not much of a feeling of *sanuk* in Chinatown, but there is much hard work. H. W. Smyth, author of *Five Years in Siam*, dismissed the Chinatown of 1898 as being 'Chinese Bangkok, malodorous and ill-mannered'. It is still much the same: bustling, rude, commercial, though the smell these days is more from dried fish piled high in bamboo panniers than from the blocked *klongs* of Smyth's time. And although the opium dens and the beckoning green lanterns outside the brothels have not been seen since the 1960s, Chinatown is still redolent with atmosphere, its narrow streets too congested for traffic, forcing one to wander and browse. Covering the area from New Road (Charoeng Krung) down to the river, this rabbit warren is worth a good day's visit. It is hard to say exactly who is Chinese in modern Thailand. Intermarriage is widespread – usually Chinese man with Thai woman – and the accurate observation of H. H. Hallett, an English traveller a hundred years ago, is still pertinent today: 'Half the population of the Menam Delta – the Bangkok area – is Chinese, and very few of the people are without some trace of Chinese blood in them.' The Chinese have been part of the scene in Thailand since at least the end of the seventeenth century, when their 3000-strong community in Ayutthaya provided valuable trading links between the city and the outside world. By the time the capital was moved to Bangkok, several thousand were coming in annually, an immigration swelled by various causes: the domestic upheavals of the Opium Wars, overpopulation and the ever-present threat of famine, and the gradual incursion of the European powers that preceded the fall of the Dragon Throne in 1922. Another huge wave of Chinese business families followed the Revolution of 1949, this latest influx being known as Shanghai Chinese.

At the same time that the Chinese were arriving in great numbers, Siam was beginning to open up to Western influence after the signing of the Bowring Treaty with Great Britain in 1855. Although this treaty ended the country's self-imposed isolation the Thais, traditionally farmers, were reluctant to enter into the newly opened trading arena, thus leaving an opportunity perfectly tailored to the Chinese commercial genius. The immigrant business families and travelling salesmen became the middlemen between Western firms in Bangkok and the indigenous peasant population. As agents for such local products as tin, rubber, shellac and agricultural commodities, they acquired a financial strength out of all proportion to their numbers. Any resentment from the native population was no doubt partly forestalled by the fact that Taksin, the first king of Bangkok, was half Chinese and one of the early queens of the Chakri dynasty was wholly Chinese. In Thailand, such royal associations would have done much to smooth the path of the whole community, and to be anti-Chinese would have been, however indirectly, anti-monarchy.

Sociologists reckon that in Thailand there are about 8 million people, 15 per cent of the population, who, in terms of blood, language, looks or culture can be classified as Chinese. Half of these live in Bangkok or its suburbs. They are now well integrated into the Thai scene, speaking Thai, and many having changed their names to Thai equivalents. They are also well established in all the professions, though many still follow the trades traditional to their linguistic group: Taichiew speakers (concentrated in Bangkok) are big wholesalers, Cantonese are mechanics and carpenters, Hainanese specialise in domestic service and the restaurant trade.

But the Chinese were really established by gold. Secure, portable, and easily convertible, the tangible quality of the yellow metal seems more to the liking of the telluric Thais than the abstractions of money. They wear it, work it, put it in banks, hide it away, cover their Buddha images with it. The Thais have always liked gold, and the Chinese have always liked selling it to them. The centre of the country's flourishing gold trade for at least a century, supplying kings and commoners alike, has been Yaowaraj Road, here in the heart of Chinatown. There are hundreds of dealers but the trade is run by a cartel of seven shops, called the Gold Traders Association. Any item bought from one of these is guaranteed as to weight, purity and resale value at any other shop in the road. The difference between the buying and selling price, fixed by the government, is exactly 100 *baht* for the standard measurement of 15.2 grams (also, confusingly for the foreigner, called a *baht*). This stability has fostered great confidence in the market, and Thais flock here from all over to put their money into gold rings and chains. If things go well, they will later exchange them for heavier ones; if things go badly, the Chinese have considerately opened plenty of pawn shops along the street. As one of their proverbs says: 'We don't mind who holds the head of the cow as long as we can milk it.'

It is thus fitting that just inside Chinatown, squashed between the junctions of New Road and Yaowaraj Road and Hualumphong Railway Station, should sit the most celebrated example of the goldsmith's art: the Golden Buddha. One of the prime tourist attractions of Bangkok, this impressive image is housed in the unprepossessing surroundings of Wat Trimitr, one of the least attractive *wats* in the whole country. At least the story behind the image is more glamorous than its present home. Some years ago when the East Asiatic Company was extending the port of Bangkok, workmen came across a huge stucco Buddha image, weighing five and a half tons and standing, or rather sitting, almost eleven feet high. Brought to Wat Trimitr, on the night before it was due to be installed in its new chapel, the image was soaked by a monsoon shower. The next day, while being moved, it fell to the ground, the softened stucco cracked and a golden gleam was revealed. The outer covering carefully removed, the image was found to be solid gold. It had probably been disguised to hide its real value from the invading Burmese in the eighteenth century. Several other sizeable gold images have been discovered treated in this way, and one wonders how many more are still hidden beneath their stucco skins.

The image belongs to the Sukhothai school of the thirteenth to the fifteenth centuries, a period generally considered the apex of Thai artistic achievement, but to my mind, with its brilliant metallic sheen and outflung chest tapering to a wasp-like waist, the figure has a brittle quality, quite devoid of that softly indrawn spirituality that infuses so many of its less illustrious contemporaries. To be sure, the setting does not help: a small, bright, modern room, lit by cheap light fittings that reflect off the tan-coloured linoleum. The Golden Buddha deserves better.

I never visit Wat Trimitr without remembering an occasion
some years ago when I was leading a group around Bangkok.
Coming down the steps here I noticed a couple of members of the
party, young American bankers, discussing something with
obvious interest. I wandered over, wondering in my professorial
way if they had started to appreciate the glory of Buddhist art, or
the subtlety of its teachings. No such luck. They were calculating
the current market value of the Golden Buddha.

Perhaps I should have taken them out of Chinatown, across
Rajadamnoen Klang Avenue and behind the Suksaphan store.
For it is here, not, as one might expect, in the Street of the
Goldbeaters (Tanon Tee Tong), that one can still see the gold
beaters at work. These muscular young men pound away at
wafers of pure gold half an inch square, sandwiched together
between pads of buffalo hide. Each sandwich contains about 500
wafers separated by greaseproof paper such as I remember from
my mother's kitchen. The trick is to keep pounding without
stopping for several hundred blows, as this continued assault
heats the gold up and spreads it out into its final shape, about four
inches across. Each flattened piece is then cut up into several
squares of finest gold leaf, which are sold, singly or in booklets, to
the faithful outside the temple. Applying the gold leaf to images is
one of the principle ways of offering worship and simultaneously
gaining merit. I have to admit I don't know the market value of
these booklets, but I do know they make lovely souvenirs.

Although there are markedly less smiles per street here than in
any purely Thai neighbourhood, Chinatown is a cheerful enough
place during its festivals, all of which serve the twin aims of
Chinese piety: ensuring the material continuity of the family and
appeasing that vast celestial bureaucracy which is the Chinese
pantheon. The New Year is the most important of these festivals,
and it is evident a week beforehand, with preparations in full
swing all over the city. During the three to five days of the actual
festival, Chinese housewives flock to the temples to offer whole
roast suckling pigs to the gods, whereas New Year's Eve sees
business for once come to a halt as the boss treats all his
employees to a slap-up feed. On the pavements and in the

shadows of the shops people can be seen spreading offerings of food, drink, incense and candles, then bowing low to the spirits of the passing year. Straight after New Year comes Lantern Day, primarily a religious celebration, when red and gold lanterns are hung out and little lions are made out of white sugar, while the family visits the temple to see if the signs are auspicious for the coming year. A little later on Cheng Meng Day, the streets are full of groups going to the cemetery with baskets of presents to offer at the tombs of their ancestors. Cemeteries are again visited *en masse* in the middle of July, when offerings are made to the ancestral spirits and the family graves are swept. The mid-autumn Moon Festival honours women; food and goods are spread out for the Moon Goddess who is believed to come forth to bless her sex. The final annual festival is the Winter Festival, celebrated on 25 November, when the family gets together for a feast. The proceedings are also visited by the household gods, who report back to heaven on the family's goings-on over the previous year, so sweets are lavishly provided to sweeten their tongues.

There is a feeling of abundance too at the very heart of Chinatown, the riverfront section of Sam Pheng. This areas was first developed at the end of the eighteenth century, when Rama 1 discovered that the site of his proposed Grand Palace was already occupied by a Chinese merchant community. He persuaded them to leave their homes and settle here, a little downriver from where his Palace now stands. At the foot of the Memorial Bridge on the Bangkok side is Pak Klong Market – a gargantuan wholesale market for fresh produce in a sprawl of cavernous buildings and umbrella-shaded stands. It was set up in 1953 to relieve the area around Wat Po, as part of the municipal authorities' unending battle to clear the streets of anarchic vendors. The market is a sensory delight and photographer's paradise, especially in the early morning when the goods are being unloaded from the river. The flowers are overwhelming. If you want a carload of orchids and still have change from 500 *baht*, this is your place: purple Pompadours, fleshy pink and yellow Vandas, spindly Scorpions, feathery Caesars – they are all here in profusion. Or you can just pick and choose from the necklaces, bands, wreaths, bracelets, brooches, stars, and, yes, flowers, made of flowers within flowers within flowers. Wriggling frogs, shrimps and squids in pink translucent heaps and miniature crabs with glistening white bellies cover stalls guarded by great spreads of smoked eels fanned above the pavements, speared between two bamboo staves. As well as all the fruit that one might expect from an oriental market, much of it familiar in recent years to European shoppers, there are varieties here whose very names are an Epicurean experience – pomelo, mangosteen, sapota, durian, rambutan – all heaped up in baskets that overflow like fragrant cornucopia. Some of these exotic edibles are still grown over the river in family plots in Thonburi, once full of orchards. The spice sections, too, have unusual items, such as *kha* – a rainbow-fleshed type of ginger, distant and unlikely relative of the banana, of which, incidentally, Thailand has eighteen varieties. *Kha* is used extensively in fish soups, one of the specialities of Bangkok cuisine. Dried lime skins (*makrood*) are another staple spice, the olive-like *makork* augments many chilli sauces, and the small fiery green berries (*makhua puang*), which are part of the aubergine family but look deceptively like peas, are an important ingredient of the typical Thai curry. Best of all is lemon grass (*takrai*) which adds the subtlest *frisson* of citron to many soups and dishes, leaving a clean, aromatic aftertaste that is, for me, a flavour quintessentially Thai.

Bangkok is humanised by her markets. They are well worth a visit, and will teach you more about the country than a thousand souvenir shops. Tewes Market, tucked away in a relatively quiet corner of the city near the National Library at the river end of Krung Kasem Road, specialises in flowers and plants; Pratunam, a huge rambling area over both sides of Ratchprarop Road, is famous for clothing and fabrics (many Indians trade here); the Sanam Luang bookstalls on the north-east corner of the ground offer a wide selection of secondhand books and magazines in Thai and English. At the Grand Palace end of this market are a few stalls specialising in aphrodisiacs – strange salves and potions, murky bottles containing pickled worms, insects and heaven knows what else. The vendors here have developed a graphic hand language all their own to extol the virtues of their products.

One of the most intriguing markets, at Wat Rachanada opposite the Golden Mount, is the Amulet Market, a dim, cramped and cluttered area offering magical protection against anything that might inadvertently befall one. Amulets play a vital part in the Thai psychological life, and most men will wear or carry some sort of protection against accidents, impotence, bullet or knife attacks. Most common are the miniature Buddha images, in bronze, stone, clay or gold. It is not uncommon to see people with several strung around their neck; they range from a few *baht* to several thousand *baht* for the antique or specially potent ones.

Less mysterious but more famous is the Week End Market, late of the Sanam Luang ground, but moved out to Chatachuk Park, near the airport, to make way for the bicentennial celebrations of 1982. Old Bangkok hands lament its passing, saying it has lost its former atmosphere. To begin with the new 29-acre drive-in plot did have a sterilised feel to it, with its cement floor and its signposted alleys. But it has mellowed over the years and assumed its own character, and its 6000 stalls still offer the most astonishing range of goods and services, from faith healers to fighting fish. It is very popular; an average Saturday or Sunday will see about 100,000 people thronging through. Not all of these are buying. Many are simply pursuing one of the favourite Thai pastimes, known as *pai-tio*, the nearest translation being, I suppose, 'wandering around'. This aimless but interested strolling, people-watching, taking the air, is a vital part of the social life of a people who find the desire for solitude well-nigh incomprehensible. Thais love to see and be seen, and at any given moment, a high proportion of the Thais you see out and about, unless they look *very* purposeful, will probably be indulging in a bit of *pai-tio*. Although the nostalgic complain, some people are relieved the market has moved from the Sanam Luang. Among these should be counted the sanitary department workers, who no longer have to clean up on a Monday morning, the lovers who like to enjoy a little romantic *pai-tio* hand-in-hand across the grass, and all those who value a week-end breathing space that relieves

congestion and sets off the vista of the Grand Palace. Not least of
the grateful must be the tamarind trees that ring the oval ground.
After the market moved more than two hundredweight of hooks
and nails were removed from their long-suffering trunks and
branches.

The Sanam Luang ('royal ground') is the centre of the old royal
Bangkok. At its southern end stand the three structures which
constitute the symbolic and historical heart of the capital: the
Grand Palace, and two adjacent temples Wat Po and Wat Phra
Keo, the latter better known as the Temple of the Emerald
Buddha. Here at last is the Thailand of *The King and I*: a clutch of
gilded and sparkling spires, visible equally from river or land, that
rise majestic and mysterious over high white walls, promising
fantasy and intrigue in equal measure. Normally this fairy-tale
skyline is set against the brilliant blue of the Bangkok heavens but
now, in early May, the sky is a dull grey-green of solid yet
indistinguishable cloud as the hot season swelters on. There have
been intermittent evening showers of late, but it is another month
before the rains will really come to clear the air. Entry is both
expensive by Thai standards (100 *baht*) and selective; only *farangs*
have to pay. A young Englishman ahead of me, armed against the
unpredictable weather with rolled umbrella and brogues, is
loudly contesting this discrepancy, drawing a comparison with
the egalitarian entrance fees of the Tower of London. (This is not
wholly appropriate, Wat Phra Keo is, after all, a place of worship
and pilgrimage for some very poor people.) The uniformed
attendant's smile is as adamantine as it is polite, 'You no like, you
no come.'

The Temple of the Emerald Buddha is the repository of the
most revered image in the kingdom and is the showpiece of
Bangkok. A dazzling and closely packed display of brilliantly
embellished buildings, the compound is a riot of colour spread
over hard gilded surfaces and ceramic and mirrored tilework.
There is no real marriage of form and content here, rather an art
of surfaces, an art of decoration, a polychrome aesthetic that
clothes the sacred in layer upon glittering layer and expresses
adoration through a process of unrestrained accumulation. Here

the Thai love of brilliance meets the Hindu-Khmer doctrine of the temple as the earthly palace of the gods. The result is a world imbued with magical influences, heavy with the sweet scent of jasmine and sandalwood joss sticks, tinkling with the sound of wind chimes hanging from the elegantly upturned eaves. This sacredotal Disneyland is entered through a gate set in cloisters whose inner walls carry murals depicting the *Ramakien*, the Thai version of the Indian *Ramayana* epic. Executed in Rama 3's time, and restored fifty years ago with the unhappy introduction of such Western conventions as perspective and 'tasteful' colours, the bold integrity of the originals has been destroyed. The courtyard, coolly flagged in grey and white marble, is watched over by fearsome *yakshas* – fifteen-foot-tall guardians armoured in brilliantly painted stucco. Their bulbous stares must immobilise all but the most recalcitrant demons.

Today the place is especially busy as crowds are already gathering to witness the arrival of the Crown Prince to present new robes to the monks in honour of Visakha Puja. The courtyard is filled not only with pilgrims and sightseers, but saffron-robed monks wearing an extra piece of orange cloth, like a padded sash, around the waist as ceremonial dress. Pavilions and pigeons, bells and offering bowls, pinks, greens, yellows, blues mingle together. It is all very clean, with none of that barnyard atmosphere found in the temples of Bali or Nepal.

Three of the Kingdom's most important buildings stand next to each other on an elevated platform. First to catch the eye is a gleaming golden dome with ringed spire, a *chedi*, modelled on those at the Royal Chapel of Ayutthaya, Wat Chedi Si Sanphet.

Next to this smoothly sheathed monument stands a square pavilion (*mondop*), which in most temples would house a Buddha image or relic. Here the *mondop* was built as a library to hold the Tripitika, the sacred scriptures, which repose in a mother-of-pearl casket within.

Lastly comes the Royal Pantheon building (Phra Thepidon) containing the lifesize statues of the first eight kings of the Chakri dynasty. It is open only each 6 April, Chakri Day, when its small interior is filled with subjects silently prostrating before the likenesses of their former rulers. The Pantheon is covered in blue and red tiles, pointed with gilded capitals and carved, gilded gables, and topped by a spire known as a *prang*. This derives from the Hindu-Khmer dynasties of Cambodia, who governed much of the country from the eleventh to the thirteenth centuries, and symbolises Mount Meru, the sacred mountain at the centre of the universe. So great was Khmer influence that Rama 4 had a model of their royal temple at Angkor Wat placed behind the gilded *chedi* as an inspiration to his people. Outside the Pantheon building stand gilded *kinnaras*, the mythological creatures half human, half bird, that so eloquently express the soaring spiritual aspiration of Thai art. Everything here tends upwards – spires, finials, slender columns, curved eaves, roof peaks – expressing the traditional and Thai view of life as an ascending hierarchy of perfection.

All of this finery is but a preparation for the centrepiece of the complex: the Emerald Buddha. Ever since its first recorded appearance in fifteenth-century Chiang Rai, this image that has become a symbol of the country has been believed to possess magical powers. When the King of Chiang Mai tried to install the Buddha in his own capital, the elephant carrying it refused to take the road to Chiang Mai, and ended up in Lampang. As the beast refused to move any further, the king accepted the omen and had a temple built to accommodate the image. Further travels took it eventually to Vientiane in Laos, from where the future Rama 1 captured it and brought it back to Bangkok. Thus the image became a symbol of the new dynasty and the new capital, and indeed much of Rama 1's popular support stemmed from his association with the little green figure. Even today the monarch approaches the Emerald Buddha at the start of each season and carefully wraps a robe around its shoulders; a gold and diamond tunic for the summer, a gilded robe flecked with blue drops for the rainy season and one of heavy gold chain encased in enamel to keep it warm throughout the cool time of year. Outside the entrance the faithful take thimble-sized cups of gold or silver filled with consecrated water, hold them between their hands as they *wai* then drink the water smoothing the last few drops over

5 Detail from the spire of the Dusit Maha Prasad, an audience hall built in 1789 as part of the Grand Palace, Bangkok. The figure is Phra Krut, the mythical bird that is the symbol of the Chakri dynasty

6 The Aisawan Tippaya Asna pavilion built in the late 19th century in the grounds of Bang Pa-In, a former summer palace of the royal family, 12 miles south of Ayutthaya

7 Buddha images in laterite and stucco from the 14th-century garrison town of old Kamphang Phet, 'City with Diamond Walls'

their face or head – the most spiritual part of the body. The interior of the *bot* is vast – rising sixty feet to a ceiling of red and dull gold, a relief after the brightness of newly restored gilt outside. The walls are peopled with lovely murals. Perhaps a hundred worshippers sit silently on the floor, legs tucked under them, absorbing the presence. Here sanctity is compounded by remoteness, for the Emerald Buddha is only about $2\frac{1}{2}$ feet high, sitting nearly forty feet up on banked tiers of gold platforms like an imperious child god, ensconced in a glass cabinet that tapers away to a gold finial and is flanked by the sacred nine-tier parasols. To many a foreign visitor, this jewel set in the heart of Bangkok may initially be a disappointment; it is too small to be seen clearly, not even emerald but probably a type of jasper and photography is strictly forbidden. But there is something very special about the place if you take the time to sit quietly and absorb the atmosphere. So much respect has been afforded this small object that has held a whole country under its thrall for centuries. Even today the great majority of Thais would ascribe it magical properties and view it with reverential awe. The Emerald Buddha is strength concentrated, the subtle energy of the seed, the taming power of the small. A tiny statue in a huge room, holding court aloofly above a throng containing highest and lowest alike, united in their submission. This alone is a type of magic.

And so to the Grand Palace, adjacent to the temple. Much of this is closed to the public, and viewing restricted to the outside. Of the three principal buildings, the first is the Amarin Winichai Hall, a reception hall with fine painted walls and ceiling, still sometimes used today when the King receives the credentials of foreign envoys or presents awards to government officials. At such occasions the throne is concealed by a curtain from the audience below until the monarch has taken his place when, with a fanfare, the curtain is drawn and Bhumipol the Great is revealed in all his majesty. Next comes the Chakri Maha Prasad, the royal residence, built by Rama 5 (Chulalongkorn) and finished in 1882 to coincide with the centenary of the dynasty. Designed by a British architect in the style of the Italian Renaissance, with a

central balcony and wide approach stairway, the Palace is topped
by a traditional Thai roof, that rises in levels to three seven-tiered
spires. Thais have dubbed this curious hybrid 'the *farang* with the
chada' ('the foreigner with the Thai dancer's headdress'). It is said
that the xenophile Chulalongkorn wanted a totally European
building, but deferred to the entreaties of the more traditional of
his advisers to include at least a roof of indigenous style. The Thai
roof was put to Thai use as well. Under its central spire rest ashes of
the eight Chakri kings to date, while those of principal members of
royal houses are under the other two.

Lastly comes the Dusit Maha Prasat Throne Hall. It was built in
1789 on the site of an earlier building struck by lightning and, like
so many of Thailand's wooden structures, destroyed by fire.
Among the firefighters was Rama 1 himself, who helped carry his
throne to safety. It is a cruciform building, with its gilded nine-tier
roof supported by mythical birds (*kruts*) and an elegant pavilion in
front, where the monarch dismounted from his elephant and
changed robes before proceeding inside. There is a unity to this
building that is emphasised by the mixed blood of its neighbour.
The Dusit Maha Prasat was used for special ceremonies, especially lying in state. Queen Saowapa, who was married to Rama 5
when she was sixteen and served as his first queen for fifteen years,
dying in 1919, spent no less than seven months here in a golden urn
awaiting the astrologically auspicious time for her cremation.

Perhaps the past of the Grand Palace is more interesting than its
present. The buildings I have just described, set in their neat lawns
with pruned trees and gold-plated street lamps from
nineteenth-century Europe, form part of what was known as the
'Outside'. Behind them lay the hidden and mysterious 'Inside', the
harem quarters. Malcolm Smith, an Englishman who was the royal
physician in the late nineteenth century describes the 'Inside' thus:

> The harem was a town complete in itself, a congested network of
> houses and narrow streets, with gardens, lawns, artificial lakes
> and shops. It had its own government, its own institutions, its
> own laws and law courts. It was a town of women, controlled by
> women.

Chief of these female controllers was a fearsome character known as the 'Directress of the Inside'. Under her were various officials in charge of the minor wives, serving maids, and the kitchens. She also ran the police force, an all-women squad dressed in blue *phaasins* and white jackets with a cream-coloured scarf across the breast. When anyone of importance entered the precincts they would run ahead and warn the people to crouch on the ground in respect. At night they patrolled the streets with lamps and torches. Their main duty was to guard the gates and to accompany and supervise the activities of any men who entered this closed world. These might be workmen or doctors, or the royal princes, allowed to live there until they reached puberty. The only man who lived in the 'Inside' was the King.

The population of the 'Inside' was probably over 3000, about a tenth of those on the royal payroll. Such a number must have led to considerable oppressiveness, especially when one considers the heat and lack of sanitation – all refuse, human and otherwise, had to be carried out in pails. Each queen had her own household of between 200 and 300 women, and her ladies-in-waiting also had their own servants. Each minor wife had a separate establishment and retinue, which would increase if and when she became a mother. But it is the figures for royal wives and children that are most astonishing today. According to the *Chronicle of the House of Chakri*, the official dynastic history, the first five kings of the dynasty fathered between them a total of 325 children and had an average of thirty-five wives, though the names of wives who had no children merit no mention. The result of such energetic polygamy was an enormously extended royal family and the most intricate system of hierarchichal status and title in the world, a fact that both catered to and perpetuated the Thai love of social gradations. Many of these ranks remain today. Once married to the king there was no divorce and no re-marriage when he died, but there was lifelong security, for no woman was ever banished from the 'Inside'. When out of favour or bereft of her erstwhile charms (of which blackened teeth and short hair brushed up into a tuft played a considerable part) she was relegated to the sexual Siberia of the apartments known as the 'Yellow Rooms'.

King Mongkut was the first monarch to allow his wives to leave
the palace precincts, but the privilege was not much exercised in
his time. Later kings followed his lead, but if a wife did leave, it
was with express permission and chaperone, and when she
returned an exact report was sent to the king, detailing her
timings, who she had met and where she had been. Clandestine
affairs were hardly possible, though there are records of one or
two that took place in the Palace itself, with fatal consequences for
both parties.

Closely confined though they were, the women of the 'Inside'
seem to have led a pleasant enough life, though their sense of
female solidarity would not, in modern eyes, compensate for their
lack of freedom. Siamese women, certainly when compared to
their Hindu or Muslim sisters, have always enjoyed a relative
degree of liberty after marriage and compared to this, the ladies of
the 'Inside' were indeed restricted. But even Anna Leonowens,
who was strongly opposed to polygamy, could not discern in these
women any longings to escape from the gilded cage in which they
spent their lives:

> The ladies of the harem amuse themselves in the early and late
> hours of the day by gathering flowers in the garden, feeding the
> birds in the aviaries and goldfish in the ponds, arranging
> bouquets, singing songs, dancing to the music of the guitar,
> listening to their slaves reading, strolling with their little ones
> through the parks and parterres and especially in bathing.
> When the heat is less oppressive they plunge into the waters of
> the pretty, retired lakes, swimming and diving like flocks of
> brown water-fowl.

Just south of the Grand Palace is the oldest and largest temple
in the city, Wat Po. It dates from the sixteenth century, but really
came into prominence at the time of the founding of modern
Bangkok, as a centre of learning and education. It was the
country's first university, and is still the place for treatment and
research in herbal medicine as well as Thai massage – the 'real
thing' its practitioners hasten to tell you, wary of Bangkok's
reputation in this respect. People flock here for treatment each

afternoon and many come to learn the ancient skills. Geological lessons were given by the mounds of stones dotted around the courtyards and many of the inscriptions deal with such diverse topics as archaeology, astronomy and military science, as well as the usual Buddhist teachings. The compound is huge and rambling, including a very large collection of Buddha images, chapels (*vihans*), an old library, a schoolroom for the teaching of Buddhism and over ninety *chedis*, some containing ashes, some studded with pieces of Chinese porcelain. Shaded by mimosas and displaying a mixture of Buddhist, Chinese and Hindu influences, Wat Po is rightly considered one of the 'musts' of Bangkok. It is also a place to pick up some of the most attractive souvenirs found in Thailand: rice paper stone – rubbings of the reliefs depicting the *Ramakien* epic engraved on the balustrades of the main chapel.

The centre of attraction here is the famous Reclining Buddha, a form of the Master especially popular in Thailand. Despite the Thai love of relaxation, the reclining posture represents not, as so often supposed, a spiritual siesta, but the Buddha's death. This is the largest such image in the country, measuring 150 feet from the face, austere and rather quizzical in the Bangkok style, to the soles of the feet. The feet of mortals are ritually unclean, but Buddha's feet are worshipped all over the land. Here the soles are ornamented in mother-of-pearl and divided into 108 panels that display the auspicious signs of the faith. Daily life goes on everywhere around this colossus, down to the red pay-phone and the lottery tickets that share his sanctuary.

Back across the Sanam Luang, originally the royal cremation ground, are several important buildings. First comes Silapakorn University, a former palace now the home of the Humanities. Past the adjacent pink National Library lies Wat Mahathat, which, like the six other temples of the same name in the country, is believed to contain a relic of the Buddha. Despite such eminence, the compound is crowded and the buildings undistinguished. King Mongkut of the eighty-one wives spent many years as abbot here; nowadays it is a centre for the reformed group of Mahanika monks he founded, distinguished by their rust-coloured robes and bare feet, and is a centre for meditation.

Between the *wat* and the National Museum lies Thammasat
University specialising in Law and Economics and known for its
radical students. The demonstrations of 1973 and 1976 were
born here. Both were violently suppressed; perhaps as an
acknowledgement of official over-reaction, the dead from the
former uprising were given a royally sanctioned cremation on the
Sanam Luang itself.

Next to the University is another former palace, now the
National Museum. It has a superb collection of Thai art, though
labelling is sparse and the lack of air-conditioning is a handicap.
There are guided tours, adequate if not inspiring, in several
languages and covering various aspects of the culture. The
architectural highlight of the collection is the Buddhaisawan
Chapel, Rama 2's private hall of worship. It has very beautiful
murals and a highly considered Buddha image from the
Sukhothai period. Nearby is a collection of the chariots that
carried the royal corpses to cremation. Before its recent renova-
tion this gallery was an eerie, cobwebbed place, but ghoulishness
has given way to fresh paint. As recently as 1986 there was a
spectacular and traditional funeral procession for the Queen of
Rama 7, that wended its way for two hours through the heart of
old Bangkok. Drummers, trumpeters, conch players and royal
pages flanked the chariots, while nine battalions and all the major
figures of the royal family accompanied the cortège to the Sanam
Luang. Here four cannons fired 300 times in salute, and the pyre,
towering ninety feet high as an ornate model of the sacred Mount
Meru, centre of the universe, was lit by the King himself.

Bangkok's modern palaces are its hotels, serving a new breed of
privileged. An inexpensive workforce, a tradition of graceful
service and a natural sense of style combine to make some of them
very special. Most celebrated of all is the Oriental, a member of
that most stylish of hotel chains: the Hong Kong-based Mandarin group. Although over-exposure and the press of tour
groups have brought changes in the last few years, the Oriental is
still one of the great institutions of Bangkok. Located on the river,
not far from the area that was the first European enclave, it enjoys

one of the most attractive views in the city, looking across the Chao Phya to Thonburi. Small by international standards and genuinely friendly, the ambience here is not so much that of a hotel but a club, where the guest feels at home yet elegantly attended. The hotel's riverside terrace is the most pleasant place in the city to breakfast or relax in the early evening and watch the sun go down. Here the staff glide past with never less than a smile and never more than a single item on their tray at once – a gold-rimmed jug of cream for the strawberries, a basket of toast wrapped in a napkin of the palest duck-egg blue, a sprig of white orchid for a table setting. Thailand is a country where service does not yet connote servility, and nothing better epitomises the attitude the Oriental represents than its laundry service. Not only is it prompt and immaculate – one gets blasé about such rarities here – but each shirt is returned to your raw silk room wrapped in pink-and-white tissue in its individual box, bound with a purple ribbon and fastened with a matching orchid. With such treatment, even the humblest traveller is made to feel like a monarch.

4

The Fallen Angels

Recently Mr Nut has been looking at me a little strangely. I thought perhaps I had offended him by breaking some invisible but vital rule of the intricate Thai etiquette, though reassured myself that by now he must be so used to *farangs* and their clumsy ways that nothing I could say or do would shock him that much. Still, in a country where to blow your nose in public is the height of bad manners, you never know. The problem started a couple of nights ago, when on my way late back to my hotel I bumped into him outside the Miami.

'You no have lady?' he asked, obviously disappointed at seeing me alone. 'Why you no have lady? Lady no ploblem.'

'Oh, you know, working, working, no time,' I mumbled, unwilling to get into the complexities of why I was unaccompanied, doubtlessly incomprehensible to his straightforward mind.

'Mmm,' he replied, obviously not convinced, 'lady no ploblem in Thailand, lady good.'

Today, after a couple of journeys of unaccustomed solemnity, it finally comes out. 'Why you no go Pattaya Beach?' he asks with sudden and unaccustomed aggression, referring to the sun, sea 'n' sex resort down the coast of the Gulf of Siam.

'I'm going next week,' I reply.

He looks relieved. 'And why you no go sex-show?' he continues, warming to his theme. 'Sex-show good: see lady and ping-pong ball, fire-eating, banana, open cola bottle, boy-girl make love.' His eyes roll with anticipation. 'Sex show OK, no ploblem, start eight o'clock, not far from here, I take you.' A pause and his jolly moon face clouds over. 'Only two sex-show left now Bangkok,' he concludes in a sad tone.

I realise Mr Nut thinks I'm a bit soft, going to all these temples and museums. Culture is all very well, but . . . So we agree that this evening I'll go on the town a bit, and enjoy some *sanuk*, like any other self-respecting tourist. First stop is the Oriental for a drink overlooking the river. Then, a couple of minutes across New Road brings me into Silom Road, the business heart of the city. This financial artery, straight and tree filled, is one of Bangkok's more attractive streets, and is its Wall Street, Bond Street, Park Lane and Fleet Street all rolled into one, with a couple of Chinese cemeteries and a Hindu temple thrown in for good measure. Even those visitors staying in the least salubrious parts of town will probably come down to Silom, for off its smoked-glass chic runs the most notorious vein of Bangkok's pervasive nightlife, Patpong Road. Now, in the early evening, there is a delicious stir of expectancy in the balmy air. All over the downtown area hundreds of neatly dressed girls wait at the bus stops, some going back home from the office, others on their way to unknown destinations and assignations. Overhead the birds are wheeling and gathering for the night, lining the wires that skein the skyline of this insomniac city, and everywhere the day shift, its energy spent, is giving way to its nocturnal successor, fresh and full of vigour for the hours ahead. Daytime roadside markets are metamorphosed into night-time food stalls and open-air 'noodle shops' – chairs and tables set up on the pavement where you can see the food sizzling in front of you and eat well and safely for under £1. In Patpong, the girls are arriving for work. They too are smartly dressed with their freshly ironed clothes and plastic handbags. Only the *farangs* allow themselves sartorial sloppiness in this city, a fact the Thais are used to by now, but still do not understand or like. The Bangkok phrase for the back-pack, budget travellers translates as 'bird-shit tourists', presumably because they have fallen from a great height. Many of the girls take their evening meal in the street, while around their feet the pavement vendors spread out paintings, watches, tee-shirts. Then, with darkness beginning to fall, the neon lights wink on one by one, the music starts up and the girls filter inside the clubs and bars. Another night of possibilities is set to begin.

In fact, there are now two Patpong Roads, numbered One and Two, and running parallel. With an irony entirely appropriate to this city of contradictions, they are situated right across Silom

Road from the high walls of the Carmelite convent with its strictly enclosed complement of twenty nuns. Outside the joints the girls cajole the passers-by with well-practised enticement. Inside, mottled by the flashing lights and pounded by the loud music, some gyrate their smooth young bodies on platforms, counters and stages that place their crotches just above the customers' heads, whilst others sit at the tables and booths around the walls, encouraging the customers to buy drinks, and pidgining their way through the ritual conversations, jokes and responses. It's all loud, garish and metallic. Every so often, more than a drink is sold, and a girl vanishes behind the scenes, reappearing in her street clothes to leave early with a man who has paid the bar a fee on top of what he has agreed with her. And so it goes on, night after night, at La Chérie, Pussy Galore, Love Nest and the hundred other bars, clubs, and discos that constitute this pulsating part of town.

Most of this stroboscopic seduction proceeds with a professional and detached cheerfulness, the sordidness alleviated by a natural Thai grace that is not entirely obliterated even here. The bars change names and hands with bewildering rapidity and the girls do likewise, moving from place to place in search of better money, more variety or escape from feuds and quarrels. Though many of them look little more than kids, by twenty they are streetwise women of the world, with a strong sense of economic reality and mutual solidarity. Despite an occasional jealous squabble over the lucrative attentions of a customer, the bar-girls of Bangkok display a protective concern for each other which acts as an invisible shield against a foreign and male world they distrust yet depend on. Suddenly on the dot of one o'clock, the blaring music stops and the flashing lights are dimmed. The girls dive behind the bar, or into a back room, to strip unselfconsciously and swap their skimpy bikinis for street clothes. They leave the bar rapidly, hopping into the fleet of waiting *tuks-tuks* and taxis, some with customers who have agreed to the going rate of 500 *baht* for the night, others in groups to eat and chat in the nearby noodle shops before heading home.

Habitués complain that nowadays Patpong has lost its edge, and that international fame as a tourist spot has brought a middle-aged cosiness and self-parody that was never there in the raunchy days a dozen years ago. It is certainly true that if topless go-go girls, ladies doing athletic things with fishes or rentable overnight companions are not your cup of tea, there is fare to be sampled that is more in keeping with Benidorm than Sodom and Gomorrah. Take, for example, Bobby's Arms, a traditional English pub run, like many of the clubs, by an ex-pat, complete with polished wood and beer tankards and a band thumping out trad jazz from an innocent era before most of the Patpong girls were even born. It's good clean fun if you can find it, tucked away on the first floor of a car park of all places. But it is still also true that you can get whatever you want in and around Patpong and although the days of such carefree indulgence must be numbered, the message doesn't seem to have sunk home yet.

Bangkok's nightlife is a compelling attraction, even for those not normally drawn to such things, and an atmosphere of partying is ever present, not confined to any one enclave, not even the three or four areas – Patpong, Sukumvit, New Petchburi Road – where the joints are concentrated. There is perhaps a pause for breath between 6 a.m. when the unsuccessful girls from the all-night coffee shops finally call it a day and return home, and 8 a.m. when the successful ones can be seen leaving the hotels heading for work or home for a few hours' rest. But there is never a break in the overall ambience of complicity, a knowingness that has seeped into the very fabric of this Asian Babylon and its economy, a sybaritic scent so pervasive that it cannot but affect the general atmosphere and social life.

Consider the facts. A survey conducted by Mahidol University in 1980 reported that in Bangkok alone there were 977 establishments – bars, clubs, disguised brothels (for prostitution has officially been illegal since 1960) – that provide 'special services' for their male customers. Added to these are the two dozen or more escort agencies, advertising openly and competitively, some of which have hundreds of girls and boys on their books, the marriage and 'introduction' agencies, and the untraceable freelancers. Many of the girls have full-time jobs and sell

themselves part-time to boost their earnings. A recent survey of
1000 massage girls caused a slight stir in the corridors of power
when it revealed that over one per cent of the interviewees were
moonlighting from government jobs!

Bangkok is an expensive city, ranked in 1980 by the American
Chamber of Commerce for Thailand as more costly to live in than
Washington. The fact that a massage girl or prostitute (the two
are not synonymous) can earn an average of 10,000 *baht* a month,
with the possibility of substantial bonuses, whereas a waitress or
factory employee might expect 800 *baht*, and a clerical worker
1300, explains how many girls who come to the city for other jobs
end up in the 'service industry'. Although a regular mainstream
job may seem to offer a longer and more secure working life, the
realities of the Thai market place often tend to militate against
this. Not a few employers follow a tradition of sacking their
female staff young, as they know that absenteeism from ill health
caused by bad working conditions will increase dramatically once
the woman is over thirty. This was especially the case in the textile
industry with its concomitant lung diseases and building workers
suffer a similar fate. In jobs where the 'image' matters, such as
a waitress or beautician, the demand for a girl drops off
remorselessly the older she gets. Most estimates agree that the
number of girls involved in prostitution at one level or another in
Bangkok is about 200,000; in the country as a whole at least twice
this. On top of all this Bangkok sports a widespread and
conspicuous gay scene. A quick glance at the entertainments page
in any of the papers reveals a profusion of gay clubs, bars, gyms
and saunas: 'Big Boy Cocktail Lounge', 'City Men Pub – We
cater to your needs', 'The Golden Cock . . . the more the
merrier', 'Adonis . . . where gallant hosts entertain you nightly'
and so on. All in all, the City of Angels reeks of sex.

If the oldest profession is universal, there is an aspect of it that
is particularly Thai, and that is the massage parlour. They are all
over the country, on the streets and in the hotels, ranging from
those grotty whorehouses where there is little pretence at
massage at all and the girls are bonded labour, to veritable palaces
of decadence, with uniformed flunkies to accompany you from

the car park, neon lights, fountains, bars and coffee bars, four or five hundred girls to choose from, and lavish rooms in a variety of décor. Some have the girls grouped according to prettiness, each group in a different costume. One offers massage, another massage and the 'whole works', a third dispenses with massage and gets straight down to the 'whole works'. Some parlours offer 'body massage' where the girl uses not just her hands but her whole body; others offer girls in tandem. The massage parlour is obviously very big business, but it should be remembered that massage-girls do not necessarily sell themselves. This freedom of choice grants them considerably more status in Thai eyes than the girls who accept all customers indiscriminately.

At about the same time the massage girl returns home after eight hours of sitting in an artificially lit fishtank with a number pinned to her chest awaiting business, Bangkok's second night-shift is clocking on for work: the girls in the all-night coffee bars. Compared to the profusion of clubs, there are not many of these establishments, but one of them is more famous than all the rest, and that is the Grace Hotel. It seems a fitting final port of call for my night on the town, and although Mr Nut has a romantic assignment elsewhere, he goes out of his way to drop me there, bidding me goodnight with a conspiratorial wink. Situated in the rich Arab ghetto that has sprung up around Soi Nana Nua at the beginning of Sukhumvit Road, the Grace is an ugly skyscraper towering above an area littered with Arab restaurants, groceries, banks and medical clinics. The shops, whose prices are as inflated as the self-esteem of their customers, all display notices in Arabic, and at one in the steamy morning the area is still humming with life. Touts of all descriptions and genders stroll the pavements, weaving in and out of the *tuk-tuks* and taxis. Above the quiet leafy lanes behind Sukhumvit, open fields until thirty years ago, tower several apartment blocks bristling with birthday cake domes and mock Moorish grille work, behind which the flats cost upwards of 40,000 *baht* a month. Inside the Grace this bizarre cultural mélange continues. The sprawling lobby is empty except for a few local girls sitting round, some of them, plump by Thai standards, kitted up for the part in long dresses, headscarves and heavy gold baubles, to mimic that overripe sumptuousness of the Middle East. Off the lobby there is a huge restaurant, where the male diners sit on the floor eating kebabs and watching a cabaret of belly dancing. Next to the restaurant is another lofty room, full of men, with billiards, snooker and ping-pong tables under cut-glass chandeliers. But through the lobby down into the basement lies the real Mecca: the coffee shop.

There are probably two hundred girls in this subterranean cavern – lining the long curved bar, draped around the pillars, lounging at the tables and wall-booths, clustered around the juke-box. The air is thick with cigarette smoke and erotic expectation in this seething pit of hungry eyes, watching and waiting in the semi-darkness. Some of the girls look like tarts, others look more like secretaries, some are dressed up, others nonchalant in jeans or shorts. Here and there sits an older woman, painted and weary, who must be a veteran from the Vietnam days and nights, while next to her may sit a nervous-looking fifteen-year-old. Every Thai ethnic and racial strain seems represented in this huge flesh market, every cut of feature, every shade of skin. Over in a far corner there is a crumpled looking girl, cocooned in the warmth of her dreams, nodding over a cold cup of coffee. I point her out to a girl standing next to me at the bar, who pulls a face and says 'Number 4 lady', referring to the type of heroin currently in favour with users. Not a few of the faces look strained and pinched, the result of the continued use of antibiotics as a preventative against the hazards of their trade. Some of the girls come here only occasionally when they need the money, others are regulars, though the Grace may lead to more than a one-night stand. Many girls find a *farang* companion and keep him company for his stay in the city, perhaps travelling around the country with him, and, who knows, maybe even ending up as his wife in far-off Düsseldorf or Hamburg. The clientele is as varied as the girls, but one thing is striking: there are no Thai men. The Grace has a reputation as the lowest of the low, the place for 'no-good' girls, it is strictly a *farang* scene. There are budget travellers, relaxed and cheerful in beach wear, who seem to treat the scene with a truly Thai light-heartedness, middle-aged businessmen, more intent, in freshly ironed safari suits and newly purchased silk shirts, and every so often the groups of northern Europeans, drunk and loud, or the sad lone drinker, lost in a fuddled isolation which sets him apart from Thais and *farangs* alike. And then there are the Arabs, floating past in their white robes like some unshaven, venal priesthood dedicated to the worship of mammon. But despite their money, the Arabs are not popular. Most of the girls avoid them, wrinkling up their snub noses in eloquent disgust at the very mention of the word. The coffee shop opinion is that they smell, and this is a very black mark with the fastidious Thais.

Each of the girls here has her story, unique yet a variation on a theme repeated all over this city. Lek tells me of her brutal husband who, when he got drunk, which was often, 'went boxing, *boxing*!' She is wide-eyed with indignation at the memory, punching her fist in the air to illustrate her point. At first I imagine a harmless addiction to the national sport, but it transpires she means he beat her up. Her friend Tum sums up her married life as: 'One husband, one me, life OK; one husband, many me, no OK.' Noi, from Korat, has two fatherless children to support, one Thai one half-American *farang*; Tui, from near Chiangmai, has a family dependent on her irregular remittances. Each story, culminates on the same rhetorical and plaintive note, spoken or unsounded: 'So what can I do? What can I do?' The answer, of course, is to come here to the Grace, and sit and wait with all the others. The regulars buy little books of tokens for food and drinks to avoid having to bother with loose change during the long hours of their nightly vigil. But as all the girls I speak to are quick to assure me, they have only been coming here for two or three months. Well, maybe five or six . . .

By 4 a.m. I have had enough of it all, and return on foot to my hotel. I need the walk to clear my head and get things in perspective. Contrary to Bangkok appearances and myths long circulated on the international tourist grapevine, Thai women are not at all promiscuous by nature. Warm hearted, relaxed, down to earth and humorous they are, free of sexual guilt within marriage they may be, but they belong to a people governed by a traditional conformity which expects modesty and decorum from women in their lives, and virginity when they marry. As a result, they are typically far more conventional in their dealings with the opposite sex than Westerners. Many a *farang* has asked a girl out in up-country Thailand only to have her turn up chaperoned by a friend; many a university student going to visit her male professor will take along a fellow student whose only function is to be there, and this is considered perfectly normal by all parties. The traditional bonds of family and religion mitigate strongly against permissiveness. In addition, much adult socialising revolves around the ritual segregation of the sexes; the men go out with the men and the women spend time with each other. Public propriety is especially important in Thai society at any level, no matter what may go on in private, thus the demeanour and behaviour of the 'Bangkok girls', as they are disparagingly known, is deeply shocking to the great majority of Thais. If they do seem tolerant of a situation that everyone realises is deeply ingrained, it is because tolerance is part of the Thai wisdom of accepting what is, rather than getting fruitlessly and impotently agitated about it. And yet, what the visitor may not initially realise is that prostitution has become an integral part of the overall economy of the country, an ineradicable feature of the social fabric, the disappearance of which would lead to considerable disruption. The girls of Patpong and the Grace are acting out of a strong sense of free choice and responsibility by engaging in an entrepreneurial move designed to sustain family units in a rural economy under increasing pressure. Many, though no doubt not as many as make the claim, are supporting parents or children back home, or paying for the education of younger family members. There are a number of things that can drive a marginal family over the financial edge – persistent drought, population pressure, un-scrupulous money-lenders or middlemen, the intrusion of outside groups that disrupt village equilibrium. A prime example of this last is the invasion of the big timber merchants who bribe local officials and indulge in illegal tree felling in the sure knowledge that the blame will fall on local peasants collecting their firewood. In the north-east, the poorest part of the country and along with the north the biggest supplier of girls to the cities, the problems are compounded by the chronic infertility of the soil and the presence of landless immigrants from Laos and Kampuchea. Within this scenario women are not just helpless dependents but puissant earning members of the family, with a clear sense of their responsibility. Many are recruited by older female relatives or friends already established in Bangkok's flesh trade. The smart clothes, city ways and apparent wealth of the procurers are often irresistible to pretty youngsters who see no way out of the cycle of village poverty. Ironically, this flaunted wealth may be only a show, maintained so as to avoid losing face on a visit home. Some parents, ground down by hardship, acquiesce in their daughter's prostitution, enjoying the new house and relatively comfortable standard of living it brings. Others turn a blind eye to what they must realise is happening. Not infrequently in recent years, government attempts to intervene in areas known to supply large numbers of girls to the 'service industry' have met with fierce resistance from the parents and families concerned. Exploited by agents some girls are, and in this they are like a proportion of prostitutes in any country, but it should be realised that many of them are responding in their own way to a problem which lays bare some of the shaky foundations on which the country's economic progress has depended.

Since the 1950s Thailand has steadfastly opted to reject the sort of tight economic planning and extensive controls that an emerging country might have been expected to follow in its desire to build up an indigenous manufacturing base. Instead, an aggressively free-market situation has been encouraged; international trade unrestricted and incentives offered to foreign and local investors to develop urban enterprises. What goods the country has produced have had to remain inexpensive to be competitive and the way chosen to ensure this was not price control but policies designed to divert investment from the countryside, thus simultaneously minimising the economic and political muscle of the farmers, the generators of the primary wealth of the country. A continually depressed rural sector can supply not only a huge 'reserve army' of cheap labour, but cheap food to feed it on. For the last twenty-five years incentives have been aimed at encouraging entrepreneurs to produce for export rather than develop a strong economic infrastructure. These exports – rice, rubber, tin, tapioca, corn, sugar – have been produced by a labour force that, by international standards, was considered 'docile'. Respect of authority is a strong and well-known trait of the Thai character, reinforced in this context, it must be said, by the high profile that the army has taken in Thai political life since the days of Pibul. More than seven out of ten Thais work on the land, yet, as a result of government strategy, more and more of them have ended up doing the same thing. The expansion of marketing and communications has not brought any real widespread development in terms of diversity, a broader-based economy or technological improvements. What benefits have accrued have been largely to the Central Plain, an easily accessible area and historically relatively prosperous anyway. For the north or north-east, or indeed anywhere at the end of a long dirt road or on the far side of a craggy hill, benefits have been slight. Those with existing social or geographical advantages may well have had them multiplied; the rest have been squeezed ever nearer the margin.

It is this priority of urban over rural investment that has spawned the growth of Bangkok, a city dominated by a small urban middle class monopolising Thailand's wealth and influence. Bangkok's supremacy is more than just that of a typical capital city. It now has a population of almost 6 million; the second most important city in the country, Chiangmai, a mere 120,000. Two important spanners have been thrown into the works of the Thai farmer: the American involvement in Vietnam (and thus Thailand) and the foreign tourist business, the latter blooming just as the former was fading. Both encouraged urban investment; both facilitated massive earning potential for rural female labour prepared to migrate to the cities. The relative scale of this earning can be astounding in terms of local expectations. In a country where the annual per capita income is about £550, a girl can earn as much in a couple of years on her back in the city as she can in a lifetime on her knees in the fields. I do not mean to imply, as some Thai intellectuals claim, that the sex business is solely the result of foreign exploitation. It is run by locals, including a large number of Chinese, and every Thai town has in addition to the establishments geared to the tourists, its local whorehouse, the vast majority of which have never been visited by a single *farang*. Throughout history Thai men who could afford it have had 'minor wives', in a polygamous situation that everyone has known about and accepted. Such a situation can easily shade off in modern times into a climate that accepts the role of the prostitute. And it is part of the Thai male's love of status and display that he be seen to have the leisure and money to indulge in extra-marital entertainment. Thus the system is geared to all income levels, from the urban labourer or taxi driver who might spend 50 *baht* in the crummiest brothel, to the businessman, government officer or foreign tourist who may spend 1000 *baht* in the swankiest. But it cannot be denied that the sudden influx of GI money and the tourist boom that followed hot on its heels was what established the current pattern. Tourist agencies, Thai and foreign, have unashamedly and often unsubtly sold sex as one of the country's principal attractions, especially in West Germany and Japan. The market has been very receptive. Moreover the tourist boom coincided with a weak Thai currency in the late 1960s and early 1970s, making the plentiful supply of commercial sex even cheaper. Thus, ironically, did cheap urban labour make its way into the foreign arena. The sex industry needs virtually no investment; the demand, both in Thailand and on the international circuit, is enormous. One out of every two visitors to Thailand is an unaccompanied male – far higher than to other tourist destinations – and although a hint of sexuality is never far from tourist promotion in many exotic countries, none of them has used it so blatantly and so consistently as the Land of Smiles.

My intention is not to strike a high moral tone over all this. People must do what they want, or feel they have to, with their bodies. Nor am I making explicitly political criticisms; how the Thais run their country is their business, not mine, and anyway, I am no economist. Prostitution, as metaphor or reality, is a fact of Thai life. It may well become a more important one in the future, not least because AIDS is knocking on the door of Asia. The spectre this conjures up, given the number of people involved, is horrifying.

Such sombre thoughts are interrupted by a double dose of the Bangkok bizarre. First, I come across the aftermath of an accident. Three cars – a taxi, a Toyota and a Citroën – are inexplicably jammed, rear to rear, at the side of the road. Two of the cars are locked tight together, whether the third rammed them, or was backed up later, I can't tell. The pavement is covered in broken glass, but there are no injured in sight. The Citroën has all of its wheels missing. A small crowd watches the proceedings with interest, while four or five people unload the Citroën through its large back window – now a gaping and jagged hole – of cartons and cartons of beer and bottle after bottle of Mekong Whisky.

Shortly after this I drop into the Ambassador Hotel to pick up an early morning copy of the *Bangkok Post*, that excellent English-language daily. I leave the hotel by its back doors into the car park, a large open space lined by trees and the cages of the hotel's miniature zoo and much frequented by ladies of the night. As I come down the steps, my attention is attracted by soft, seductive noises coming from the shadows. Wondering if I am being propositioned for the umpteenth time this evening, I wander over towards the sound to investigate. It transpires that the source of the gentle clucking and cooing is nothing more salacious than a flock of pink and white South American flamingos. I think it's time I left this city.

II

THE HEARTLAND

5

Beyond Bangkok

There are a number of places near Bangkok that can be seen in a day-trip from the city. Squarely on the tourist map is the famous floating market at Damnoen Saduak in Ratchaburi Province, about an hour's drive south-west of the capital. The road passes through an area of salt flats – an empty, waterlogged landscape dotted with white heaps – ghostly in the early morning light. The market is a remnant of what was once the commercial pattern of the country: sampans paddled by women in wide-brimmed straw hats, the long sleeves of their blue tops pulled down well over their hands to shield them from the sun, for like all Thais, the boat-women dislike dark skin. The boats are laden with fresh fruit, vegetables and meat; many of them are mobile kitchens, ready to cook whatever you might want. There is also a land-based extension to the market, selling manufactured goods. Sadly, this is growing rapidly under the impact of tourism, and plastic is fast replacing bamboo. But Damnoen Saduak is still a vital place, best visited in the early morning, and far superior to the floating market in Thonburi, which has already been ruined by over-exposure. Easily combined with Damnoen Saduak is one of the country's most important historical sites: the massive *chedi* at Nakhon Pathom, thirty-five miles west of Bangkok. This whole area was one of the earliest settlements in Thailand, populated since the fourth century BC by the Mons, an ethnic group originating in north-east India who still exist in a few scattered communities along the Chao Phya River. The *chedi* is believed to mark the spot where the teachings of Buddhism first arrived in Thailand, brought from India by missionaries dispatched by Emperor Ashoka, the Constantine of Buddhism, 2300 years ago. At this time, Nakhon Pathom was a capital of the ancient kingdom of Suvarnabhumi, the 'Golden Land', which stretched from

Burma to Vietnam, and south into modern Malaysia. Whether the teachings did arrive this early is open to question, but Nakhon Pathom has yielded a few Buddhist remains from the second century BC, and a great number from when it was the capital of the later, Dvaravati empire (sixth to eleventh centuries AD), itself stretching from Burma to Cambodia. These artefacts show that the Mons were the first people to break away from Indian artistic models and develop a Buddhist art uniquely South-East Asian. Though the origins of the *chedi* are lost in the past it is known that it was sacked by the Burmese in 1057, abandoned for hundreds of years, and finally restored when Rama 4 ascended the throne in 1851, the present dome being erected over the ruined original. Rama 5 continued the restoration, but even he didn't live to see the work completed. The town finally came to life again after the railway was built here in 1900; now it is a thriving centre of a fertile area famous for its bananas, coconuts, watermelons, oranges and custard apples.

As befits its historical and religious importance, the *chedi* is the largest in the Buddhist world, rising 400 feet to dominate the surrounding park and countryside, though the massiveness of the orange-tiled structure disguises its height. As a major centre of pilgrimage, it is a colourful place, especially during its three-day festival each November, when there are astrologers, entertainers, side-stalls and all the usual pilgrim paraphernalia.

Kanchanaburi, the main town of the province of the same name and about eighty miles north-west of Bangkok, is a prosperous little town set in the lush valley of the Mae Klong River, one of whose tributaries is the River Kwai. Its income derives from gemstones (especially the blue sapphires from the world-famous Bor-Ploy mines nearby), teak trading with neighbouring Burma, and above all sugarcane, that graceful plant whose silvery-lilac fronds turn plantations into shimmering seas of feathery softness each autumn. First established as a border defence against the Burmese by Rama 1, the modern Kanchanaburi has a restful and pleasant provincial atmosphere, unruffled by the trickle of tourists who visit. The Thais come largely for the many waterfalls that sprinkle the surrounding valleys, but the purpose of the visiting *farangs* is an altogether more sober affair. For despite the charms of the modern town, Kanchanaburi is notable chiefly for providing one of the very few rents in that seamless cloak of smiles which cocoons the average tourist's stay in Thailand. It may be hard to imagine now, but this was the site of the infamous Death Railway, borne by the Bridge over the River Kwai, that the Japanese had built by slave labour to provide a bridgehead into Burma for their unexpected and devastating advance west. The scale as well as the speed of the Japanese advance was astonishing, over three million cubic metres of rock had to be shifted, and almost nine miles of bridges built. The toll for such an ambitious project was terrible. It is estimated that over 12,000 Allied POWs and nearly 100,000 indented coolies, mainly from Indonesia and Malaysia, died while working on the railway, victims both of the ravages of dysentery, malaria and gangrene, and the brutalities of their captors. The hardships the prisoners underwent are tellingly documented in the JEATH museum adjacent to Wat Chaichunpon (JEATH being a rather unfortunate acronym of the countries involved: Japan, England, America and Australia, Thailand, Holland and, I presume, rhyming with 'death'), inspired and maintained by the energy of its chief monk, Phra Maha Tomson Tongproh. Unfortunately, my visit coincides with his absence, and I am left wondering at his historical concern to commemorate this particular piece of human folly and suffering, a concern which, in its naïve belief that mankind can learn from its mistakes, strikes me as being somehow more Christian than Buddhist. Whatever the inspiration, the museum, a bamboo hut (replicating the camp accommodation), does its job with sobering efficiency. It is filled with memorabilia, photographs and paintings documenting such horrors as the hacksaw operations performed without anaesthetic, the logs over the cesspits where the men squatted among the squirming maggots, and the *ad hoc* treatment of sitting in the river and letting the fish nibble away the worst of the puss and rotting flesh that, like the frilly tendrils of some virulent sea anemone, fringed a gaping and putrescent crater open to the bone beneath. The comments column in the museum's visitors' book is, for the most part, eloquently empty.

Yet the appalling conditions of the Kanchanaburi camp threw up heroes as well. One of them was the Australian surgeon, Edward 'Weary' Dunlop, a man of quiet courage and indomitable will who saved hundreds of lives against enormous odds, and was to the prisoners in Thailand what Frank Pantridge was to those on the Burmese side of the border – a source of hope and inspiration. Another was Bunpong Sirivij, a Thai who worked ostensibly as a river trader in eggs and bananas, but who risked his life daily to smuggle in life-saving drugs to Dunlop and his team. As a memorial to the triumph of human spirit over such adversity, a Dunlop/Bunpong medical exchange is getting underway between Thailand and Australia. It will send senior Australian surgeons to Thailand each year, and will enable Thai doctors to train in Australia.

My hired Toyota takes me along the river for a couple of miles to the actual Bridge: a functional structure of girdered sections on heavy concrete piers, inelegant and undistinguished. Absurdly perhaps, I am disappointed, expecting a bridge that would carry not just trains and pedestrians, but some of the weight of its terrible mythology. I have missed by a couple of weeks the *son et lumière* show mounted at the beginning of each December to commemorate the destruction of the original bridge by Allied bombs in 1945. By all accounts this is a highly dramatic spectacle much frequented by Thais who, perhaps betraying their Chinese blood, are easily lured by the prospect of fireworks. So has history slid inexorably into pageant. Throughout the rest of the year the river here provides the setting for a more typically Thai entertainment: floating restaurants which, in a lovely setting, serve excellent food and seemingly limitless quantities of drink.

A worthwhile stop on the way back into town is the Kanchanaburi War Cemetery. Immaculately maintained, it houses the named remains of 6932 Allied soldiers and an unknown number of unidentified dead, each nationality neatly in its own plot around the central monument. The tombstones are low, flat and the colour of earth, each bearing its poignant legend promising a heavenly reunion. This sombre chequered board of dun and green is very different from the Chinese cemetery adjoining, with its huge colourfully painted mausolea, yet they are united in their hope of consolation after death, and their utter ignorance of what it really promises. The visitors here are visibly shaken, sitting silent and pensive in the few patches of shade; it is a quiet, moving place whose powerful understatement touches even those too young to remember the horrors it commemorates.

A bridge of a different sort, from the realm of history to the realm of myth, is provided by the Lak Muang or City Pillar, not far from the main market area. This shrine, set up in the middle of the road, contains a bulbous pillar, perhaps five feet high, which, covered in gold leaf and garlands and the object of much adoration, symbolically unites the earth with the heavens. It is the symbolic centre of the community, a collective Jacob's Ladder through which people can ascend to intercede with the celestial powers that are believed to govern life. The Lak Muang is found in many cities, and is a Thai version of a universal urge. Each culture has developed its own *axis mundi*, but in Thailand such a divine totem pole is not merely a quaint reminder of a distant and more credulous past, but part of the living psychic life of the people. Only a couple of days after my visit to Kanchanaburi, I read in the *Bangkok Post* that the northern city of Chiang Rai is to have its sacred centre (called in the north the Sadeu Muang, or 'navel of the city') reconsecrated. The granite pillar has been carefully brought to Bangkok where, in a ceremony presided over by Buddhist dignitaries and civil authorities, no lesser person than the King, himself the supreme symbolic link between the celestial and the mundane, will anoint it. Then after a tour through the district of Chiang Rai to bless the local inhabitants, the pillar will be ceremoniously reinstalled.

To penetrate the heart of Thailand, you must travel along its main artery, inland from Bangkok up the Chao Phya River, back along the lazy brown ribbon as it uncurls its way through field after field of lush green paddy, back through history. For a few hours north of the present capital lies its celebrated predecessor, a ruined city that has thrown its shadow over all subsequent Thai history: the wondrous kingdom of Ayutthaya. Ayutthaya was not the first united kingdom of Thailand, nor did it produce the country's finest art or architecture, but it has become established in the Thai imagination as the Golden Age of prosperity, stability and good government; it has become a sustaining myth. Named after Ayodhya, the divine city of the Indian epic, the *Ramayana*, Ayutthaya was founded in 1350, after the Thai nation had been driven south from Sukhothai. It lasted for 417 years, through five dynasties and stretched from the north of modern Thailand to Johore and Singapore in the south, at its height including the Shan states of Burma and Cambodia as well. It was to Ayutthaya that foreigners first flocked, sailing up the Chao Phya as traders and envoys, and all were united in their praise of the city they saw. The Portuguese commented that in 1511, the Chinese community already had the monopoly on profitable trade in 'rice, hides, tin, pepper, ebony and rosewood'. The Japanese came in search of guns, ammunition and gunpowder, developed by the Thais in their continuing wars against the Burmese and renowned all over Asia, and became so well established at the court that there was even a band of Samurai attached to the King's Guard. The first British ships anchored here in 1612, the East India Company setting up a post within the year. There were also sizeable communities of Dutch, Spanish, Indians, Persians and Malays, each in its own enclave. From the mid sixteenth century the court of Ayutthaya pursued a policy of conscious internationalism within a Siamese framework; foreigners even being invited to fill important government posts if they had the necessary skills and knowledge.

There was even a Greek, Constantine Phaulcon, who ended up as Prime Minister to King Narai the Great, the most renowned monarch of Ayutthaya. An employee of the East India Company, Phaulcon was shipwrecked off the Malabar coast. The only other survivor turned out to be the Thai ambassador to Persia, and the Greek never looked back.

The French, later to extend their grip over Thailand's eastern neighbours, were particularly represented at Ayutthaya. It was the time of Louis XIV's domination of Europe, and the Siamese were keen to extend contacts with a king whose style most approximated that of an autocratic and extravagant oriental potentate. Narai the Great invited French architects, engineers, military advisers, and soldiers to his court. He was encouraged in this preference by Phaulcon, who realised shrewdly that the French could be used to keep at bay the Dutch who had less to offer. Narai had a Siamese Versailles built, and because the French naturally brought their wily Jesuits, churches of the Society of Jesus flourished. There was even a French Catholic school called the College of Nations, where the students were instructed in Christianity and foreign languages, especially French. The standard was high; six Asian students were sent to France to sit in competitive examinations, and by no means disgraced themselves. For their part, the French gained an entrepôt, for China and Japan had recently closed their ports to foreigners. Thailand thus became the perfectly placed staging post for Europeans to leave their wares to be picked up by Chinese junks and taken east. It was at this time that the word *farang* entered the Thai vocabulary; derived from *ferenghi*, the Indian for 'French', it came to be applied to any white foreigner, as it still is.

As Ayutthaya is only forty-six miles north of Bangkok, most tourists see it in a day trip from the capital. This can be done with a drive one way and a river journey the other, a popular combination being to drive up and enjoy a leisurely afternoon boat-ride back, avoiding the evening rush-hour.

And so on 7 April, 200 years to the day that the ancient capital was destroyed (a pleasing piece of symmetry) I join a party in a gleaming new Mercedes coach with icy air-conditioning. Travel by coach is, by and large, a comfortable and well-organised affair in Thailand, punctuated by drinks on demand and pleasantly scented cool face towels. As we leave Bangkok, the opposite side of the smoothly tarmacked road is clogged with a queue of lorries stretching for a couple of miles. They are laden with rice, fruit, cement and gravel, and are forbidden entrance to the city until ten o'clock, in an attempt to alleviate the early morning traffic jams.

Our guide is a smooth character with dark glasses and a mid-Pacific accent. He tells us that the people around Ayutthaya are 'the poorest in Thailand'. This is not true. I have certainly seen poorer soil and poorer people than what greets me out of the window now. Although it is the parched hot season at the moment, the land we are travelling through is the garden of the country, producing tangerines, sweetcorn, bananas, mangoes, mangosteen, and rice. I wonder if the guide's speech is a public relations operation to impress the tourists. I may have misheard him – my hearing is somewhat impaired by my neighbour, a twelve-year-old with a red baseball cap and stereo headphones that hum like a mosquito just out of range, a computer game that keeps bleeping and a book entitled *Great Trials of the World* that includes Charles I and the Yorkshire Ripper. I suspect that my neighbour may turn out to be a trial himself.

Our first stop is Bang Pa-In, the erstwhile summer residence first of the Ayutthayan and later the Bangkok kings, who would sail up here for picnics and outings to escape the stuffy heat of the city. Rama 5 would travel along these *klongs* for weeks on end, with a fleet of up to 600 boats, into which were sometimes packed 4000 people. The villages through which the royal retinue passed would build temporary accommodation of straw and bamboo, decorated with a profusion of flowers.

The Bangkok theme of Siamese Victoriana is carried on here in pleasant enough gardens that contain a real gem of Thai architecture: a little pavilion in the centre of an artificial lake, called the Aisawan Tippaya Asna. It must be one of the most photographed structures in the kingdom, and deservedly so. But behind the rather vapid prettiness of Bang Pa-In lies tragedy. In 1881, Queen Sunanda, Rama 5's half sister and favourite wife, was on a boat trip here with her young daughter. She was twenty-one, and expecting her second child. Somehow, the boat capsized and, because of a law that no commoner was allowed to touch a member of the royal family, her attendants stood around helplessly as both mother and daughter drowned. The king was devastated, and erected a baroque Victorian memorial that would not look out of place in Highgate cemetery. As our guide finishes recounting the sad tale, Baseball Cap screws up his not very attractive face. 'Hmm. They sure were dumb,' he comments loudly to no one in particular. I'm beginning to wish he were.

A further level of irony in the sad tale of Bang Pa-In is that Rama 5 began his reign by abolishing the law that decreed all subjects must keep their head below the level of the monarch's feet, and continued throughout his life to desanctify the Kingship. It is quite possible that the tragedy was one of the prime motivators of his desire to reform Thai customs. It is worth quoting (from *Siamese State Ceremonies* by H. G. Quaritch Wales) the actual law that was the cause of the drowning, as it gives insight into a code of practice the modern mind can barely comprehend: 'If a boat founders, the boatmen must swim away; if they remain near the boat they are to be executed . . . If they lay hold of him [the royal person] to rescue him, they are to be executed . . . If the barge sinks and someone else sees the coconuts (lifebelts) thrown and goes to save the royal person, the punishment is double and all his family is to be exterminated. If the barge founders and someone throws the coconuts so that they float towards the shore [away from the royal person], his throat is to be cut and his home confiscated.'

About thirteen miles later we reach Ayutthaya, an island about four miles by two, formed from the confluence of three rivers. Though the modern city is renowned for little save its propensity to produce gangsters, and a devastating fire that recently destroyed most of its wooden buildings, the old part is an open-air museum of temples, *chedis*, palaces and huge stuccoed Buddhas who gaze down resignedly on the ruins of their former home. This is a living gallery of the art of nostalgia, and an eloquent testament to the extraordinary burst of creative energy with which the capital was founded; most of its 400 *wats* and major monuments were built in the first 150 years of its existence. In its urge to create a national idiom and a mighty empire, Ayutthaya was a society of builders rather than sculptors. The Buddha images characteristic of the period tend to be hieratic and formalised, each with their long, curved aquiline nose, and quizzically arched eyebrows creating an expression of haughtiness. Power is what is to be conveyed, in a stylised idiom that at its best is confidently authoritative, and at its worst becomes cold and bland, presaging the lifeless figures of the Bangkok period.

Ayutthaya must have been a place of extraordinary magnificence. Travellers describe the city as having more than 300 gilded and towered temples and we know that multi-coloured mosaic was practised at this time, and that there were over thirty miles of waterways along which the royal barges travelled carved in the highly coloured shapes of fabulous creatures – garudas, sea monsters, dragons, serpent kings – along with many humbler craft. There was the same length of paved roads, thronged by elephants and palanquins, and a six-mile wall guarded by numerous bastions and fortresses. The King glided throughout his kingdom in an atmosphere of ritualistic secrecy and holy dread. To assure that the King was always elevated above his subjects, no houses outside the palace area could be built more than one storey high, and when he travelled, the populace, on hearing the royal musicians announce his appearance, had to hide themselves behind a hedge of canes, close all doors and windows and keep silent until he had passed. Nevertheless, *sanuk* was not entirely vanquished by such protocol. One English traveller finishes off his glowing report of the capital by saying that 'the inhabitants of this kingdom are much given to pleasure and ryot'.

But it was riots of a different sort that spelled the end of Ayutthaya's open-door policy. In 1688, Narai fell gravely ill. A strong anti-French lobby, long frustrated, seized the chance to act. With the King confined to his palace, his 'Greek favourite', hugely unpopular for his extravagance and suspected designs on the throne, was captured and executed. The following month Narai died. The French troops were immediately expelled, and Ayutthaya's gates virtually closed to foreigners. The once international court embarked on a policy of isolation that was to remain through the decadent and unsettled reigns that led to its final sacking by the Burmese a hundred years later.

The eclectic nature of the Ayutthayan building style is observable everywhere. Wat Yai Chai Mongkol, the oldest

8 Worshippers kneel in front of the Phra Buddha Chinaraj in Wat Mahathat, Phitsanulok, one of the country's best-loved sanctuaries

9 Varied architectural styles at Ayutthaya, the capital of the Thai kingdom from 1350 until 1767, when it was destroyed by the Burmese. The spire on the left is built in the style of the Khmers of Cambodia

10 A typical pavement fruit stall. At the far end can be seen the large spiky durian, which, despite its overpowering smell, is highly prized

11 Transplanting seedlings in the paddy fields of central Thailand, the rice bowl of the country

building on the site, was constructed in 1357 to celebrate the return of some monks from Ceylon who had brought with them the teachings of Hinayana Buddhism, an animistic form of which is still the religion of 95 per cent of the population. Here there is a reclining Buddha, restored in a pristine white coat of stucco, lying stiffly like T. S. Eliot's 'patient etherised upon a table'. He is surrounded by the remnants of a covered walkway. Both the figure and its setting are derived from Ceylonese prototypes. It is a pleasant site, a quiet open-air courtyard near the main *chedi* sprinkled with yellow and white from the sweetly scented frangipani and orange from the flame trees, onto whose trunks are tacked little notices with Buddhist homilies: '*The wise should keep vigil*', '*Nirvana is the highest happiness*', '*By yourself censor yourself*' and '*The victor begets hate*'. The *chedi* itself is ringed by new cement images donated by the faithful, at 5000 *baht* for a small one and twice that for a large one. Both figures and monument are draped in yellow cloth proclaiming a festival. Eclecticism is evident, too, in the evolution of the characteristic Ayutthayan *chedi*, the best examples of which are at Wat Phra Sri Sanphet, which was the royal temple within the palace compound. Built in 1491, this was to be the model for Rama 1's Temple of the Emerald Buddha in Bangkok. The three main *chedis*, containing royal ashes, stand like silent sentinels, Singhalese in their diminishing rings leading to a bell-shaped dome, Burmese in their delicately elongated and ringed spire. Nearby sits one of the most impressive images at Ayutthaya, the giant bronze Buddha of Wat Phra Mongkol Bopitr. Originally set in the open air – a common practice in Ayutthayan times – this obsidian colossus with its sparkling mother-of-pearl eyes is a jungle totem, hinting at the animism not far below the moral and ethical surface of Thai Buddhism. Both the image and the pleasingly proportioned building which houses it were restored thirty years ago with the help of the penitent Burmese. During the process many hundreds of miniature bronze Buddhas were found within the main figure and buried in the surrounding ground. These were donated by laymen to gain merit and magically to protect the place.

The centre of Ayutthaya's stage belonged to Wat Maha That (1384) believed to have been built on the site of a buried Buddha relic that the King's brother saw glowing under the ground. Little now remains apart from the base of a huge Khmer-inspired *prang* that rose like an elongated artichoke of brick, laterite and plaster 165 feet above the plain. But the sense of scale, the feeling of majestic, imperial self-confidence is still undeniable.

Outside the old Citadel I come across two places of interest. One is the temple of Wat Phanan Choeng, on the river just south of the island. It dates from 1324, a little before the founding of the capital and, much patronised by the Chinese, is full of red and gold lanterns and paper banners with dancing black characters. The place is humming with life. Outside a collection of stalls sells a wide range of votive plaques – featuring miniature Buddhas and cast in clay, terracotta or resin – inside a *ranad-ek*, a type of wooden xylophone, keeps up a bubbling hypnotic tune not unlike the *gamelan* of Indonesia. Worshippers come and go in the curling mist of sandalwood joss-sticks, some offering flowers and candles, some kneeling and prostrating. One group bears a pig's head – favourite offering of the Chinese – its downy ears softly pointed over sightless pink eyes and leering grin. The gilded brick image is superb, about forty-five feet high and retreating mysteriously into the half-light high up into the back of the hall. The whole setting has been perfectly stage-managed to produce an atmosphere of awe-inspiring majesty. It takes some seconds in the dark to make out the imperious gaze under half-lowered lids and bejewelled third eye of wisdom, the lips full and sensuous yet tempered by a self-control born of discrimination rather than strain. This tremendous figure was understandably one of the most revered images in the city, and people believe that tears sprang from its eyes when the Burmese invaded. The massive knees and right hand, extending downwards in the 'Earth Touching Posture', are thick with layer upon layer of gossamer gold leaf squares, placed by the faithful. This is normally applied with the heat of the hand though sometimes a little garlic (a magical herb here as in Europe) is used as an adhesive. Such worship brings merit: good luck in this life or a favourable reincarnation. (If you do good secretly the Thais call it 'applying gold leaf to the back of a Buddha image'.) The air scintillates with specks of gold, detached by the cooling breeze from the fans and wafted like celestial fireflies to alight with thistledown caresses on one's skin and clothing. It is a lovely place, full of people, colour and unselfconscious piety.

My other find is the railway station. I like such places for their Toytown quality and, in a country where the railway is still the popular means of transport, they are invaluable for watching and meeting people. Now, nearing lunchtime, the station is deserted apart from a few sleepers slumped along benches and some equally prostrate dogs. I poke my head into the unmanned ticket office and catch sight of a notice on the wall that speaks volumes about Thai psychology. It reads like this:

REMINDER TO ALL PERSONNEL
THIS IS YOUR RESPONSIBILITY

1 Smile at all times.
2 Speak clearly, pleasantly and courteously.
3 Dress neat and clean.
4 Be nice, charming, gentle and graceful.
5 Give the best service to the best of your ability.
6 You are not supposed to say 'Yes' all the time, but try your best to avoid saying 'No', there are many other ways to say so.
7 To deal with difficult customers: Advise, explain, say 'Sorry' or better keep your mouth shut, as the case may be. Do not argue, talk back or raise your voice. If you can't manage, call your next available superior.
8 Nobody wins an argument.
9 Keep your temper to keep your job.
10 The customer is always right.

The boat-ride back to Bangkok glides smoothly. We pass cluster after cluster of wooden houses on stilts with green corrugated iron roofs. The grey-brown afternoon haze is startled intermittently by the odd *wat* or *chedi*, each with its own jetty, blazing a spanking new cream, orange, red and gold. Groups of svelte brown children splash at the water's edge, shrieking white-toothed and soundless. Riverside shops run into verandas festooned with washing, house plants potted in old tins, and Chinese ceramic water containers – tall, dun-coloured and emblazoned with pale yellow dragons. Lemon acacia droops languidly over the brown water, here and there a sudden burst of red or orange bougainvilia. Caravans of rice barges, each long and wooden with a curved roof of corrugated iron, are pulled along by tugs. Some have been converted into houseboats, many have five or six flat barges in tow bearing rice, or tapioca, or sand, or coal. Every so often the water's silky flow is slubbed by clumps of water hyacinth with its demurely mauve flower and dark fleshy leaves. Despite the clumps of it along the flat banks, it seems well under control. A number of rusted tankers are busily devouring it: the plant fed up a stepped conveyor belt at the prow and then shredded down into the hold. Perhaps Thailand has found a use for this ubiquitous plant that is busy clogging up half the rivers and waterways of the world.

It's all very soporific and peaceful until the arrival of tea. Ice cream galvanises even the laziest into action. My neighbour in the queue is my old friend Baseball Cap. We smile warily at each other.

6

Rice and Royalty

At the astrologically auspicious time of 8.49 a.m. on 8 May 1987, a yellow Rolls-Royce bearing His Majesty King Bhumipol the Great, his son and heir Prince Vajiralongkorn and his favourite daughter Princess Sirindhorn, draws up at the Sanam Luang park in the heart of old Bangkok. A few minutes later, seated in a pavilion draped with brilliant blue and gold silk, His Majesty receives the long, low bow of the Lord of the Ploughing, a portly, bespectacled man dressed in white and gold robes with a scarlet sash, heavy rows of medals on his chest and a tall white conical crown on his head. His formal respects paid, the Lord of the Ploughing takes up position in a group of people that looks like something out of the more splendid days of the medieval Papacy. To the sound of the *pinphat* orchestra – shawms, gongs, drums and a bubbling wooden xylophone – the strange procession moves off across the park ringed with white marquees that fly flags of every colour under the sun. The annual Ploughing Ceremony, dating back to the time of the Buddha and revived by the present King thirty years ago, has begun.

First comes a white-robed brahmin priest, scattering sanctified water and intoning mantras, for this ceremony, like much of the Court ritual, has a Hindu origin. Next follow five other priests also wearing white, representing the five elements and attended by two bearers with red ceremonial parasols, the symbol of both spiritual and secular majesty. Then, flanked by twelve attendants in scarlet tunics with breeches, cuffs and caps trimmed in gold, come two massive white bulls, drawing a ceremonial red plough. Both the animals and the plough have been anointed with gold leaf that glitters fitfully in the morning sun. Behind the plough strides the Lord of the Ploughing, in everyday life the Director-General of the Department of Agriculture, scattering seeds from four baskets – two silver and two golden – carried Chinese-style from poles slung across the shoulders of four women. In normal life they, too, are employees of the Department of Agriculture; today, dressed in shimmering silk *phaasin* suits of green, pink, purple and cream, they represent the four *theps* – the goddesses of the four directions. At the tail of the group come two more priests and two more bearers of the red parasol. For perhaps thirty minutes the procession winds slow concentric circles round the Sanam Luang, ploughing four great furrows into which the seeds of six kinds of rice are scattered. Then, its last turn completed, the procession halts in front of the royal pavilion. Two trays of food are presented to the King before being offered to the bulls. Which food their long pink tongues lap up will be read by the Court Astrologer as an omen of the next harvest and the country's general prosperity over the coming year. Licked clean, the trays are taken to a nearby marquee and ceremoniously laid in front of a statue of a Hindu deity, the Dancing Shiva. Then the official report of the Astrologer's prediction is read to the King, and speeches follow. The outstanding farmers of the previous year are presented to His Majesty, each of them in the traditional up-country uniform of blue receives an award from him and, in a gesture that typifies the human touch of this wise and much-loved monarch, some seed rice from his own experimental plots at the Chitralada Palace. Then, ceremonies over, the royal party departs to the strains of the National Anthem. As the last note dies away, the huge crowd that has silently watched the whole lengthy proceedings, bursts through the boundary ropes and rushes into the grass arena, to see if it can retrieve some of the sacred rice from the great black furrows. Thus, each year, does the world's largest exporter of rice ensure its crop.

The Central Plains of Thailand are the rice bowl of Asia: flat green fields stretching for mile after mile to a flat horizon. Around Ayutthaya they open out, like some vast and subtly chequered mosaic, a Paul Klee canvas come alive, composed of innumerable plots, perhaps forty years each side, gently terraced to compensate for irregularities in the terrain and to facilitate irrigation. Shallow drainage ditches and earth walls no more than a foot high divide plot from plot, giving a walkway for the farmers and relief to the eye. The landscape is more obviously broken up by clumps of fruit trees, coconut and sago palms and the occasional bamboo, that enclose the thatched hamlets where the farmers live. Every so often a spirit house rises rickety from the ground like a roofed bird-table, bearing untidy offerings of flowers and joss-sticks to appease the spirits of the field. Now, in spring, the mosaic is predominantly chocolate and yellowy-brown, as the first seed beds, freshly ploughed, alternate with the dried stubble of fields left untouched since the last harvest. After a few weeks, seedlings will cover the ground in a soft emerald pelt, the lushness of the nursery plots heightened by the mirror-like surfaces of their neighbours, which, stubble burnt off, ploughed and flooded, now await the planting out of the young shoots. It is a wonderful time of the year; the air is full of promise and the fecund land tingles with the energy of new growth. The water in the fields is so calm that plants and sky lie side by side, plot after plot, as far as the eye can see. Soon humans will enter the scene in a typical Asian tableau: village women in straw hats arched straight-legged over the back-breaking task of gathering the young plants, binding them into bundles with a sliver of bamboo, untangling and dipping the wispy white roots into fertiliser and then planting them out again, tops pruned and widely spaced, into waterlogged fields that begin to resemble a series of bald hairbrushes, sparsely tufted with brilliant green. This is the last chance for the water-buffalo, born without sweat pores and always happy to laze in water, to enjoy their daily bath, for soon the only thing in the fields apart from rice will be small children, perfecting their catapult skills as human bird-scarers, or fishing for edible paddy frogs. As the paddy bends under the rains, it thickens into growth – green, moist and glittering in the intermittent sun. Then, after anything between ten and twenty weeks, depending on the type of paddy, the fields are drained, the plants flower and the plots, now dry if Nature has complied and halted the rains, coalesce into one vast and seamless swathe, bushy and golden, ready to be harvested.

There probably isn't a simpler or more expressive name for the grain that supports half the world than the one the Thais have given it: *khao suay* – 'beautiful rice'. Rice nourishes these people body and soul; whether it is white, red, sticky, fine quality, poor quality, unhusked or ground, it is their life. In Thai mythology, Mae Phosop (Mother Rice) becomes pregnant each year when the rice flowers bloom. Her offspring, Rice, has a soul, so its gathering must be a ritual affair and its journey to the granary a communal *rite de passage*. Whoever buys the grain must return a handful to the farmer, so that the soul may impregnate the next crop and the cycle of life go on.

Eight out of every ten Thais is a rice farmer; each year the country grows thirteen million tons of the stuff. Of this, over four million are exported – mainly to Africa, China, Iran and the Middle East – so that rice has been not only the staple of Thailand throughout history but, up until very recently, her biggest earner of foreign exchange. It is rice that has kept the country stable enough to enjoy its current position as the healthiest economy in South-East Asia, with an annual inflation rate that has rarely crept above 3 per cent since 1980, and it is rice, along with textiles and tapioca, that has formed the basis of a solid and consistent export achievement over the last few years. It is Japan that is the barometer of economic fortunes in South-East Asia. Whereas up until ten years ago she considered Thailand as too small and corruptible a market, preferring Indonesia as a country rich in raw materials and potential, today she praises the Land of Smiles as 'the rising star of the Asian nations', backing the accolade with widespread investment.

But for the rice farmers themselves, such a success story must seem rather academic. As mere producers they are but the bottom level of a pyramid composed of successive tiers of middlemen and government exporters, and as such they are in no position to effect the price the results of their labours fetches on the open market. For this they must rely on the wisdom, or otherwise, of whatever government is in power in Bangkok. The uncertainties inherent in a fluctuating world market have been exacerbated since April 1986, when Washington, bowing to the muscle of the American rice industry, announced massive subsidies for rice growers. The export price of American rice fell by almost a half, dealing a further blow to Thailand's hopes of competing with the Superpower at a time of growing protectionism. The issue created an unprecedented rupture in the habitually cordial relations of the two countries. The situation was further complicated by the American farmers' plans to produce the round grain favoured by the Japanese, who, looking to import, offer a potentially lucrative market that could increase world demand by over a third. Thailand, which can grow the long but not the round grain, sees herself being squeezed out of the first league of rice producers. Washington's reply to Bangkok's charges of 'unfair' subsidies that penalise a developing country is to accuse the Thai government of failing to have a consistent or clearly thought-out policy on rice farming, and of relying on *ad hoc* decisions, often not announced until midway through the growing season, by which time the farmers have had to commit themselves to planting a crop, unsure of what returns it may bring. And planting a crop can be a costly business, in a bad year actually costing more than it will fetch. Each year many a farmer finds he is spending the money set aside for planting on daily living, and when seed time comes around, he goes even further into debt. Ironically, the two crops a year achieved in the Central Plains and held up as a model of agricultural efficiency only compound the problem: by doubling the debts incurred in planting and doubling the risk of the harvested crop not securing a decent price.

An important part of this spiral of debt is the price of fertiliser and pesticide. The big chemical fertiliser companies encourage greater and greater use of their products, comparing Thailand's low use of inorganic fertiliser to Indonesia, China or the Philippines, and gaining government support for the necessity of boosting production as a hedge against the projected population increase over the next twenty years. But fertiliser, as both the big companies and the small farmers well know, costs a lot of money. Much of Thailand's soil is poor; even the relatively fertile Central Plains are bedevilled by a stultifying acidity. Although Thailand produces a third of the world's rice, the yield per acre is very low, perhaps a third of that enjoyed in the United States or Japan, and it is only the sheer numbers of people in the fields that keeps Thailand competitive on a world basis. There is, however, one bright star on the paddy horizon, and that is the recent discovery of marl: a natural deposit of mixed clays that occurs in considerable quantities in the Central Plains, especially around Saraburi, Lopburi and Nakhon Sawan. Marl is highly alkaline, neutralises acidity and, being plentiful and readily available with minimum transport costs, looks like providing a relatively inexpensive fertiliser that would also nourish, rather than deplete, the soil it augments.

A survey conducted in 1987 by the distinguished economist Professor Praves Wasi concluded that 80 per cent of Thailand's 50,000 villages are in debt to the average tune of over two million *baht* per village and that the great majority of farmers are suffering chronic hardship. Professor Praves is spearheading a move-ment to reverse the dependency on cash crop farming and to convince the farmers to grow food, not 'profits'. He sees self-sufficiency as a safer and more integrated goal than producing for export, and advocates a combination of diversified crops and animal husbandry, intended primarily for the families' own consumption. Only the adoption of what he calls 'Buddhist agriculture' can hope to reverse the trend of landlessness, poverty and the collapse of family and village. His approach provides an interesting contrast to the Marxist solutions to similar problems so rashly embraced by Thailand's neighbours over the last few decades. Seeking to invigorate, rather than destroy, the traditional bulwark of Thai life, her Buddhist religion, he adapts the traditional Buddhist teaching of *benjakhant* – the five co-ordinated factors that make up human life – to the five related elements that compose a healthy society: mind and spirit; agriculture or technology; community life (which includes religion and culture); self-sufficiency; and the balance of nature. As Professor Praves warns: 'If one factor is missing, the whole system may collapse.'

Though the relevance of 'Buddhist agriculture' might seem irrelevant to the ruthless world of international agribusiness, its appeal to a substratum of the Thai personality is probably considerable. Apart from its demonstrable good sense in material terms, the philosophy would resonate with beliefs still held by many country folk. One has only to visit some of the temples in the Central Plains to see this. Take as an example Wat Thepithak, twenty-seven miles east of Saraburi and on the edge of the area that serves as Bangkok's vegetable garden. In the fields here thatched maize seedlings spike the rich red earth with green, and along the road custard apple bushes are shaded by the large, spatulate leaves of the papaya palm and the profuse, dark foliage of mango trees. Here and there vivid, pointilliste laburnum blossom adds an unexpectedly English touch to the parched countryside. Half-way up one of the sugarloaf hills that dot the area sits a gigantic Buddha, visible for miles around, gleaming brilliant white against the backdrop of the hillside. Built by an ex-prime minister with funds from the lottery department, the Buddha sits 157 feet high and 125 feet across at the knees. Even an ear – long-lobed as a sign of wisdom – measures twenty-three feet. Wat Thepithak, the temple at the foot of the hill, is today full of people sitting around, chatting quietly. I learn that they are families and friends of a group of young novices who are at the moment in the *bot* undergoing their ordination, a ceremony that ideally takes place at the age of twenty. To the Thais, a monk in the family is a source of great status and spiritual merit both for the boy himself and his parents, and the family and community at large. Indeed, assuming the robe is considered the most efficacious way to repay the filial debt to one's parents. The vows are not binding for life and, anyway, time spent in the monastery provides an access to education and contacts that may later be of use in the outside world. The ordination is clearly a precious moment for all concerned, and while the lads in the *bot* are reciting the 227 vows that will henceforth order their lives, their well-wishers enjoy a time of pride, a time of quiet reflection on the losses and gains in life. One of the chidren, probably a younger sister, comes up and offers me a shy smile and a bunch of pink and mauve bougainvilia as large as her head.

A different aspect of contemporary Thai life is provided by Wat Tahm Krabok, a temple in Saraburi province run by Phra Chamroon Parnchand. Over the past few years the *wat* has become

famous as a treatment centre for drug addicts, of which Thailand
is estimated to have well over half a million, of which many are
young country people unable to cope with the competitive
pressures of urban life. The detoxification programme is harsh.
No substitute drugs are used, but instead a concoction of a
hundred locally gathered herbs that Phra Chamroon has devised.
Each day the addicts line up in the compound in front of a bucket
of water and a large spitoon. The medicine is administered and to
the ritualistic accompaniment of drums and gongs, the patients
start to drink the water, a combination that has them vomiting
violently time and time again. The tortured cycle of drinking and
spewing goes on for about fifteen minutes until they are almost
too exhausted to walk back to their dormitories. The daily purge,
together with a detoxifying herbal steam-bath known as the
'sauna', a rota of hard work and instruction in Buddhism and
meditation, has a very high success rate. 'I've not seen a person
who walked out of here not cured,' says Phra Gordon, a lanky
black from Harlem who, after three years in Vietnam and many
months trying to readjust, finally settled here as a monk. It was
Vietnam that indirectly caused the Thai drug explosion. By 1971
an estimated one out of every five GIs based in Thailand was
regularly using heroin. When the Americans finally pulled out in
1974, the local population fell victim to the vast amount of drugs
available. Though foreigners with drug problems come here, too,
the *wat* does not charge for treatment and is always short of funds.
Some medical authorities in Bangkok may be sceptical of Phra
Chamroon's claims, but there are no recidivists. If a person
released as clean goes back to his habit, he has broken the most
important of the vows that he makes here, and will not be re-
admitted. Phra Gordon is matter-of-fact about the seriousness of
what is involved. 'It's not true that the treatment will kill the
second time. What is true is that once he has taken the medicine
for a particular drug addiction, it stays in his system for the rest of
his life. If he goes back to drugs, he'll be dead within thirty days.
You become clean and you have to stay clean. That's all there is to
it.'

    On the outskirts of Saraburi, a more traditional temple is Phra

Buddhabat, the shrine believed to hold the footprint of the Buddha. A long stairway, flanked by the five-headed protective dragons known as *nagas*, leads up to a number of small temples set at different levels in a Chinese-style compound amidst ornamental shrubs, trees and rocks. The temple with the footprint has exquisite mother-of-pearl doors that open onto a rectangular pit, perhaps four feet by two feet and surmounted by a pinnacled canopy in which is set a rock with the footprint indentation. Around the pit lie solid silver mats, which, the attendant monk tells me with some pride, were presented by the King himself, and weigh no less than ninety pounds each. The place has a pleasant atmosphere, and though the idea of the Master's footprint, like the hair of the Prophet, may not impress the cynic, this focus of devotion draws a steady trickle of pilgrims daily and in February, at the annual festival, large and happy crowds.

The main town in the area to the east of Highway 1, which runs from Bangkok to Nakhon Sawan, is Lopburi. There is something here to interest most visitors. Neolithic and Bronze Age remnants have been found in the area and the town has been consistently inhabited since the Dvaravati period, many artefacts from which can be seen in the Narai National Museum within the Narai Palace. From the tenth century Lopburi served as a provincial capital of the Khmers of Cambodia, an Indianised people who followed both Hinduism and Mahayana Buddhism, built Angkor Wat, and ruled over much of Thailand until the rise of Sukhothai, the first united Thai kingdom, 300 years later. Two structures date from the Khmer period: the Phra Prang Sam Yod ('Sacred Three Spires'), a Hindu-cum-Buddhist laterite temple built in the thirteenth century by Jayavarman 7, the last great king of Angkor, and the Prang Khaek ('Hindu Spire') also built of laterite and which, standing rather squashed on an elongated traffic island in the middle of the town, is probably from the eighth century. The architects of Khmer temples conceived of them in the Hindu fashion as early abodes of the gods, and their distinctive plump spire (*prang*) symbolised Mount Meru, centre of the universe and home of the gods. The *prang* was adopted by the Buddhists to symbolise the thirty-three stages of perfection, culminating in *nirvana*. Both these sites have traces of the fine carving and stucco decoration that characterise Khmer artistry. Tourists are sometimes directed to another temple, near the railway track, San Phra Kan ('Rama Temple'), but it is an unimpressive place, overrun by scabby monkeys and redeemed only by the temple dancing that is occasionally performed there.

Lopburi is famed as the birthplace of a distinctive and highly accomplished school of sculpture that specialised in both Mahayana and Theravada figures. Made of bronze and, later, sandstone, Lopburi Buddhas are often marvellously authoritative, with solid, energised bodies, the flat ethnic feature of Cambodia, and diadems enclosing a conical *ushnisha* – the protuberance on the crown of the head signifying enlightenment. The Khmers believed in the divinity of the king and Lopburi Buddhas are the first to be portrayed in regal attire. A favourite subject, encouraged no doubt by Cambodian snake cults, is the Buddha seated on the coils of Muchalinda, the serpent king, whose five or seven hoods formed a protective canopy over the Master's head – an image illustrating the legend that Muchalinda once protected the Buddha from a violent storm.

King Narai of Ayutthaya favoured Lopburi as a summer retreat from the humidity of his capital, and palaces were built here for both him and his chief minister Phaulcon. Narai played out the final scenes of his rather unhappy life here in the Suttha Sawan Pavilion. As he lay usurped and dying in the spring of 1688, he was surrounded by his last ten faithful retainers. Realising that as soon as he died they would be massacred, Narai had them ordained as Buddhist monks. He secured the protection of the saffron robe by donating the Pavilion to the monastery, and when Rama 4 came to reinstate Lopburi as a summer palace in the nineteenth century, he had to provide another building to rehouse the monastic order. Narai's palace (officially known as the Narai Raja Niwes Palace) dominates the centre of the town, contains the Narai National Museum and has some fine buildings left. Best preserved is the Dusit Maha Prasat Hall, built for an audience granted to an ambassador from Louis XIV in

1685. Two buildings are attributed to Rama 4: the Chantra Paisan Pavilion that he restored, with a curved base and sweeping tiered roof in the Ayutthayan style, and the Phiman Mongkut Pavilion, a three-storeyed mansion that he built in the colonial style of the mid nineteenth century. The palace of the Greek favourite, to the north of Narai's palace, is terribly neglected.

Lopburi gained some notoriety as the scene of a huge massacre of *farangs* in Narai's time. A large group of merchants suspected of attempting to manipulate the court was summoned from Ayutthaya for a dinner in the palace. Half-way through the meal, the doors of the banqueting pavilion were locked and the entire building was burnt to the ground. My own memory of meals in Lopburi is a happier one. Not long ago I shared a table in the excellent Po Ngam Restaurant with a couple and their six-year-old daughter. The father, a bear of a man who works for Esso and is based in Singapore, was explaining to me some of the difficulties in dealing with Thai bureaucracy. His little girl, very fair-skinned with a lovely head of long blonde hair, was a source of fascination for the uniformly black-haired Thais and especially the waitressses. After they had served the meal, two or three of them came up behind her and quite spontaneously began to weave her hair into long plaits, singing softly as they did so. It was a charming scene. That particular family turned out to be a good source of *sanuk* for the locals. After the meal, as the father lumbered his considerable frame towards the door, one of the diminutive waitresses, hardly half his size, ran behind him playing hide-and-seek with her colleagues, to the uninhibited and quite unmalicious hilarity of the whole restaurant.

One legacy the Khmers bequeathed to their Thai successors was their reverence for the Crown. No visitor to the country can fail to be impressed by the extraordinary love, pride and respect in which the Thai people enshrine their ruler. To be sure, His Majesty King Bhumipol Adulyadej is an extraordinary man. His birth on 5 December 1927 in Cambridge, Massachusetts, raised no great interest, indeed it took the *Bangkok Times* ten days to report the happy event in a couple of terse sentences. At that time

the young Bhumipol seemed to have very little chance of ever
becoming king, as any children of the reigning monarch Rama 7,
his own father Prince Mahidol, and his elder brother, Prince
Ananda, all stood between him and the throne. But his father died
young in 1929, Rama 7 died childless in 1941, and Ananda died
mysteriously in 1946. Thus did fate haul the eighteen-year-old
Bhumipol onto the throne. Since then he has remained the potent
and steadfast unifier of a country otherwise taut with the energies
of disparate political, military and economic groups – a tautness
that has erupted into fourteen coups or attempted coups over
the last fifty years. That none of these has shaken the stable
foundations of the country is due largely to the quietly authoritative figure of its King. Virtually every home, shop and business in
the land displays a picture of King Bhumipol with his lovely
Queen Sirikit. The affection is genuine, unforced and intense,
and the one thing the otherwise easy-going Thais will not tolerate
is any disrespect paid to their monarch. The British may consider
themselves lovers of royalty but the sort of crude and often cruel
satire the British media commonly directs at its royal family would
be quite unthinkable in Thailand. Not only would the authorities
immediately clamp down on such blatant cases of *lèse-majesté*, but
no Thai would want to produce, read or watch such childish
nastiness. Even objects bearing the King's likeness, such as
banknotes, are treated with respect by at least the traditional older
generation, and these feelings should never be underestimated by
a visitor to the Kingdom.

This sensitive, bespectacled and frail-looking man has
become the living symbol of his country. On formal state
occasions, weighed down by ceremonial braid and crowned in a
plumed helmet, he evokes the past of the glorious House of
Chakri, in its time perhaps the most ritualistic and exotic of all
Courts, where, only a hundred years ago, the subjects could not
even *look* at their King. Today, for one so revered, he is highly
visible, and a more human and familiar image is of a man in
fatigues or an open-necked shirt, binoculars and camera around
his neck, notebook and map in hand, hurrying to board a
helicopter, or down on bended knee listening to the requests and

opinions of the poorest peasants in the land. King Bhumipol takes very seriously the traditional role of Raj Dharma – the duties and obligations of a King according to Buddhist principles. Like any other Thai male he has done his time as a monk, going out barefoot on the early morning alms round with the rest of the community, and many of his important public ceremonies are to do with honouring the Buddhist monkhood. One such is Kathin – the occasion of the famous Royal Barge Procession – when new robes are presented to the monks of Wat Arun in Bangkok each October at the end of the rainy season. But Bhumipol is an active as well as a moral force. Over the past thirty years he has set in motion more than 1500 Royal Projects ranging from fish-farming to artificial rain-making, and he spends over half each year on working tours up-country encouraging the villagers to be their own masters. There is a story that illustrates the natural bond between the King and his subjects. During the early days of the opium substitution project in the far north, King Bhumipol presented a set of fruit tree pruning and grafting knives to hilltribesmen who had completed a training course in Chiang Mai. To his surprise a sum of money was sent to him by the tribesmen. It was so small that it could not be considered payment for the tools. Inquiries revealed that the tribesmen were acting according to an old Thai custom. A sharp tool such as a knife is a potential weapon and cannot be given to a friend as it could destroy the friendship. It has to be bought; hence the payment.

The only criticism I have ever heard voiced of the King, if criticism it can be called, is that he is so devoted to the cause of the poor peasants that he barely has the time for other pressing concerns. This devotion nearly killed him some years ago when he contracted a blood infection on an up-country tour and almost died. Those with a sense of history remembered the death of another beloved and innovative king, Rama 4, who contracted malaria on a field trip. Since that illness, his health has been the cause of much concern to his people, but his workload has not diminished. Many Thais I have spoken to fear their King drives himself too hard. Yet there is another side to Rama 9, a truly Thai love of *sanuk*. Well known for his sense of humour, the King is a painter, who has exhibited his works on a number of occasions, and an accomplished musician playing woodwinds, trumpet and piano. He has composed over forty works, some of which, like 'Hungry Man's Blues' and 'Falling Rain' have become Thai standards. For many years he and his band had a regular radio spot each Thursday, and during a state visit to Vienna in 1964 his three-movement *Monohra Ballet* received its première. But he is most at home with jazz, and has swung alongside some of the veteran jazzmen, names such as Benny Goodman and Lionel Hampton, both in the Royal Palace in Bangkok and abroad. The King is also a skilled dinghy sailor who designs and builds his own boats. All in all, he is a man of many talents.

It is said that he suffered a great personal sadness when his eldest daughter, Princess Ubolratana, married an American engineer and went to live in the United States. Since that time his right hand has been his second daughter, Princess Sirindhorn, popularly known as Phra Thep – 'the Goddess'. As her soubriquet implies, she is universally adored. A devout Buddhist, she appears wedded to the welfare of the people, remaining single and living a life of dedication, either working with her father on his projects or undertaking many of her own. In addition, she has a genuine interest in traditional Thai culture, being a classical musician and holding degrees in Pali and Sanskrit and archaeological inscriptions. Her life and popularity would seem to single her out as the natural successor to the throne. She would undoubtedly be the choice of the people, many of whom would die for her, and the constitution would in theory allow a woman to rule the Kingdom.

The Thai love of spectacle endears them to all monarchies, and they seem to feel a particular affinity with the British on this score. There was tremendous interest in the 1988 visit of the heir to the British throne and his wife to mark the celebrations of King Bhumipol's sixtieth birthday. This was a particularly auspicious occasion, being also the end of his fifth twelve-year cycle and only a few months away from his becoming the longest reigning member of the Chakri dynasty. The sartorially acute Thais were much taken with Princess Diana, praising her fairness and her glamorous style. While watching the visit on television in a bar, I got chatting to my neighbour. He was delighted to learn that he was drinking with a Scot, but saddened to hear that Scotland no longer had its own King. After my brief synopsis of the dramas of Jacobite history, he fell silent for a moment. 'Hmm. Scotland no have King. Have President?' he asked hopefully. I had to admit that it does not. He looked glum, sympathising with my loss of face. Then, as it so often does in these cases, football came to our rescue. A wide grin split his face, and he announced, 'Ah! No have President, have Kenny Dalglish!'

7

Ancient Capitals

From Lopburi a majestic steam engine, manufactured, according to its sparkling plate, in 1913 by the North British Locomotive Company, proceeds at a leisurely pace to Nakhon Sawan, a modern town of some 90,000 inhabitants. Just north of here three rivers – the Yom, Ping and Nan – converge to form the mighty Chao Phya. In the old days these waterways were vital links in the chain of teak that stretched from the forests of the north to the port of Bangkok, when the logs were lashed together into great rafts and floated downriver in an almost continuous caravan. Nowadays the teak business is in decline and the slow-growing trees are disappearing from up-country, though the occasional raft can still be seen. The rivers' main function today is to irrigate the surrounding paddy fields. Strategically placed in the middle of the Central Plains, Nakhon Sawan is the wholesale rice market and the main distribution point of the milled grain.

The railway line continues north-east from Nakhon Sawan to Phitsanulok, but after a little over sixty miles to the north-west on Highway 1 you reach the first of the three deserted capitals which lie like discarded jewels at the heart of the country's history. This is Kamphang Phet ('The diamond wall') built by King Li Thai of Sukhothai in the mid-fourteenth century to serve, as its name implies, as a garrison town for his capital forty-five miles to the north. The defensive wall is still standing twenty feet above the moat, its earthen ramparts fortified with laterite, a local volcanic rock whose dull reddish-purple surface is pitted with tiny holes. Within the enclosed citadel lie the ruins of two major structures: Wat Phra Keo and Wat Phra That, and a small but very good museum. Motor transport is a must here, as the best known ruins are outside the city walls. Wat Phra Sri Iriyaboth, amidst the usual arrangement of *chedis* and *viharns*, has a central square sanctuary with each of its sides depicting one of the four classical poses of the Buddha: sitting, standing, reclining and walking. Only this last is in good repair, but it is still a fine example of the fluid gracefulness that characterises Sukhothai art. Nearby is Wat Chang Rob, 'The shrine surrounded by elephants', a huge laterite *chedi* with its base ringed by large elephant caryatids, one row of which is still well preserved. Though the spire has long since tumbled, the view from the top is well worth the climb. Unrestored since Ayutthayan times and relatively unvisited today, Kamphang Phet has kept an elemental quality. A sense of wild grandeur hovers over the wilderness of fresh shooting greenery scattered with crumbled stones like the bones of a fallen giant. Time has worked its magic with many of the Buddhas too: their stucco coats eroded, they sit with laterite sinews exposed, skeletal Giacometti figures whose stark abstraction has a haunting beauty.

From Kamphang Phet Highway 1 continues north-east to Tak, fifty miles from the Burmese border. Once a prosperous junction in the river trade, Tak is now a centre for smuggling: drugs, teak and gems from the Burmese side, guns and virtually any consumer goods from the Thai. The area west of Tak, around the border town of Mae Sot, was a hotbed of Communist insurgence in the turbulent 1970s. In those days the road south of Mae Sot to Um Phang was known as 'Death Highway' not, as one might expect, from the way Thais drive, but because of the constant guerrilla activity. Times have changed. The ex-leader of the local CPT is now profitably involved in building hotels and doing his bit to encourage the visitors who come to trek and hunt in the hills surrounding the Long Sang National Park, and the area is generally struggling to put itself on the tourist map. But it has not completely outgrown its wild past. There are not infrequent reports of violent clashes between the Thai Army Rangers, the crack border police, and 'illegal loggers' caught in the Park. The Rangers have been called in because of local police corruption; the going rate to turn a blind eye to teak smuggling is said to be 125,000 *baht* a truckload. The smugglers tend to move at night, not only to minimise the risk of detection, but because the lorries' tyres are so bald they would blow in the fierce daytime heat. Nor is

all the hunting legal: tiger and elephant are poached by organised
gangs, the ivory ending up on the Japanese market, the fur in
Singapore. As with most places on the Thai periphery, there is
lawlessness in the air.

Western Tak province is heavily influenced by Burmese
culture, and is host to a number of groups of Karens – 17,000 in
unofficial refugee camps alone – driven over the border from
Burma as a result of the running battle the Karen National Union
has been waging with the Rangoon government ever since the
country's independence from the British in 1948. Many older
Karen served with the British, for the colonists ended for them a
hundred years of Burmese persecution, and a 10,000-strong
Karen army fought the Japanese invaders in the Second World
War, distinguishing themselves particularly at Imphal, where the
Japanese advance was finally halted. Once the Burmese were
given power in Rangoon, retribution against the Karen was swift,
and the tribespeople were forced back to the borderlands and
their independent state of Kawtulay. Many Karen now earn their
living from smuggling, especially guns to aid their cause in
Burma, and levy tolls on smuggled goods coming into Thailand,
such as teak and livestock. Anti-Communist and Christian led,
unlike many of the dozen or so groups ranged against Rangoon,
they are strictly moralistic (ten years' imprisonment for premar-
ital sex is not unheard of) and claim to have no connection with
the lucrative opium trade. As an aspiring tourist destination, Tak
rather plays on its reputation as the capital of Thailand's Wild
West. The best hotel in town refuses Travellers' Cheques, saying
it trusts only cash, and the high spot of the evening cabaret is a
cowboy riding into the bar on a horse. But in Mae Sot, the border
town shadowed by the undulating hills of Burma, the potential
danger feels more real. 'Enjoy yourself, but if you carry a gun
you'll end up in jail' warn notices in Thai, and the sight of the
black-uniformed Rangers strolling through the town with that
sinister leisure of border officials, M16s in their hands and strings
of opium poppies around their necks, gives one a certain *frisson*.

Culturally Mae Sot is an intriguing mixture. The temples are
mainly Burmese in style, writhing with ornate woodwork; the

streets carry signs in Thai, Chinese and Burmese. Beneath this dancing jumble of rounded and square scripts, Christian Karens in colourful ethnic dress walk alongside Muslim Indian merchants sporting beards, and sartorially impeccable Burmese in the traditional chequered sarong they call the *lungyi* and short, collarless jackets. The Burmese are largely Muslim too, and both women and men enjoy what Kipling called 'whackin' great cheroots'. Taxi trucks (*songtheows*) go to the river bank that is the Thai side of the border and legal Burmese goods can be bought in the market here: foodstuffs, teak carvings, lacquerware, gems.

Sukhothai, birthplace of the Thai nation, is the second of the three ancient cities you reach travelling north through the Central Plains. Lying at the apex of a roughly equilateral triangle formed by Tak, over sixty miles to the west, and Kamphang Phet, over fifty miles to the south, Sukhothai can be approached from either. To reach the old town, the visitor must run the gauntlet of the new. This was almost entirely rebuilt after a devastating fire thirty years ago, and is a prime example of that featureless homogeneity all too common in urban Thailand: 1960s 'World Bank architecture' laid out on a grid. The basic unit of this dreary scene is the shophouse, a three- or four-storey block, one room wide, devised by Chinese merchants to make the most economical use of costly urban space. The ground floor serves as a shop, restaurant or office and is protected after hours by a metal roller-door or sliding grille that gives the night-time buildings an air of sad abandon. The floors above provide accommodation for the family or tenants; as many Thais leave their country homes to work in the towns, such lodgings are in high demand. Wooden shophouses first appeared in Bangkok's Chinatown in the 1890s; nowadays the concrete version is to be found on every street in the land. But eight miles and 600 years down the road, the old city presents a different vista. The Sukhothai Historical Park, a huge rectangle protected by three rows of earthen ramparts and a double moat, contains the remnants of twenty separate temple complexes. These were the core of the Sukhothai kingdom which, though it lasted a mere 200 years, is considered the fragile peak of Thai civilisation.

This brief but brilliant period is inextricably bound up with the rather enigmatic beginnings of the Thai nation. The first references to the Siamese are in inscriptions, one from eleventh-century Vietnam and another from the twelfth-century Angkor Wat, where a group of foreign soldiers called the 'Syam' served at the court of the God King Jayavarman. For perhaps two centuries prior to this, the Thais had been filtering into modern Thailand from the provinces of Yunnan and Sechuan in south-west China. This gradual influx was greatly accelerated at the end of the thirteenth century, when shock waves from Kublai Khan's devastating invasion pushed a number of groups over the Empire's borders. Taking advantage of the warmer weather and richer soil, the displaced Siamese coalesced into two main groups: one staying in the northern territories irrigated by the Mekong River, the other coming south to the headwaters of the Chao Phya, where they eventually established Sukhothai and its satellite towns. To do so they had to defeat the already weakened Khmers, and it appears Sukhothai was laid out originally upon Khmer lines, as a microcosmic map of the universe drawn up in accord with the Hindu rules of sacred architecture. Under its first king, Intradit, the new capital was named Sukhothai, 'the dawn of happiness', and to judge from the twenty stone inscriptions so far uncovered, it was indeed a contented and peaceful time. We are told that Intradit's son, Ramkamhaeng the Great, would sit on his stone throne on the Palace Mound, the symbolic centre of the citadel, and dispense justice. A massive bell was set up so that any subject, noble or commoner, could ring it and summon his monarch for a fair hearing. Ramkamhaeng maintained peace at home, extended his frontiers and opened up relations with China. As one inscription says: 'In the water there are fish, in the paddies rice. The lord of the land does not raise taxes for his people taking cattle over his fields or horses over his lands. Those who want to play, play. Those who want to sing, sing. Those who want to laugh, laugh.'

The constitution of this Eastern Camelot is the stone stela attributed to Ramkamhaeng which is now displayed in the National Museum in Bangkok. Inscribed in 1292, which, as a

Year of the Dragon, was one of momentous changes according to Chinese belief, the inscription is Thailand's Magna Charta, containing a wealth of information on subjects as varied as the King's invention of the Thai script, his conquests, political philosophy, taxation, and the worship of spirits. The stela was discovered by the then Crown Prince Mongkut in 1833 and its contents influenced the future Rama 4 to shift from the old Hindu/Khmer concept of a divine god-king to the Buddhist/ Thai vision of the monarch as a wise and paternalistic leader. There are those scholars who cast doubt on the authenticity of much of the inscription, thereby implying that it is something of a royal exercise in public relations, but I would not care to be the one to prove that the stela is a fake. Sukhothai burns like a brilliant and fugitive flame in the surrounding obscurity of Thai history. The kingdom lasted a mere 200 years before being eclipsed by the rising star of Ayutthaya; yet it witnessed a flowering of all that is best in classical Thai culture, reaching heights of artistic expression never again attained.

The best way to begin a tour of the park, which is divided into five separate zones, is to visit the Ramkamhaeng National Museum, just inside the Kamphang-hek ('Broken Wall') gate. Especially noteworthy here is the orientation model of the site, the copy of Ramkamhaeng's stela with an explanation of his alphabet, and, in the second of the two buildings, a marvellous display of Buddha images. These, to my mind, are the supreme achievement of Sukhothai. No other figure, Buddhist or otherwise, has ever achieved such a balance of the spiritual and the sensual, or so fully expressed beatitude. Sukhothai Buddhas seem to float rather than sit, their bronze bodies weightless. With delicate oval faces, aristocratically aquiline noses and lowered eyes that look down from an Olympian height, they radiate calm, suffused at the same time by a pleasure which is at once sensuous and incorporeal. The major innovation of the school was the Walking Buddha, a figure poised between space and solidity. These images sway into movement with a feline and luxuriant ease, the shoulders broad and the limbs elongated, tumescent as a sap-filled plant. This stylisation, disquieting to some Western eyes, is not concerned with mere adherence to outer form, but aims to express, from the inside, the actual feeling of the Buddha's transfiguration. The result is an androgynous grace in which contrasting energies are perfectly balanced. The Sukhothai smile celebrates the marriage of inner divinity with outer realisation: the knowledge that even the febrile melodrama of human life, when viewed aright, is nothing less than the play of Infinity: full, uncontaminated and blissful. Here is the spiritual archetype of *mai pen rai* – the harmony of all things. Beside this transcendent sublimity the enigmatic Giaconda smile seems an earthy, almost flirtatious allurement. The fragile bloom of the Sukhothai Buddha flowered for little more than fifty years. By the second half of the fourteenth century, a superciliousness had begun to pucker its lips, in time degenerating into a self-satisfied smirk that paved the way for the haughty and detached expression of the Ayutthayan and Bangkok periods.

The park contains a variety of building styles – Khmer, Mon, Sri Lankan – all of which were preparations for the typical Sukhothai *chedi*, a tall and elegant tower with an elongated 'lotus bud' finial. The magical and spiritual centre of the kingdom was Wat Mahathat, which contains no less than 200 *chedis* and many other assorted buildings. It is especially beautiful at dawn or dusk, when the principal Buddhas are silhouetted against a purple and aquamarine sky. At the Festival of Lights (Loy Krathong) the ruins are covered with hundreds of tiny candles, as the local women gather in traditional dress under the November full moon, to float banana-leaf cups (*krathong*) laden with flowers, incense and candles as offerings to the water spirits. Of the six or seven other most frequented *wats* here, Wat Sri Chum with its giant Buddha and Wat Saphan Hin on a hill overlooking the site should be seen. Thanks to the attentions of UNESCO, the Thai Fine Arts Department and latterly the Japanese, Sukhothai is now all red brick restoration and neatly manicured lawns. It is a pretty place, with flame trees and ponds crowned by pink lotuses, but I must confess, I prefer my archaeological sites untamed, left as unkempt spaces in which to wander, discover and dream.

*

The Old Sukhothai Cultural Centre, thatched bamboo accommodation just outside the Kamphang-hek Gate, is a lovely place
to stay, though advance booking is necessary from October to
April. I spent four or five peaceful days here, touring the site in
the early morning and late afternoon, returning for lunch and a
siesta in my cabin bungalow. The sightseeing is done on a lady's
bicycle, somewhat battered, improbably named the Golden Bull,
that I hire from a large and rather formidable woman who sits
outside her shop all day, working her way through a large pile of
punctured inner tubes, victims of the thorns that lurk in the dry
grass. She obviously has me down as an unreliable character, as
each time I wobble past she assails me with the refrain: 'On the
road! On the road!' Despite such warnings, her misgivings turn
out to be justified. On my last day, in search of a photograph, I
stray off the path and end up with not one, but both wheels
punctured. Shamefacedly, I wheel my gilded ox back to its owner.
Even the outrageous compensation she demands and gets, fails to
bring a smile to her face. I hope she has no influence with the local
authorities, or by the next time I visit Sukhothai, the park will be
tarmacked.

My evenings are spent in the large open restaurant, owned and
run by Khun Nam Kang ('Mrs Dewdrop'), a supremely elegant
woman who enjoys much status as an ex-beauty queen. How she
retains such an air of coolness in this heat is a miracle, especially
as being a restaurateur in Thailand is hard work. Thais are quite
happy to sit down to a full-blown meal – fish, meat, rice, noodles,
vegetables – at any time of the day or night, and restaurants seem
happy to serve them. The place has a relaxed and friendly feel,
operating like an amorphous extended family. I am happy to join
it, become part of the furniture and sink into a familiarity that
distances me from the periodic invasions of tour groups, those
universal ambassadors of crimplene and Kodak, hot and tired
from a bout of rapid, but rigorous temple-bashing. Observing
such groups, I sympathise with the common Thai opinion that of
all *farangs* the French are the most difficult to deal with. By and
large the British appear timid and well behaved, the Italians noisy,
the Germans beerily boisterous, but it is the French who most

indulge in the one vice the oriental finds incomprehensible – impatience. Apparently unaware of the *sotto voce* lubricant that keeps Thai society running smoothly, the French display a rudeness that in this polite setting is gross. Thais place great importance on the tone of voice, and loudness is interpreted as not only impolite, but threatening danger. Thus most Thais sound like the tinkle of a Fabergé clock chiming the quarters. The sheer volume of an irate *farang* can almost knock one of the locals off his feet, and it is an ugly thing to witness. Apart from the tour groups the Centre is a quiet place; the loudest sound of an evening is usually the croaking of the bull frogs by the lotus pond. As yet mercifully free of neon lights and thumping discos it is an example of a type of ambience the Thais would do well to develop in their tourist spots. Evening entertainment is sometimes provided in the form of classical dance by students from the local academy of performing arts. This is of a high standard, and concentrates on the Sukhothai style of slower dance rather than a mixture of 'folk' styles. With luck these shows will not degenerate into those mutually embarrassing displays in which there is always one sulker and one giggler in a bored troupe who, half-blinded by camera flashes, go through the motions of a wooden and lacklustre performance. Thailand has her share of these but the show at Sukhothai is not one.

By the end of March, the skies are beginning to fill up with kites. Introduced from China at about the same time as paper, kite flying has a long history in Thailand, and in a country where people will gamble on fights between fish, beetles, cocks, humans and bulls, kite fighting was bound to catch on. King Intradit's wife records that her husband gave the sport his blessing, and the Sukhothai kings liked it so much that it figures prominently in the literature of the period. The craze had reached such a height by the time of Ayutthaya that a royal edict was issued in 1358 stipulating that no flying was allowed in the vicinity of the palace. Nowadays, at the climax of the season in April, huge kite battles are waged between the male *chula* – a star-shaped giant that takes a team of ten to launch – and the female *pakpao*, small, triangular and far more manoeuvrable. The kites are flown over a field divided by a rope into 'male' and 'female' zones, the object being to snare your opponent and drag it into your territory. The adults love kites as much as the children: long-tailed snakes, fish, owls, supermen and butterflies – all are highly coloured and decorated, and as the hot season progresses the roadsides flutter with stalls, and the telegraph wires sag with casualties.

It was King Narai of Ayutthaya who first used kites to gauge the pre-monsoon winds, and today their appearance seems to tease the first showers of the year out of the April sky. On my last evening in Sukhothai, a warm wind rises up from nowhere, whipping the dust into angry whorls, rattling loose fixtures and hurtling unripe mangoes down onto the corrugated iron roofs with cracks like pistol shots. The local animals, who like to congregate in the restaurant, are jittery: the dogs shift restlessly from one end of the room to another, the cats prowl round its periphery like caged panthers. Then with one or two heavy warning drops, a violent downpour ensues, driving clouds of steam up from the hot earth. Everyone in the restaurant cheers and laughs, the tension at last relieved. Later I eat with a friend in his house. The men sit on the floor around a cloth spread with a succession of dishes issuing from the kitchen, while the females who are not cooking squat by the kitchen door, watching silently. The food is so good I can hardly restrain myself from attacking it without ceremony, but my Thai companions eat little and slowly, treating the food as an aperitif for the rice whisky, which they consume with gusto. In due course we move outside to sit on bamboo beds. The stars in the rain-washed sky are brilliant, visible for the first time in days. One of the group is an educationist, organising a conference of head-teachers currently being held at the Centre. A gentle and intelligent man in his forties, he studied twenty years ago in the United States, and returned to become one of the regular contributors to the *Social Science Review*, then Thailand's leading intellectual magazine and a lone voice of protest against the Vietnam war. The talk turns to tourism, and he tells me that it is precisely because Thailand has never been colonised – a source of great national pride – that she is now so easily seduced by all things Western. Fascinated to hear such uncommon opinions, I think of all the Thais I have heard deprecate their own country as underdeveloped, contrasting it enviously with Japan. Thanks to tourists many Thais are convinced that all *farangs* are fabulously rich.

'People say my country is economically backward,' says my companion in faultless English. 'It is not; it is economically unbalanced. More televisions and make-up will not help my people. What we need is education. Why doesn't some of the money go into universities instead of hotels? What is the point of trying to mimic the bigshots like America?' No one answers. He smiles. 'The farmers in my country have a proverb: "To watch an elephant shit and then to try and do the same is a dangerous business."' After the laughter dies down he fixes me with a friendly smile. 'You tourists', he says softly, 'you are the colonists now.'

If you follow the river Yom north of Sukhothai, you reach her sister city, Si Satchenalai, that dates from the same period. The new town belies the name, being little more than a few rows of wooden, and not unattractive shophouses. Behind this façade, traditional village life goes on in hamlets with such engaging names as 'Wild Banana village' or 'Palace of the Numerous Maternal Grandmothers village'. Here the wooden houses crammed together are raised on stilts, providing wet-season protection against floods and a dry-season gathering place. Sheltered from the stunning heat, whole families spend much of the day here; the children running in and out among domestic animals and the women weaving the red and black cotton *sarongs* for which the area is famous. Life here is quiet, unhurried and simple. Eight miles back down river lies the old city of Si Satchenalai, built probably on the site of a former Khmer settlement called Chaliang. This collection of overgrown ruins was first put on the map in the 1930s by a retired British Consular official called Reginald le May. Like many after him, he fell quite in love with Thailand, and, retiring early, devoted himself to her exploration. In those days it took him eleven days to get from

Bangkok to Chiang Mai (now a sixty-minute plane hop) and he made his way around the country by train, bus, bicycle, elephant, pony and foot, convinced that no other traveller would describe the view again. A self-taught and passionate art historian, he couldn't find 'a single material soul' who knew anything about his special love, Si Satchenalai, or its sacred centre, Wat Mahathat. He wandered freely around the deserted capital for weeks, every so often picking up exquisite little Buddha heads that lay strewn in the long grass. He wrote as he wandered, and in his *Buddhist Art in Siam* correctly surmised that Wat Chang Lom, better preserved than its namesake at Sukhothai, owed its elephant buttressing to Singhalese influence. He was right, for Ramkamhaeng summoned monks from Ceylon who brought not only Pali scriptures, but architectural ideas and iconographical rules to inspire the Theravada Buddhism that has remained Thailand's official religion to this day. As his stela proudly tells us, the King built 'the Elephant-girded *chedi*' in 1285 to house relics of the Buddha. With its stairway mimicking a ladder to heaven, its two terraces as artificial mountains linking the mundane to the celestial and its bell-shaped spire signifying enlightenment, Wat Chang Lom was the prototype of hundreds of *chedis* that were to follow, their domes swelling like spiritual breasts to nourish the faithful. Le May loved Thailand passionately, but the world did not reward his devotion. He returned to England to write up all he had discovered, and published several books, eking out a living by selling off his collection of antiques. In the last years of his life, the only reputation he gained was of being a cantankerous old man who would threaten fellow drinkers in the pub he frequented with blows from a silver-topped cane if they disagreed with him. Opinionated he must have been, but to those whose company he suffered he never once spoke of Thailand.

Although Si Satchenalai crept slowly onto the tourist map, it remained virtually unchanged from le May's time to the present, a magical wilderness of ruins, accessible until recently only by a ferry across the river Yom. Then, in 1987, as part of the Visit Thailand Tourist Promotion Year, the place began to be transformed. The Park's usual annual budget of 1 million *baht* was increased nineteen-fold, with the instruction that if this money was not all spent in six months, it must be repaid to the Government. Bulldozers moved in, levelling off the land and doing untold damage to whatever remains lay undiscovered beneath the surface. Si Satchenalai was to be tidied up, made into another Sukhothai, landscaped for tourism. Tourism! The word was on everyone's lips, like some mantra promising universal prosperity. Never mind 700 years of history in a country that has effaced much of its past already, let's get the tourists in! Invading armies may not have been able to breach Si Satchenalai's walls and destroy her character, but the great Mercedes coaches, those Trojan horses of tourism, will surely do so.

The River Yom not only filled the city's canals and irrigated its fields, it also provided clay for the grey-green ceramic ware known as Sawankalok, a highly renowned type of pottery named after a local village. It was le May who introduced celadon Sawankalok to Britain but it had already been valued for hundreds of years elsewhere. Multi-purpose storage jars, similar to the amphorae of the Mediterranean world, had been exported to India for sale in the West, and, particularly favoured as burial urns, Sawankalok pots have been discovered as far apart as graves on the Thai/Burmese border and pits in the Philippines and Indonesia. The traditional wisdom is that when Sukhothai was founded at the end of the thirteenth century, fifty potters were imported from China to teach the locals, setting up kilns that were later transferred to Si Satchenalai. This theory fitted with the prevailing attitude of China as the purveyor of 'high' culture, and Thailand the undeveloped recipient. Since 1980 archaeological digging in the area has shed a different light on the subject. The Thai Ceramics Archaeological Project, a Thai/Australian venture involving the Department of Fine Arts and the University of Adelaide, had discovered over 200 kilns on both sides of the Yom, and evidence sufficient to posit the existence of perhaps 800 more. All of these are in a three-mile area between the old and new towns of Si Satchenalai, specifically located in and around the little village of Ban Ko Noi. As well as the kilns, the team has uncovered twenty-seven metal furnaces and evidence for perhaps

12 Houseboats on the River Nan at Phitsanulok have TV sets, even if few other amenities

13 'Lest we forget': a gardener tends some of the graves in the Kanchanaburi War Cemetery, the burial place of 6982 Allied POWs who died in captivity in the Second World War

14 Buddhist monks from the Mahanika sect on their early-morning alms round; they collect food, and the donors gain merit

15 Temple dancers taking a rest at Wat Mahathat, Phitsanulok. They are paid to perform classical dances by worshippers giving thanks for having their prayers answered

another eighty, a *chedi*, habitation sites, graves, canals and a
riverside quay – altogether evidence of a major centre of
production and distribution. According to the latest
palaeomagnetic techniques of dating, the kilns appear to go back
to about AD 900, at least 400 years before the Chinese are
supposed to have taught the Thais to pot, and considerably earlier
than any Chinese ware found in the area. The range of the
Si Satchenalai finds is huge: jars, lidded pots, bowls, bottles,
architectural pieces, lamps, figurines and toys. Some of the
underglaze painting of fish and plant forms is very fine, and it now
appears that the Thais may well have had considerable influence
on Chinese ceramics rather than the other way around.

That the story of ceramics in South-East Asia is being turned
on its head is exciting enough for the specialists, but the
importance of Ban Ko Noi goes far beyond that. The village,
numbering about 500 people or, as the locals calculate,
'seventy-five roofs', is a typical poor, up-country community
struggling to survive in changing times. When the archaeological
project moved in, it installed electricity in exchange for a promise
that the local people would stop looting exposed sites. This had
previously been rife and is a widespread problem all over
Thailand. (The burial sites at Tak have already been totally lost to
the looters, and Sukhothai is said to have lost 70 per cent of its
Buddha figures to foreign museums and collectors.) The people
of Ban Ko Noi not only kept their side of the bargain, they began
to show a genuine interest in the project, hurrying to tell the two
resident members, Don Hein and his wife Toni, whenever a
piece was overturned by the plough or a new kiln accidentally
stumbled upon. In an area where a day's work in the fields earns
only enough money to buy a chicken, such honesty is incredible.
As a result of the genuine affection that has grown between the
Heins and the villagers, and the hard work put in by those living
here and the scientists who visit from time to time to lend their
expertise, the dusty little hamlet positively hums with pride and
purpose. For the villagers the discovery is not just pots and kilns,
but their own history, their sense of identity and self-worth, and
effective participation in a future which can combat the drift to

the towns and the consequent destruction of community. The Heins have encouraged the villagers to rediscover the art of potting too, and many families are learning to produce modern copies of traditional Sawankalok ware as a means of supplementing their meagre agricultural income. Small scale, but integrated tourism is also on the books, with groups coming to live in the village for a few days to have an authentic experience of how eight out of every ten Thais live. In 1987 Princess Sirindhorn, a keen supporter of the project, opened an excellent museum and study centre at Ban Ko Noi, and a couple of months later the integration of the Heins' project seemed complete when their son Peter married a local girl.

But when I last visited Ban Ko Noi in February 1988, an air of gloom hung over the place. There was talk of government displeasure with Don and his team, and the possibility of not only support being withdrawn but work permits too. This was the result of a campaign that had silently been gathering momentum over the previous few months, spearheaded by a series of critical newspaper articles alleging, of all absurdities, that these dedicated people were involved in antique smuggling. Perhaps this quietly intense couple had inadvertently crossed someone in Bangkok's bureaucracy, perhaps the Department of Fine Arts had felt its thunder being stolen by the acclaim the *farangs* were getting, perhaps a powerful smuggler had had his pitch queered. Whatever the reason, should the exploration be terminated, it would be a tragedy for all concerned: for international research, for the village of Ban Ko Noi and for all those who have invested so much time, labour and love in the project.

III

THE NORTH

8

Water and Worship

Northern Thailand can be said to begin above an imaginary line drawn from Tak in the west to Phitsanulok in the east. The area so delineated is sliced vertically by four major rivers: the Ping, which passes through Chiang Mai and is the longest in the country, the Wang, the Nan and the Yom. The land between the river valleys is hill country, covered in jungle and forest. This elevation makes the north more temperate than Bangkok or the Central Plains, but the hot season, from March until June, still averages a blistering 86°F. The rainy season lasts from June to the end of the wettest month, September, and the cool period, the pleasantest time for a visit, runs from October to February.

All of the north was once the kingdom of Lanna ('the million rice fields'), a loosely knit political and cultural entity that endured longer than either of its more celebrated sisters, Sukhothai and Ayutthaya. Indeed, Lanna lost its semi-autonomous status as *Chao* ('prince-governor') only when it came under the direct rule of Bangkok in 1939. Though many are unaware of this history of independence, the northerners remember it with pride, and point to Lanna's distinct cultural forms, most notable in sculpture and temple architecture. Although early chronicles speak of its beginnings in the seventh century, Lanna can realistically be dated from the accession of King Mengrai to the throne of Chiang Saen in 1259. Within ten years, this resourceful and ambitious man had extended his small kingdom on the borders of Laos to include the southern outposts of Chiang Rai and Fang. Not satisfied with these conquests, he advanced on the powerful centre of Mon culture, Haripunchai, the modern Lamphun. (This is sixteen tree-lined miles south of Chiang Mai, and full of archaeological interest. It is best visited on a day-trip from that city, which should include Wat Phra That Haripunchai (1157), one of the loveliest temples in the country, and the excellent museum behind it, as well as the nearby village of Pasang, famed for its cotton products and the beauty of its girls.) Mengrai was a tactical genius. Astutely recognising his army was no match for the enemy, he infiltrated spies to undermine Haripunchai from within. It took eight years of patient subterfuge, but in 1281 he was at last able to march into the city virtually unresisted. With the capture of Haripunchai, the kingdom of Lanna became a reality. Mengrai lost no time in establishing friendly relations with Ramkamhaeng of Sukhothai and, like that monarch, encouraged the spread of Theravada Buddhism by inviting monks from Ceylon to unify his new kingdom. He also sought the Sukhothai ruler's advice in drawing up plans for what was to be the symbol and crowning glory of his achievement, the capital he called simply the 'New City' – Chiang Mai.

Lanna's history is one of internal conflicts, but the fourteenth and fifteenth centuries were also times of external threat. The greatest rival was Ayutthaya, the southern kingdom that was to eclipse Sukhothai in 1438, and throughout Thai history this north/south conflict plays an important and persistent part. But even this was temporarily eclipsed in the sixteenth century when the Burmese, who themselves were finally to destroy Ayutthaya, turned their aggressive attentions to Lanna. They were to occupy much of the Thai kingdom over the next two centuries, and the distinctive flavour of northern culture derives partly from their influence. In sculpture, Burma provided a strong link with the traditions of India, the home of Buddhism, and in architecture she bequeathed a legacy of highly embellished wooden structures, often open-sided and with decorated pediments and gables. By the time Ayutthaya fell to the Burmese in 1767, the population of Chiang Mai had been decimated, worn out by almost constant conflict. Indeed, the city was abandoned for twenty years, fully revived only at the beginning of the nineteenth century as the administrative centre of what was known as the 'Nothern Circle' of the Siamese nation.

Chiang Mai, 'Rose of the North', is the city in Thailand that has changed most rapidly in recent years. I remember it not so long ago as small and relaxed with an almost perfect climate, a town set in lovely wooded surroundings dominated by Doi Suthep Mountain with its sparkling gold *chedi*. Doi Suthep and some of the trees are still there, but the town itself has fast developed into a thriving commercial centre. It is also a hub of tourism, and used as the jumping-off point for the tribes and for the treks further north. The Night Bazaar epitomises this change: formerly an ethnic mud-floored market it is now a concrete shopping arcade, an oriental Oxford Street blaring out pop music. Fortunately, Chiang Mai has not lost all of its character, though what remains looks fragile. The heart of the original town was protected by a square moat that today encompasses some of the oldest and best buildings, such as Wat Phra Singh, Wat Chedi Luang and Wat Chiang Man, the oldest temple in the city. The main artery of the new city is Thapae Road. This connects the moat, fringed by flame trees and fished by crossbows, with the River Ping. Most visitors will spend some time in Thapae Road's banks, souvenir shops, tourist agencies and airline offices, and some may even stumble across the little-known Wat Saeng Fang, a gem of Burmese architecture, down a lane opposite the better known, but less attractive, Wat Buparam.

Nearby is one of the finest buildings in Chiang Mai, the eighteenth-century wooden cultural centre attached to the Diamond Hotel on Charoen Pathet Road. Beyond the river lies a pleasant administrative area containing the General Post Office and the Railway Station. Here, as in many parts of the city, are many attractive houses, built in wood on the traditional northern style, with high, crossed gables. From this side of the river the Super Highway loops back in an arc over the north of the city to join Huai Khao Road, which has some of the town's older high-class hotels, and leads to the National Museum, Doi Suthep and the University. All three are worth a visit. The display in the National Museum is excellent, though its staff, like the staff of many museums in Thailand, are unfriendly. I don't know whether bad pay or boredom creates this syndrome, but it does seem to exist. Like most of the country's universities, Chiang Mai has a well-laid-out campus, its 600 acres set against a backdrop of verdant hills. I find it an inspiring place, serving 10,000 students and it well reflects the esteem that education commands in a country where it has not yet been taken for granted. This esteem is obvious from the status teachers enjoy in the community: addressed by the honorific title *achaan* (from the Pali word meaning 'spiritual preceptor') they are the inheritors of a tradition that still invests education with an almost religious value. Indeed, teachers are so respected that questions may well not follow a lecture, as this might imply the delivery of the topic was unclear or at fault in some way, but be brought up by a student only days later, and then indirectly. Vigorous disagreement or argument with an academic superior is unheard of in Thailand, and many a visiting Western academic has had to learn to adjust to this lack of accustomed feedback.

Chiang Mai is easy to negotiate. *Songthaew* pickups serve as party-taxis and will take you anywhere in town for a couple of *baht*. *Tuk-tuks*, *samlors* and regular taxis are also available, and both push- and motor-bikes can be hired cheaply and easily. Mobility is very much a feature of Thai life. The country has probably the most varied public transport system in the world, with over fifteen different forms, and the typical informal greeting is '*Pai nai?*' ('Where are you going?') This mobility is the result partly of the practice of pilgrimage, and partly the result of migration from home in search of work. It also helps explain the extraordinary proliferation of informal eating places. A traditional Thai meal takes time and many ingredients to prepare, and serves many people. For a migrant worker, probably living singly with limited cooking facilities, it makes better sense to eat at a roadside noodle-shop, where a good meal costs only fifteen *baht* and there is both company and *sanuk*. I am reminded of the Lancashire pie-shops in the days of the cotton trade.

Thailand really gets on the move at festival time, when families come together from distant ends of the country. Anyone wishing to travel at such times should reserve both accommodation and transport as far in advance as possible. The main festivals in Chiang Mai are the November Loy Krathong and the Flower Carnival in February, but the most exciting of all is Songkran, which takes place in the middle of April each year. Songkran ('changeover') celebrates the astrological New Year, when the sun passes from the constellation of Aries to Taurus. It was originally an occasion to pay genteel homage to one's elders and betters, usually by pouring scented water over their hands, and lustrating the ashes of the ancestors. This is another example of the sacramental part played by water in Thai life. Rivers are known as Mae Nam ('Mother Water') and, like 'Mother Rice', provide a sustenance that is divine as well as material. Songkran, like the other festivals, also provides a short-term order to a world that is, in the Thai imagination, always vulnerable to chaos or unpredictable change. In a society governed by the rhythms and vagaries of Nature the festival is a dependable sign of regularity, which acts as a social, even cosmic, reassurance. Such animistic patterns of thought lie deep in the Thai psyche, buttressed by the Buddhist teachings on the impermanence of all created things. To the Western mind consoled by the hope of progress and control of the environment, such a world view might smack of pessimism; in traditional societies such as Thailand, it seems rather to have engendered a wholehearted ability to live in the present and enjoy whatever it has to offer.

Nowadays Songkran lasts for four days, from 13 to 16 April, and each day has its own pattern. The first is devoted to cleaning the house and getting new clothes; the second to preparing food for the monks and presents for elders and respected superiors. This is also a day of prayer and offering at the temple. Sand from the Ping is brought in silver bowls and by the bucketful into the temple compound, where it is shaped into rows of miniature *chedis* which are decorated with coloured paper flags marked with zodiacal signs and supplications to the gods for longevity and good luck. The custom allows each person who cannot afford to gain Buddhist merit by actually constructing a *chedi* to make a symbolic one until such time as his fortunes improve. The third day is the main time of merit-making. Food and robes are offered to the monks, the temples turned into ecclesiastical fairgrounds by groups of vendors selling birds in tiny bamboo cages, or fishes, eels or turtles in water-filled polythene bags, all of which can be bought and released as another way of gaining merit. The fourth day is the official time for paying respects. There is a huge procession, composed of representatives of the province's many varied communities, which ends at the Governor's residence in a spectacular cultural show. Many other processions have been held during the previous three days, but this is the most splendid. There are musicians in the coarse blue wear of the north, tribal people in their black dress colourfully embroidered and weighed down with heavy silver jewellery, shimmering dancers in Chiang Mai's famous silk. Here an old-timer beats a giant drum with deft jabs of his feet, knees and elbows – executing a performance with all the panache of a Thai boxer, there a group of girls weaves dreamily through the slow-motion Faun Lep ('Fingernail') dance. Elderly women in Burmese dress walk alongside boys whose faces are painted ghostly white with festival powder. And no Thai celebration would be complete without its beauty queen. Earlier in the festival all the prettiest girls in the area have been drawn through the town in a bicycle rickshaw procession under brilliant parasols, and the winning Miss Songkran now rides in a giant flower-bedecked float, surrounded by billowing clouds, mythical birds and a retinue of slaves and followed by a chariot bearing a huge image of the Buddha. The Thais love beauty contests, and will organise one at the slightest excuse. As well as the regular town and district competitions, the arrival of seasonal fruits is celebrated by a Miss Pineapple or a Miss Mango Queen and in Lopburi a 'Most Beautiful Widow or Divorcee of the Province' contest recently became an annual fixture. Even the small villages hold their beauty parades, though in the impoverished north the first prize may turn out to include an introduction into the 'service industry' of the nearest big town.

Throughout the four days of Songkran, things get steadily wilder and steadily wetter. By the last day the festival has become a boisterous water-battle, an uninhibited way for people to let off steam. The revelry gets more uproarious each year, to the dismay of the conservative members of the Chiang Mai community who write in alarm to the local papers. In the true tradition of carnival, misrule is lord, all the usual protocol that silently directs Thai society is temporarily suspended. Songkran is a social safety-valve, and *farangs* are prime targets, so if you go out onto the streets, you must be prepared to spend the whole day soaked to the skin. Nothing you read or hear about this festival can prepare you for the reality.

The mayhem reaches its height on the last day. The centre of the action is the circuit around the city moat. My hotel is well placed by the Chang Peuk ('White Elephant') Gate, whose windows overlook the canal and provide a perfect vantage-point from which to drench the passers-by below. In the street in front of the hotel, the staff have set up a front-line position with a couple of hoses. These are used to fill up a succession of plastic buckets, obtainable in various sizes from an improvised stall up the road, or, better still, turned directly onto the traffic driving past. The crowds on the canal side of the road draw their ammunition directly from the moat. Running this gauntlet is a steady stream of assorted vehicles. There are pick-up trucks jammed with twenty or thirty shrieking people, who scoop their water out of huge *klong* jars, and fire-fighting trucks with pumps mounted to squirt jets over the roadside crowds. Some motorbikes have one driver and two water-throwers, others have their side-car converted into a water tank holding fifty gallons or more. Many of the cars are smeared with a yellowy powder, the cosmetic of Songkran, their occupants running the risk of a bucketful tipped into their lap if they leave the windows open a second too long after delivering a salvo themselves. Some of the cars get so waterlogged they are temporarily abandoned. Gangs of people have even commandeered some of the city buses, which cruise past like stately battleships, water jars lined up along the aisle, passengers delivering broadsides from ten windows at a time. Individuals attack the vehicles and each other with whatever comes to hand – buckets, bowls, scoops, hoses, water pistols, bicycle pumps. Woe betide the truck that runs out of water, its passengers having to abandon their elevated position and brave the crowds to refill their jars.

Hour after hour the convoy drives round the circuit. The din is deafening: blaring car horns provide brassy punctuation to the hypnotic, manic rhythm of the lorries full of tom-tom beaters and the general singing and chanting, amidst which can be heard shouts of 'Sawadee Pimai' ('Happy New Year'). The loudest shrieks are caused by the iced water, for the noodleshops are doing a brisk trade in huge blocks of ice that give the water a freezing edge. They are also the source of a continuous supply of chicken kebabs and rice whisky, liberally dispensed to fortify the front-line troops. At one stage the crowds are parted by an airport bus arriving at the hotel, its dapper Japanese passengers wide-eyed with disbelief at the scene in front of them. Cunningly, they plead age to avoid a drenching, but the younger members of the party are soon spotted and initiated by enthusiastic members of the hotel staff. Everybody joins in, no matter what their age or rank. Next to me is a military policeman, his uniform a glistening skin, using his helmet as a bucket. Nearby I recognise a senior official from a local bank being pursued by his female staff, squealing with delight. And despite the fact that alcohol is flowing almost as freely as the water, there seems to be no violence or aggression, only unrestrained enjoyment. To be sure, it is a very liberating experience to be able to walk up to a complete stranger and tip a bowl of water all over him, participating in a celebration of water that the West leaves behind with childhood.

Then as the light begins to fade and the afternoon cools into evening, the iced water suddenly starts to feel too cold for comfort. Exhausted by their revels, the crowds with one mind begin to thin out and disperse. The cars disappear, the noise dies down and suddenly it is all over. The old belief is that the rains spring from the *nagas*, the celestial serpents which play among themselves, spouting water drawn from the cool Himalayan lakes as they snake voluptuously up the steps, along the walls or down the roofs of the temples. Songkran began as an imitation of the *nagas*, and perhaps they are pleased with such abandon, perhaps they admire the reckless squandering of water at the height of the dry season. Whatever the reason, about thirty minutes after everything has died down, it begins to rain for the first time in weeks. A few shunting rumbles of thunder, and the rain comes down in spears onto the puddles and abandoned buckets, while a cool breeze riffles through the silver streets, carrying with it the sweet evening scent of moist jasmine.

At Wat Buparam on Thapae Road, it is the abbot's birthday. He is sixty-two, and has been in the robe for forty years, one of the 40,000-odd permanent monks in the country. In a glass-doored reception hall behind the new *vihan* he sits on a raised platform above the polished teak floor. Behind him is a huge modern mural depicting the Buddha's first sermon. The room is lined with tables bearing papers, bundles of files and untidy piles of ledgers, much like any Third World office. The abbot himself is surrounded by his presents: trays of fruit wrapped in orange cellophane, coconuts, packets of washing powder, sweets, garish packets of joss-sticks. But for his imperturbable air, he could be a merchant, sitting patiently in the bazaar. Calmly fanning himself, he reads a typed manuscript and awaits the next batch of well-wishers. They are not long in coming. A group of monks, robes clinging wetly to their bodies, comes into the compound, followed by some women, three or four of whom are doing a wild version of the *ramwong*, a circling dance performed with arms outstretched. As they enter the hall, a pick-up truck lurches into the yard bearing a gang of men in dark glasses, who clutch bottles of Mekhong and beat tom-toms. The truck slews to a halt, disgorging its unsteady crew in front of the *vihan*. More women arrive in a procession, presents borne aloft, and the reception hall fills up. Trays and bowls of water are carried in, the presents offered, and with the monks on one side and the lay people on the other, the abbot begins a long blessing in Pali. It is a rich and ancient sound. Somewhere near the end, I hear the word *farang*, and several of the congregation turn to look at me, presumably I have been included in the blessing. After some brief responses and more chants, the audience is over. There are giggles all round – a common ending to Thai religious rites – and the crowd sways out into the evening, piles into trucks and disappears. The abbot picks up his paper and fan, and the compound returns to a temporary peace and quiet. A dog arrives, sniffing at discarded food, and a young monk starts to walk around the compound, very slowly, practising the discipline of maintaining mindfulness at all times.

In a side chapel an old lady performs her devotions in front of a Buddha image twice her size. Her skin gleams like parchment in the half-light, stretched tightly over fine bones, and her hair is cropped short in the manner of the elderly. She conducts a running conversation with the image while lighting three large candles, orange paper rolled loosely round a slow-burning core, that look like bumper ecclesiastical cheroots. She explains who the candles represent, pointing to each one and naming it clearly. The last is hers. She does this deliberately, several times and with patience, as if the image were hard of hearing or perhaps a little slow on the uptake. Then kneeling into a tiny bundle, she continues her prayers in a voice that is sometimes cajoling, sometimes indignant, sometimes light with laughter. The dialogue is utterly real. She offers flowers and leaves, then rises to pour two or three silver bowls of water over the image, speaking all the time in a soft reassuring tone like a mother bathing her child. She kneels again, carefully picking up the grains of rice and leaves that have fallen to the floor. I watched enthralled for ten minutes, caught in her simple spell. Suddenly, someone else comes in. She turns, sees me for the first time, and smiles, her face as open as a child's. I step outside into the twilight, as the glass mosaic on the façade of the *wat* begins to sparkle in the headlamps of the cars heading for the Night Bazaar.

Later, returning to the hotel, I pause to chat with the security guard. We recognise each other as veterans from the water-battle, though he is now immaculate in his brown uniform complete with handcuffs. He takes me by the arm and leads me to the hotel spirit-house, a splendid white and gold shrine that looks like a cross between a bird-table and a birthday cake, erected to house the lord of place (*phi phum*) displaced by the building of the hotel. It is piled high with the *malai* garlands, made from waxy jasmine buds, that are a common offering in small shrines. He *wais* deeply, and has me do the same, an action much approved by a group nearby to judge by the murmurs of *saway* ('beautiful'). We chat a little, and I admire his uniform. He makes me put on his cap and blow his whistle, and joining in I pretend to crack his baton over some imaginary offender. But he takes it, turns it into a microphone, and breaks into song with 'We are the world, we are the people . . .' Looking at his baton more closely, I see that he has carved on it a delicate picture of the *bo* tree, symbol of the Buddha's enlightenment.

Chiang Mai is famed as a centre for handicrafts, especially wood carving, silverware, jewellery, lacquerware, silk and ceramics. The whole business is very well organised and the crafts concentrated in the village of San Kamphaeng, thirteen miles south-east of the city. This is virtually one long straight road, lined by huge emporia with workshops behind. Here the various stages of production take place, involving painstaking and, all too often, eye-straining work. The tourist buses make a continuous and triumphal procession along this Credit Card Avenue, moving voraciously from one vast air-conditioned showroom to another. I have no idea how much money San Kamphaeng takes in an average day, but by Thai standards it must be colossal. Silk seems to be the favourite buy, the wooden furniture too heavy for European taste, though Americans seem to like it. Between San Kamphaeng and Chiang Mai lies the village of Bor Sang, the centre of umbrella production, where brightly painted parasols are made from mulberry paper stretched over bamboo frames. Here a lot of the work is done in less cramped conditions than seem to operate at San Kamphaeng. Although the centralising of 'cottage industries' obviously makes good marketing sense, it is a far cry from the old system of each family working at home, and I doubt if the workers have gained much from the change. Fortunately, there are still a few older establishments in Chiang Mai itself that produce on a smaller scale and have a less impersonal atmosphere. It is worth seeking them out, as the quality of their work is generally as good as that obtainable at the souvenir supermarkets, and their prices are often more reasonable.

Chiang Mai's most important *wat*, Wat Phra Singh, is also its most beautiful. Like most Thai temples, it faces east, and is best visited in the early morning when the rising sun adds a touch of magic to the glittering façade, and the spacious compound is likely to be full of orange-robed monks. The *wat* was founded in 1345 to house the valuable Phra Singh ('Ceylonese Buddha'), an image reputed to have come from Sri Lanka 1500 years ago, and to have spent time at a number of places before ending up in Chiang Mai. Such peripatetic histories are not uncommon for the most important Thai Buddhas, as they passed from ruler to ruler, capital to capital, as magic talismans ensuring the success of the owner. Whatever its origins (it may well have been brought north by missionaries summoned to Mengrai's court) the Phra Singh is a majestic piece, showing strong Sukhothai influence. It is paraded at Songkran and lustrated by the crowds, who believe that it has the power to bring rain. For the rest of the year the image receives quieter worship from its throne in the wooden chapel known as the Lai Kham Vihan. This is one of the most beautiful buildings in the country. Dating from the eighteenth century, it has the low sweeping eaves characteristic of northern architecture, a feature no doubt derived from Yunan, the original home of the Siamese people, and a lovely carved wooden façade showing Burmese influence. Inside are some unusually well-preserved murals showing eighteenth-century life, as well as the standard scenes of the Buddha and his previous births. As with all Lanna painting, the style is less intellectual than that of the Bangkok school, with a wealth of homely detail and a *joi de vivre* in the depiction of everyday life. A discreet sensuality enlivens the realism of scenes portraying an ideal of human rather than divine beauty. Another distinctive building at Wat Phra Sing, contemporary with the Lai Kham Vihan, is the library, a wooden building inset with mother-of-peal and elevated on a stuccoed brick base.

The finest Buddha image in the city is considered to be the eighteen-foot-high gilded bronze giant that presides over Wat Suan Dork. This temple, completed in 1510, is also worth a visit for its collection of graceful *chedis* containing the ashes of Chiang Mai's royal family. Their elegant spires, rising like needles to the heavens, are especially lovely at sunset. Under a huge and intricate ceiling, the Buddha is seated in the 'earth touching' position with his right hand extended to the ground, a posture that recalls the Master's victory over the temptations of Mara, the Buddhist Satan. It is the position most favoured by Thai sculptors; perhaps because the defeat of Mara became associated with Buddhism's displacing the indigenous animistic cults, encouraging the triumphant 'earth-touching' Buddha to become easily recognisable as the lord of lesser gods. The solidity of the image, with its outflung chest, shows it to belong to the school of sculpture known as Chiang Saen, one of the most accomplished Lanna styles. Unusually, it rests back-to-back with a huge standing figure which has clear fertility connections. A bundle of rice straw is often placed in its open right hand and the hair, rather than conforming to the 'snail-shell curls' as laid down in Buddhist texts on iconography, is more akin to the spiky outer skin of the jackfruit or durian, two fruits highly prized throughout the country.

For those interested in temple architecture, Chiang Mai provides a variety not equalled in any other city. Wat Ku Tao has a *chedi* shaped like a pile of alms bowls one on top of the other, while Wat Chet Yot, near the Museum, is modelled on the original temple at the site of the Buddha's enlightenment in Bodh Gaya in India. It is a tranquil place with some lovely stucco figures decorating the outside of the buildings. Wat Umong has traces of fine Lanna murals, their beauty enhanced by their fragility, and Wat Doi Suthep, on top of the hill overlooking the city, should be visited as an example of a living temple colourful and rowdy on most days, its fairground atmosphere augmented by the recent introduction of a cable car for lazy pilgrims. In 1545, Chiang Mai was shaken by a violent earthquake, and one of the casualties was the 500-year-old *chedi* of Wat Chedi Luang, which, standing almost 300 feet high, must have been one of the most substantial buildings in the north. The *chedi* was never repaired, a curious fact as the *wat* must have been one of the most sacred in the city, having accommodated the Emerald Buddha for almost a century, and being the site of the Lak Muang pillar. This can be seen today, sheltered in a small building close to a sacred gum tree which is believed to enshrine the guardian spirit of the city's fortunes. Added to which, King Mengrai is believed to have died here, struck by a bolt of lightning. When Mengrai died he would have received the traditional Lanna cremation, in which the *prasat*, an elaborately painted and decorated wooden pavilion that houses the coffin, is packed with gunpowder and ignited with fireworks. Nowadays this costly ritual to celebrate the most important of Thai life-ceremonies is rare.

More typical is the ceremony I stumble across in Wat Chedi Luang some days after Songkran. This is the funeral of a well-known local dance teacher, Kin Thong ('Golden Xylophone'). In a *sala* at the back of the compound, an ornate white and gilt coffin draped with fairy lights and surrounded by bouquets is set up on a table. Next to it stands a large photograph of the dead woman in the official white uniform of a civil servant. Seven or eight women are busy filling orange plastic buckets with offerings to be presented to the presiding monks – packets of soap powder, toothpaste, lavatory paper, chillies, garlic, biscuits. A young man sits at the door taking donations in envelopes from the mourners as they arrive. I learn he studied English for a couple of years in Michigan, and now runs a bookshop in town. He makes no secret of his feelings about religion: to him it is an excuse to exploit the ignorant and the superstitious. He would rather see help given to the poor, the small farmers, or the students than to the monks, who have more than enough as it is. I think of the old lady worshipping the other evening at Wat Buparam, and cannot agree with his opinion that the people get nothing worthwhile out of their religion. But when the presiding monk arrives a few minutes later, a tall, rangy figure with dark glasses and a cigarette dangling laconically out of one corner of his mouth, I have to admit he hardly looks like an ecclesiastical dignitary.

The *sala* is filling up with people, and much *wai*-ing is in evidence, the assembled company bobbing up and down like corks on a sea of sociability. The *wai* means far more than the handshake, for it is not just a gesture of greeting or even equality, but one of respect. The general rule is that the inferior initiates the *wai*, and the recipient returns a lesser one or, if the social distance between the two is great, just smiles or nods in acknowledgement. This essential Thai ritual can cause problems for the visitor, unsure of the complex rules of etiquette. *Wai*-ing an obvious inferior – labourer, servant or child – will make you look ridiculous in Thai eyes; on the other hand, the very old and the monk are usually a safe recipient of a *wai* from a *farang*.

The theatrical nature of Thai society is very apparent at gatherings such as these, and the Thais appear a people who are kept together by being kept apart. Yet despite the ritualised formality many aspects of Thai life are informal by Western standards. Socialising is generally easy-going, especially where food is concerned, though I suspect that underneath the *bonhomie* there must be some tension generated by the desire to avoid infringing social rules and giving offence. Social lubricants such as 'please', 'thank you' or even 'hallo' are not considered necessary except in exceptional circumstances, and despite the fact that there are at least ten words used for 'you' depending on who you are talking to, all Thais are known by their first name, indeed surnames only became a legal requirement in the 1920s. In addition, most have nicknames, a hangover from the belief that if a baby's real name is used, the spirits may gain power over it. These monosyllabic sobriquets are hardly formal: 'pig', 'small' and 'fatty' being some of the most common.

Eventually, things are ready to begin. Thirteen monks, the most auspicious number for such occasions, sit ranged on sofas against the back wall. Faces hidden behind the ceremonial fans which show the level of a monk's rank they begin to chant. As the Pali rises rich and sonorous into the heat, my mind feels heavy and I can hardly keep my eyes open. Not all are so absorbed. I notice one bored-looked chain-smoker, and some women gossiping behind the shield of their raised hands. The bookshop owner is nowhere to be seen. Two young men, heads freshly shaved, kneel before the chief monk, who is now nonchalantly chewing betel nut. They are to become monks for a few days, to speed their mother into heaven and to earn merit for themselves. They offer robes, which are blessed and returned to them and then, with that skilful modesty at changing clothes in public all Thais seem to possess, they swap their jeans for the orange robe. After the ceremony, the food. The monks eat first, though they display little interest in the steaming dishes set before them, eating in a controlled and silent manner. I wander outside and bump into someone who invites me to stay for the meal. We sit and wait under canopies for perhaps thirty minutes. At last the food comes, but even then it sits on the tables for another ten minutes. It is now well after noon, and, having had breakfast at 5.30 a.m., I can hardly contain my hunger. At last, without a word, people all at once stop chatting or gazing into space, and draw up chairs to eat. As usual in a Thai gathering, everything seems to proceed according to some pattern invisible to the outsider, who can only wait and exercise the noble Buddhist virtue of patience.

The Thais, of course, have a natural skill in this, which they call *krengjai*. This is normally translated as 'consideration for others', but it is more than that, rather an intuitive grasp of the nuances of any particular situation that enables them to handle it with the minimum of friction, something the society definitely dislikes. The Western question at this point might well be: 'Then what happens to natural aggression?' That it doesn't just evaporate is suggested by the figures from the last census (1976) which reported that petty crime was rife, there was a prison population of 1.5 per 1000 of the population and also a very high murder rate. Some 1200 were reported in that year, many of them *crimes passionnels*. Interestingly, a high proportion of these took place not in the heat of the moment but a considerable time after the event, indicating that resentment in Thailand can burn with a long fuse.

After lunch my companion takes me to see a small cemetery behind the *sala*. He points out a tomb in which his father, who died two months ago, must wait for another eighteen months until the astrologically favourable time for cremation. A faded airmail envelope is taped to the tomb; it is a letter from England that arrived after the death, its contents thus conveyed to the inert body within. A lorry turns up, coffin and flowers are loaded on and, headed by the monks in a Volkswagen van, the cortège sets off for the cremation ground. I have been invited to the 'burning', and our car joins the procession, serenaded by Country-and-Western music from the radio. The scene at the crematorium resembles a race meeting. There are a couple of large stands to accommodate spectators, a performance of sacred *khon* masked dance performed by some of the Golden Xylophone's pupils, and tray after tray of iced Coca-Cola for everyone. More chanting and blessings and, as the monks pile back into their van, people crowd into the small building with a tall chimney to pay their last respects. One or two white handkerchiefs make a discreet appearance, but what grief there is is very well hidden. Because of the dramatic performance, artists' funerals are considered 'happy' in Thailand. Certainly compared to a funeral in the West, the Golden Xylophone's send-off is a cheerful event, and she must be well speeded to her next reincarnation.

Mae Hong Son, the 'city veiled by mist', is aptly named. Tucked away from the world in a lush valley between densely wooded hills, the town is almost covered in cloud four months of the year, a fact which adds to its feeling of isolation. Yet Mae Hong Son is only thirty-five minutes by air from the bustle of Chiang Mai, and since 1965 the two places have been connected by a tortuous but stunningly beautiful road that winds for eight hours up through the hills. Mae Hong Son province – named as is usual after the chief town – is Thailand's least populated, with less than 150,000 inhabitants, who are distributed between the ethnic group known as the Thai Yai and various hill tribes. It is also probably the least spoilt, being 90 per cent rugged, hilly and mountain terrain largely unaffected by the illegal logging and slash-and-burn agriculture that has denuded much of the upland country elsewhere. The town itself is a ragged patchwork of one- and two-storey shophouses and wooden homes thatched with banana leaves. The quietness of the place is striking. There are no whining motorbikes, no public transport. The streets are too hilly for the *samlor* pedicab, so people just walk. Black Chinese trousers and collarless shirts are commonly worn, as are bamboo hats, similar to those found in Vietnam. Burmese influence is clear in the wooden carving of the temples such as Wat Hun Wiang, which houses the most sacred image and backs onto a bustling early-morning market, or Wat Jong Klang with its wooden dolls carved as animals and humans to tell the story of the *Jataka* tales. Doi Kungmu gives a spectacular view over the town, spread miniaturist below like some Himalayan hill-station. So removed is Mae Hong Son that it was once dubbed the 'Siberia of Thailand', its isolation from Bangkok making it the ideal dumping ground for disgraced or troublesome officials.

Entertainment here is traditional and low key, a far cry from the Bavarian pubs and pasta parlours springing up in Chiang Mai. At about the time the 'Rose of the North' is celebrating her riotous Songkran, Mae Hong Son enjoys another quieter festival, Buat Luk Kaew, 'Ordaining the Beloved Sons'. Perhaps twenty boys, aged between ten and thirteen, become novice monks, thus repaying their parents for the gift of life as the Buddha recommended. This is the prime debt of gratitude in a society still largely structured by reciprocal favours. The focal point of the three-day festivities is Wat Chiong Kham, picturesquely located by a small tree-fringed lake on the southern edge of town. Buat Luk Kaew is always a community affair. Members of the richest family are chosen to lead the procession, they in turn will bear the lion's share of paying for the pageant, an act of merit-earning charity required by their status. After the novices-to-be (*nahks*) have received gifts and blessings from their elders, the townspeople carry 'offering trees' – bamboo poles festooned with presents, toilet articles, gaily coloured pennants and money – to the temple. The third day is the highlight, with the procession of the *nahks*. In the clear air the colours are brilliant. The boys wear sequinned costumes of red, gold, and orange silk, draped with scarlet rosettes and gold and silver medallions, their turbans covered in bright yellow flowers, the sacred parasols hung with jasmine and wild orchids. Looking strangely girlish with faces made up, the *nahks* are carried on the shoulders of their older friends, who prance and sway like horses, enacting the night the Buddha rode out of his palace to begin his new life as a seeker after truth. the gentle music at the procession's head contrasts with the driving rhythm of the long drums at the rear. As the procession winds the two miles to the lakeside temple, everyone in the town joins in. And after the ritual presentation of food and gifts to the monks, the ordination begins, and another batch of little boys is set to become novices, earn great respect, and view the world from the detachment of the saffron robe.

9

Into the Golden Triangle

Early in the morning of 21 January 1982, a squad of 800 Border Patrol Police (BPP), Thailand's frontline counter-insurgency force, closed in on Hin Taek, a tiny village north-west of Chiang Rai and five miles inside the Thai/Burmese border. The attack was the climax of many weeks' planning and practice. Some months before, Thai government troops had tried to intercept one of the regular opium caravans that criss-cross the Golden Triangle – the remote area where the borders of Thailand, Laos and Burma meet. This particular caravan was large – 200 mules laden and escorted by members of the Shan United Army (SUA), one of the many Burmese-backed groups that operate in the Golden Triangle, financing their independence struggle against Rangoon by dealing in drugs. The SUA responded fiercely with mortars and machine-guns, and as Thai government reinforcements came to the rescue, the SUA withdrew over the border to Burma. Its cargo of drugs, estimated by Thai experts to be enough to supply every addict in the world for six months, was virtually untouched. Embarrassed and angry, Bangkok immediately put a price of half a million *baht* on the head of the man known to be in control of the SUA, the self-styled king of the Golden Triangle, warlord Khun Sa. Not unsurprisingly, given the man's reputation, there were no takers. Instead, Khun Sa announced his own reward for the death of any American Drug Enforcement Agency official operating on behalf of the Thai government in north Thailand. This campaign proved more successful: between July and December eight people connected with the DEA were assassinated.

At the beginning of 1982, two of Thailand's most powerful men, General Prachuab Suntarangkul, the Deputy Premier and former police chief, and Major-General Chavalit Yongchaiyuth, the head of the army, met to devise a top-security plan to flush out the man whom the media have dubbed the 'drug kingpin'. Keeping the details of the plan to themselves, the two supervised practice manoeuvres in the province of Tak, where the rugged hill terrain is similar to that of Hin Taek, rumoured to be Khun Sa's current headquarters. Practice over, the squad moved north, still unaware of their final destination, so tight was security. The plan was for the Border Police to install themselves in Hin Taek before dawn, lull the rebels' suspicions by engaging Khun Sa and his Chief of Staff in negotiations, and then to launch a surprise attack, supported by aircraft. Things did not go quite as planned. To begin with, the support aircraft, a vital part of the strategy, failed to turn up on time. His troops exposed by the morning light, Commander Thong-oon Charoensom decided to go ahead with his approach to the rebel leaders. At 8.15 he set off for the house used as staff headquarters. The SUA guards were waiting, and opened fire on the police motorcycle cavalcade, killing several troopers. The battle for Hin Taek had begun.

Further down in the village, the main body of government troops came under fire from a large contingent of rebels situated in their arms depot situated on an elevated rise overlooking the main part of the village. As the day wore on, this was to become the core of the rebel resistance. The combat gathered momentum, and four or five Hin Taek children ran from the village school in an attempt to reach their homes. The school uniforms – khaki with long sleeves – made them indistinguishable from the SUA. They, and one of their teachers, were cut down in the cross-fire. At about ten o'clock, the long-awaited air support arrived and began bombing SUA strongholds in and around the village. It was only the eventual arrival of helicopter gunships that finally tipped the scales in favour of the government forces. Nevertheless, the battle continued all day, and as dusk fell the SUA, sensing defeat, set their arsenal ablaze. It was to burn for two days. Hundreds of charred M16s were later found, but more than fifteen tons of equipment survived the flames, including 200 walkie-talkies, 300 hand grenades, and over 50,000 rounds of ammunition. According to government figures, the battle had claimed seventeen lives and fifty casualties on the government side, while the SUA had suffered eighty-two dead and 'a great number of wounded'. Of Khun Sa and his deputy there was no sign. They had slipped back across the border to safety, leaving behind them the ruins of what must have been north Thailand's best-serviced village, complete with its own swimming pool and ice-making plant.

That a maverick band of gun-slinging drug-runners could have taken control of a town well inside the Thai border was galling enough, but the Golden Triangle has long been a thorn in Bangkok's side. Stories of the drug barons make a perfect complement to the capital's sex industry as material for sensationalist media reports, and the Kingdom has become understandably sensitive on such scores. But though the Golden Triangle has remained a problem in the period since Hin Taek, it is not one that can be laid solely at Thailand's door. It is largely the result of foreign interference in the area, and the governments of France, China and the United States all share some responsibility for a situation of intractable complexity that has been thirty years or more in the making. No single figure better exemplifies the convoluted international interests that have woven the story of the Golden Triangle than the man who now rules it, the warlord Khun Sa.

The future 'prince of poppy' was born in 1932, just west of the Salween river in the Shan states of north-east Burma. His father was Chinese, his mother Shan, and the baby was given the Burmese name of Kwan Kywa. In 1947, the fifteen-year-old Kwan Kywa's father was executed on the orders of a local princeling; no one today remembers why. It was a time of upheaval in the area. Burma was moving towards her independence from Britain, and her minority peoples, such as the Chin, Karen and Shan were eager to assert theirs' from the Burmese-dominated socialist group that was set to take over the running of the country. The Shans had moved centuries ago from southern China into north-east Burma and northern Thailand – indeed the word Shan is the Burmese version of Siam – and these people shared a sense of ethnic solidarity that far transcended any arbitrary political borders. Shan princes had been recognised by the British and, although initially willing participants in Burmese republicanism, were determined to retain their freedom. The civil war in China was nearing an end, and small communist bands were already active in the Burmese areas adjoining China. Soon after his father's death, Kwan Kywa's mother married a local Shan warlord and the lad was renamed Khun Sa. The name *khun*, not to be confused with the common Thai word meaning 'mister' (which has a different tone and spelling in Thai), proved to be prophetic. It is the title traditionally given to a Shan princeling-warlord, one of the rulers of the numerous petty kingdoms strung out along the Thai border before the unification of the country under Rama 4 at the end of the nineteenth century. *Khun*, fittingly enough, is also the name given to the king in Thai chess. While still a teenager, Khun Sa joined up with the remnants of Jiang Jieshi's Nationalist Army, the Guomindang, who had fled into northern Burma to escape the victorious communists in 1949. The Guomindang, desperate to replenish their warchests, soon learned to use opium to finance their rearguard action against Mao Zedong's forces. It was they who encouraged the Burmese hill tribes on the west of the Golden Triangle, such as the Wa, to grow, on a commercial basis, the opium they had always modestly cultivated for their own consumption. Hill tribesmen were recruited into the Guomindang, their arms coming from the sale of opium, their military training from experts from Taiwan. It was the Guomindang who first set up jungle laboratories with Chinese chemists to refine raw opium into easily transportable heroin. It was the Guomindang who first made the Triangle Golden.

This entanglement of the opium poppy with international power politics was to become the pattern for the future. When the French were attempting to halt the communist advance in Indo-China in the mid 1950s, they turned to the Hmong tribes, traditional opium cultivators on the Laotian side of the Golden Triangle. The French financed an anti-communist Hmong army, and recruited 3000 of the tribesmen into their own forces. And when the United States assumed the mantle of the anti-communist crusade in South-East Asia, she continued the pattern, though with some additional refinements. Ostensibly the US was against anything to do with the opium trade. Morally indignant condemnations were made of their enemies' involvement in it, and American authorities held several public burnings of opium pipes on the streets of Saigon. But while this was going on, the CIA was covertly equipping a secret army in Laos, and to enlist the support of the tribes, especially the Hmong, it entered the opium trade, just as the French had done before. Cultivation was increased and with the proceeds an anti-communist buffer force was formed. Having bought the opium, the CIA was faced with what to do with it. The answer had been found before: manufacture heroin on the spot in improvised laboratories. Incredibly, much of this 98 per cent heroin found its way back to American troops in Vietnam, of which an estimated one in five were regularly using drugs by the time America eventually pulled out of Vietnam. (Where the rest of the heroin was sold can only be speculated; some extent of the extraordinarily devious role the United States played in this area can be gained from looking at *The Politics of Heroin in South-East Asia* (1972) by Albert McCoy.) What is certain is that vast drug-based fortunes left Saigon along with the exit of South Vietnamese officers, probably with Americans as well. There is a poignant end to the story of the Hmong's involvement in all this. Persecuted by the government of Laos for their co-operation with the United States, many thousands were given sanctuary in America after its withdrawal from Vietnam. There they stalked the streets of Philadelphia, confused and disoriented, catapulting pigeons for food. Apparently they are now more happily settled as grape-pickers in Napa valley, California.

As host by default to much of this double-dealing, Thailand was placed in an unenviable position. A capitalist island in a sea of communism, her northern borders were under continuous threat from insurgents. If opium-growing private armies were the only way to keep them out, then so be it. Thailand opted for what it perceived as the lesser of two evils as a way of dealing with the immediate problem.

Khun Sa, meanwhile, had grown to be one of the most powerful warlords in the Golden Triangle. He had learnt to handle men, guns and mountains, and had served with General Lee Wen-Huan, commander of the notorious 93rd Division of the Guomindang 3rd Army. Moreover, he had seen at first hand how lucrative the drug business could become. His importance was soon recognised by the Burmese government, who appointed him commander of a special 'volunteer defence corps' to combat communist insurgents backed by both the Chinese and the rebel Shans. Later, the warlord would use the administrative power and contacts conferred by this position to declare himself the leader of a Shan independence struggle. Roaming at will through the border lands, he was able to recruit members for his Shan United Army, whose numbers grew like the poppies it cultivated. By 1967 Khun Sa was in a position to put together what must be the greatest drug caravan in history: 300 mules carrying sixteen tons of opium and escorted by 500 men. For their part, the Guomindang were determined to eliminate the warlord's challenge to their domination of the opium trade and thus the two met in an epic confrontation at Ban Kwan in Laos, a battle that has since passed into the local mythology as the 1967 Opium War. Khun Sa's men held their improvised teak stockade for two days, finally routed by napalm stolen from the Americans and paratroopers of the Royal Laotian Army. The defeat seemed to mark the end for Khun Sa. Three months later he was arrested for alleged extortion, rape and other crimes but was eventually released from prison for his 'good faith' in persuading his men to release two Soviet technicians kidnapped in Taunggyi, the capital of the Shan states.

By the late 1970s, political alignments in the Golden Triangle were changing once again. Beijing, in line with the new, 'smiling' face it was now presenting to the world, withdrew its support from the anti-Rangoon Communist groups it had been backing, thus virtually stranding as many as 10,000 guerrillas scattered around the prime growing area of the Golden Triangle. When drought destroyed two years' opium crop from 1979 to 1981, thus cutting off the supply to Khun Sa's heroin laboratories, the supplies-

short communists and opium-short SUA suddenly became allies
by default. Communist-gathered opium was delivered to Khun
Sa's factories and storehouses, and by 1981 intelligence agencies
were reporting the regular visits by communist accountants sent
to audit deliveries and revenues. Bangkok decided it was time to
move against the warlord: the result was the storming of
Hin Taek.

Today, the opium trail plays a less direct role in the fabric of
Thai political and criminal life. Khun Sa is still alive and well, but
now operating from back inside the Shan states. Since Hin Taek
(now re-named Ban Thert Thai – 'Independence-upholding
village') he has joined forces with yet another separatist group,
though one which has been waging a more genuinely political war
than the organisations that have fronted Khun Sa's commercial
drug ventures. The resulting Shan State Army held a passing-out
parade for a new batch of recruits at a village situated just over the
border from Mae Hong Son. Several hundred Shan guests from
both sides of the border were invited to join the celebrations along
with a dozen or so Thai and foreign journalists. Khun Sa, a
portly, avuncular figure, seemed well and confident, handling the
media with wit and cheeky ingenuousness. He claims to have
foresworn drug-running. American drug-enforcement agents
working in Thailand treat such claims with scepticism, replying
that he is still responsible for 80 per cent of the refining of raw
opium in the triangle. His army of 15,000 armed and 20,000
trained but unarmed reserves now takes a staggering 12 million
baht a month to maintain; what else but the drug business could
provide such money?

But for all his personality and power, the man is now in a
precarious position. With the Burmese army on one side and the
DEA and Thai army on the other, Khun Sa's future looks
uncertain. Meanwhile, his new image notwithstanding, the
realities of the drug trade can still be horrifying. In 1987 a
gruesome method of beating the Thai/Malaysian customs came
to light. This is a particularly tricky border for the smugglers,
joining as it does the countries which, along with neighbouring
Malaysia, make up three out of the only five countries in the world

that have the mandatory death penalty for drug trafficking. The scheme was to buy (ostensibly for adoption), or kidnap, babies from poor peasants on the Thai side of the border. These were killed, gutted and stuffed with packets of heroin. The whole operation depended on very rapid timing, so that the tiny bodies, wrapped in shawls, could be carried through the customs by their doting 'mothers' before they began to show any obvious signs of death.

Khun Sa is not the cause of the problem, only its most spectacular symptom. There remain several intractable factors in Thailand's genuine attempts to deal with the situation. One is the simple fact that nothing earns as much money as drugs. For the last decade the Thai government has been pursuing a vigorous plan of crop substitution, encouraging the hill tribes to grow such varied things as peaches, lychees, potatoes, maize, kidney beans, tea and coffee. Roads have been driven into the remote areas, schools and hospitals opened, and King Bhumipol has devoted much of his considerable energy to the scheme, considering it one of his priorities. But although the official story is that opium production is now down some 70 per cent, the fact remains that there is still more money to be made in poppy cultivation than anything else. And anyway, it was never the hill tribes who were really making the money out of opium, but the rebel bands who transported and refined the crop, and the dealers who distributed it internationally. The number of people involved, and their ability to move across borders, compounds Thailand's difficulties of being the natural crossroads of the area. Bangkok has been supported, not to say pressured, by Washington, to increase her efforts against the drug trade, though the Thais must be well aware of the irony that it was the United States' fostering of poppy cultivation twenty years ago that is partly responsible for the problem today. It could reasonably be argued that the fault lies not so much with the poor peasants who live along Thailand's uncontrollable borders as with the constant demand on the streets of urban America. By far the most lucrative business in the United States is illegal narcotics, and although America's taste has changed in recent years to cocaine (a drug not cultivated in

Asia) her addicts still look to South-East Asia for 25 per cent of their heroin. In some ways, Thailand has been made to carry the can for what is a domestic crisis in the American way of life. Washington has recently supplied the Burmese government with aircraft and equipment to spray the poppy fields with a chemical called 2,4-d, closely related to the defoliant 'agent orange' used in Vietnam. 2,4-d has the effect of killing all vegetation and is highly toxic to humans and animals. Despite US pressure, Thailand, to her credit, has refused to use it 'for humanitarian reasons'.

For a period up until the mid 1980s the so-called Golden Crescent – the border areas of Iran, Afghanistan and Pakistan – took over as the world's major supplier of heroin, and this, together with the well-established Turkey/Sicily route controlled by the Mafia looked like eclipsing the importance of the Golden Triangle. But more recently, the advances made by the Thai authorities seem to be slipping. Throughout 1987 and early 1988 the Bangkok newspapers were full of reports of jungle laboratories discovered, and sporadic gun battles along the northern borders. Now that the refining is always done on the spot, transportation becomes much easier, as heroin is a tenth of the bulk of raw opium. Perhaps as part of her new-found enthusiasm for capitalist endeavour, China appears to be taking a renewed interest in the drug trade. Routes are opening up through Yunnan, along relatively good rail, air and road links to Guangzhon and thence to Hong Kong, and the Chinese are also the main suppliers of acetic anhyldride, the chemical crucial to the refining process. Local communist governments are also looking to bolster their floundering economies with the poppy. Laos has recently become a major producer, harvesting 300 tons of opium in 1987 alone, her government's claims that all of this was for 'medicinal purposes' and legitimate export to Eastern Europe being met with understandable scepticism. The Vietnamese provide gold and silver in exchange for Laotian opium, they also supply the port of Da Nang. A part of their purchases may be to feed domestic habits; Ho Chi Minh City alone is said to have 4000 addicts.

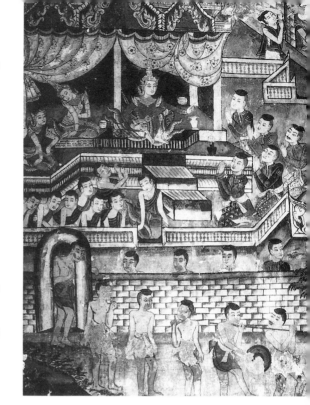

16 Detail of an 18th-century mural depicting life at the Court, from the Lai Kham Vihan, a chapel at Wat Phra Singh in Chiang Mai

17 General view of Wat Phra Singh, Chiang Mai's most important temple. The Lai Kham Vihan, the building on the left, is one of the stellar examples of northern architecture

18 Bathtime at an elephant training school in the forests north of Chiang Mai; elephants are used mainly for shifting teak logs

19 Celebrating Songkran, the riotous water festival that marks the New Year at the peak of the hot season each April

Thailand is the only country in the area where international drug enforcement officers can work and co-operate relatively unhindered. Yet in February 1988, a record 1½ tons of heroin was seized aboard a ship in Bangkok bound for New York. Such finds indicate the vast amount of drugs that are escaping detection. 1988 also saw a bumper harvest in the Golden Triangle: almost 1500 tons, enough to make 150 tons of pure heroin, were gathered from areas beyond the reach of the authorities. Whatever goes on in the remote hillsides, the same Sino/Thai syndicates are still in business, distributing the heroin through Hong Kong, Taiwan and Singapore, and any city in the West with a well-established Chinese business community: Amsterdam, London, San Francisco, Vancouver, New York. Detecting the transfer of funds is virtually impossible as a result of the unique 'chit' system of banking operated by the secretive Chinese networks. A man walks into a Chinese gold shop in New York with a million dollars. The same day, someone else collects an equivalent sum from a gold shop in Bangkok's Chinatown, and the normal banking system has been completely bypassed. At a time when banks are at last beginning to co-operate with police on international drug money, the Chinese connection remains virtually untraceable.

To confound the situation, Thailand now faces a new phenomenon: marijuana syndicates controlled not by Thais or Chinese but by foreigners, mostly Americans. In recent years a number of these groups have set up in Thailand, supplying farmers with fertilisers and seeds and buying their crop for export as the well-known 'Thai sticks', highly rated among the drug cognoscenti. While the opium poppy is confined to the cool mountain slopes of the north, marijuana can be grown almost anywhere. 'The problem with marijuana is finding where it is grown,' says General Chavalit Yodmani, head of the Narcotics Control Board. 'Our main job at the moment is intelligence gathering. I think we are winning a little bit.' Not everybody shares the General's optimism.

10

Tribes and Tourists

For Thailand 1987 was a doubly important year. Not only did it mark the sixtieth birthday of her much-loved King Bhumipol the Great, but it also witnessed the 'Visit Thailand Year' of tourist promotion. That these two coincided was somehow apt, for tourism has come to play a vital part in the life of the country, not only in economic terms, but as a measure of self-esteem and even national identity. The promotion campaign paid off handsomely. Over 3 million visitors arrived, bringing with them 1.75 billion dollars, roughly twice what rice exports earned in the same period. Whatever the long-term wisdom of such a sense of priorities might be, in the short term some 600,000 jobs were created, and the country seems everywhere gripped by a commercial fever that breaks out in a rash of new hotels and guest houses here, new bars and clubs there. This enthusiasm is not surprising. For most tourists, Thailand is a country of attractive, smiling people, delicious food, clean accommodation, and efficient transport. It has beaches and beer, mountains and mist, and, for those who are interested, the remnants of an ancient cultural heritage. The final ingredients of relatively low prices, brilliant blue skies from October to March and an infectiously convivial atmosphere, all help to make for an ideal holiday destination. From the Thais' point of view, the attraction is obvious, for the tourists must appear to have more money than they know what to do with. This is partly as a consequence of the first waves of tourists being Americans, but it is also as the result of the economic realities that persist today. A man who spends ten hours a day bent double beating silver in a Chiang Mai workshop has a job that is relatively stable by local standards, yet his monthly wage of 1000 *baht* is about half of what the average tourist spends each day of his holiday.

The possibility of extra or part-time jobs opening up through tourism would fit very well into the established Thai pattern of most people having more than one job already. This is particularly so for those in the lower levels of a government service that by 1980 was employing one person in every forty-eight, a figure that does not include some 400,000 employees of state industries and the armed forces. I have never seen a country in which one person turns his or her hands to so many things, a versatility attributable partly to economic necessity, partly to a low boredom threshold and partly to a natural entrepreneurial streak which may be something to do with Chinese blood.

Even among the rich, many jobs means much status, and I cannot resist quoting the story of Field Marshal Prapass in this context. In 1973, the Field Marshal gave a speech on the subject of employment entitled 'One Job is Enough', in which he urged his compatriots to abandon their habit of holding several jobs and to concentrate on doing one job well. The press report that covered his speech referred to the Field Marshal as Deputy Prime Minister, Interior Minister, Acting Director-General of the Police Department, Deputy Supreme Commander of the Armed Forces, Commander-in-Chief of the Royal Thai Army, Chairman of the Board of Directors of the Bangkok Bank, and Chairman of the Hill Tribes Development Committee in the Communist Suppression Operation Command. Shortly after this speech, the Field Marshal fell from power.

Of all the communities that make up northern Thailand, it is the hill tribes that are the most vulnerable to the tourist invasion. There are perhaps half a million tribes-people scattered in a wide arc across the north of the country. They are slash-and-burn cultivators who move their villages every three or five years in search of fresh forests to clear, and belong to the Sino-Tibetan language group. Until the last decade they had largely resisted the religious and cultural influences of the lowlands, remaining animists steeped in the ancient ways and beliefs that have sustained their communities since they arrived from the hills of neighbouring Burma and south China in a succession of waves during the last century. Most numerous, and so well established as to be considered indigenous, are the Karen. Originally from Burma, they account for over half of all the tribes and are thus at the opposite end of the scale from the tiny Lawa tribe, which numbers a mere 12,000. Farming the low hills and high valleys, the Karen practise an ecologically sensitive method of cyclical and shifting cultivation, and prefer where possible to establish wet paddy fields. They do not grow opium, which grows best at an altitude of over 3000 feet, though they may hire themselves out as labourers at the time of the harvest each January. They often own and work elephants, and traditionally have been involved in the teak trade. The best integrated of Thailand's hill-people, many of them are Christians, though a healthy animism still persists not far below the surface. The other main group of hill-tribes comprise the Hmong (also known as the Meo), the Yao, the Akha and the Lahu, all of whom live on the upper levels of the hills and are slash-and-burn opium cultivators. They are later arrivals than the Karen, most of them having arrived in Thailand in the early years of this century following political disturbances in their homelands on the borders of Laos and south China. Many Hmong are still arriving today, and are a cause of difficulty to Thailand, already unwilling host to refugees from Burma and Kampuchea.

All of the hill-tribes are organised around the basic unit of the village: there is no tribal leader. Each village is ruled by its headman (with perhaps a council of elders), who is responsible for maintaining order, settling disputes and liaising with government authorities. The next most important figure in the village is the shaman or priest, who propitiates the local spirits and exorcises the forces of evil, often by means of lengthy and wild trance sessions. After the headman, it is the household that organises the community, whether in its extended version with the polygamous Hmong and Yao, or with the nuclear family in the case of the other, monogamous, tribes.

Independent and lacking any sense of overall unity, the *chaokhao*, or 'mountain people', have always remained distinct from the rest of Thailand, in language, religion and customs, and their levels of education and health care are minimal. Up until 1959 they led a life unfettered by the attentions of central government, but in that year the National Committee for the Hill Tribes was formed, partly as a result of the growing threat of political destabilisation within the Golden Triangle. Two years later, free trade in opium was made illegal. Today there are numerous bodies devoted to the physical and spiritual welfare of the hill-people: government and private agencies, missionary and military bodies and, not least, the Royal Development Project. The general policy is to integrate the *chaokhao* into the mainstream of Thai national life, while allowing them freedom of religion and custom. How successful such a policy can be remains to be seen.

One immediate effect it has had is that most of the men have abandoned their traditional dress in favour of the blue garb of the Thai farmer, but the women are still colourfully attired – the Lisu in brilliant blue and green striped dresses, and the Hmong in vivid geometric patterned tunics. Perhaps the most spectacular clothes are the pants worn by the Yao women, who can take up to two years working on one pair. The quality of these designs, a combination of traditional motifs such as 'tiger's paw', 'spider's web' and 'rice grain', has influenced many a Yao man in his choice of wife. Dress is a keen reflector of self-image. The Karen still choose to weave all their cloth from homespun or market produced cotton, while the other tribes, operating on an opium-based cash economy, have generally abandoned their traditional hemp-fibre or cotton cloth for ready-woven material from the lowlands which they embellish with appliquéd or embroidered patterns unique to their tribe. One notable exception is the material some of the Hmong weave from cannabis fibres which is among the finest of all tribal handicrafts. Clothes, shoulder bags and blankets are the work of women, often done by the light of a smoky kerosene lamp after a day's work in the fields, but men produce handicrafts too. Akha and Lihu men produce some of the best basketwork in Asia. A finely woven bamboo basket with tight fitting lid can take weeks to complete, but once it is smoked or glazed with black lacquer, it lasts for decades. Each tribe has its own way of carrying baskets. The Akhu carry theirs on a wooden shoulder yoke, Chinese style, the Lisu and Lahu use a forehead and chest strap like the Sherpas of Nepal, while the Hmong baskets are always fixed with leather shoulder straps.

One thing that unites the sartorially varied tribes is their love of silver. Gold, so prized by most other Asian cultures, is used only to fill *chaokhao* teeth, and even if they could afford more of it, they would still find the weight, bulk and appearance of silver more alluring. Much jewellery is worn since childhood, becoming virtually part of the body. Thus when the Lahu worship their spirits, they remove their jewellery and add it to the offerings, saying that it represents themselves. In the hills, silver is status, and any tribal gathering will be marked by the envious and admiring glances cast upon all the jewellery worn. The main source of the silver has been coins – Indian rupees from the days of the British Raj in Burma, and old French coins from Indo-China. Even today Chinese traders pay for opium with silver coins long since out of circulation, though silver ingots shipped from Hong Kong are becoming the norm.

No single individual exemplifies the declining fortunes of the hill-people more clearly than the silversmith. Once he ranked alongside the shaman as one of the linchpins of the village. He was certainly its wealthiest member, being the source of credit, the pawnbroker, and the financial adviser. His house was the centre for inter-tribal transactions and, being in contact with other tribes, he was also chief gossip-monger, arbiter of fashion and setter of styles. Each village had its own silversmith in the old days, now one smith trades with all the tribes over a wide area, and the art is dying, for many are unwilling to train young men as apprentices for fear of competition.

Hill-tribe silver is cleaned only once a year, before the New Year celebrations. Most tribes rub it with ash and polish with cloth, but the Karen have developed a method of boiling their silver in water and tamarind, and then polishing it with strings of high-fired glass beads brought from India by itinerant traders. Because of the growing poverty in many areas, it is becoming rarer to see the whole family collection risked in open display, but it is still possible to come across a breathtaking assortment of neck-rings, buttons, bracelets, arm-rings, belts, buckles, and studs adorning a woman as she labours in the fields. The fanciest earrings, pipes and betel-nut boxes are generally kept for festivals, when the best finery is proudly displayed. Colour decoration plays little part, and the *chaokhao* put virtually no value on stones. The Yao language, for example, has only one word to cover all gemstones, and though they do differentiate between jade and pearls, they neither value nor use them. Silver has power. The Hmong believe it binds a man's souls together, and as illness indicates that the souls may be about to leave the body, heavy silver neck-rings are worn to keep them weighed down in the body. Every Akha man desires a silver pipe and tobacco box for courting purposes. Without such status symbols, he will be lucky to attract much female interest.

New Year festivals are also the time to experience tribal music and dance. Some of the instruments are works of art in themselves, such as the three-stringed fiddle of the Lisu, covered in lizard skin and intricate carvings, or the skin horns and drums of the Karen. Most evocative of all are the bamboo pipes of the Hmong, producing an eerie and energising contrapuntal sound somewhere between an organ and the uilleann pipes. These pipes, known as *ken*, are played in spirit dances where the musician rolls over and over on the ground, never missing a note. The tribal people are less governed by astrology than the Thais, and New Year is celebrated sometime during the first three months, towards the end of the cool season. Each group chooses its own time according to local workload, and each tribe has its own way of celebrating. The Lahu and Lisu are inspired dancers, while the Karen prefer singing to the accompaniment of drums and gongs. The Hmong concentrate on elaborate courting games and conduct long spirit ceremonies and massive feasts of sacrificial pork and chicken. All the celebrations are fuelled by considerable quantities of rice or maize liquor.

Twenty years ago the hill-tribes spoke little northern Thai – a language most of them have since learned, for they are good linguists – and their lack of roads and radio seemed to ensure an

isolation penetrated only by Christian missionaries whose con-
version campaigns entailed many years of patient reconnaissance
and planning. In the last two decades there has been an eruption
of tribal tourism. This has not been initiated by the tribes
themselves nor have they had a say in its organisation, direction or
development. Many villages are now not only on roads accessible
by mini-bus, but firmly on the tourist track. The 'White' Karen
village at Li, in Tak province, is virtually a tribal reservation
sponsored by the government. The settlement is well laid out with
wide, dusty streets, along which cycle young unmarried girls in
the white dresses from which the tribe gets its name. The wooden
stilted houses are thatched in bamboo straw, but many new
buildings are being built from sandstone, dug out in great blocks
from pits at the edge of the village. Banana plants, pink pineapple
and papaya trees are much in evidence, for the White Karen are
vegetarians. At noon the place is utterly quiet, becalmed in the
midday heat, and hot-season seed-pods crack underfoot. Somewhere a radio is playing, the high-pitched song serving only to
accentuate an almost eerie peacefulness. Small groups of Karen
stand around their houses, unconcerned by the tourists. The
children are extraordinarily well behaved, gazing at the strangers
with large, incurious eyes, even their requests for sweets are
restrained. Vendors hold up their wares without a word: silver
pipes that curl into dragon heads, lengths of cloth whose artificial
dyes are garish in the bright sun. Yet here and there the passivity
breaks into genuine smiles, and as the mini-bus prepares to leave,
the selling becomes a little more animated. But all in all, the
White Karen of Li seem almost uncannily gentle.

The Akha village of Sam Yek outside Chiang Rai tells a
different story. Untidily thatched houses straggle along a dusty
street that descends the hillside sharply. Up by the main road,
groups of villagers hang around awaiting the tour buses. A tribe
known for its fierce independence only five years ago now whines
carefully rehearsed phrases in English, French and German,
while the snotty-nosed children wheedle and beg. 'They like the
Swiss candy best,' counsels the Thai guide. A young woman, bare
breasted over the traditional short black skirt and wearing a

headdress glittering with silver rupee pieces, stands poised sulkily by her loom in the street, demanding two *baht* off the photographers for every time she begins to weave. The Akha are the least integrated of all the tribes, a small, mongrel-looking people, in-bred and truculent. In October, at the end of the rainy season, they sow the poppy seeds, which will need no more water than the hillside dew provides. In December the flowers dot the hillsides with white, pink and purple, and by the end of January the crop is ready. Each morning the seed pods are scratched with a special curved knife, the daytime sun dries the white milky sap into a dark brown sticky resin, ready to be gathered in the evening or following day. This sickly-sweet gum is the raw opium. Another important crop for the Akha is tobacco, which they take down to the valleys to trade for the dogs which are a staple part of their diet. In Sam Yek, the addiction seems to be to money rather than opium. The main street is littered with rusty cans, sweet papers and lined with thatched booths selling souvenirs. Bargaining turns to bickering, bickering to shouting. Someone has blundered too far into a house and is pursued by stones. Visitors to Sam Yek have an armed guard these days, to protect them not from the desperadoes of Golden Triangle myth, but from the anger of the Akha. It is a sorry scene indeed.

The Yao village further along the road that winds up out of Chiang Rai is much less of a human zoo. In marked contrast to the Akha, the Yao are a jolly lot, the women particularly handsome, straight backed and moon faced in their black or dark blue turbans spiced with geometric designs and fluffy red ruffs around their necks. They seem aware of the absurdity of selling dolls of themselves, and the bargaining is all laughter laced with a judicious hint of flirtation. This village's exposure to tourism seems to have had little negative effect, and its people retain their dignity and composure.

The trouble is that even in the villages frequented by tourists, there remain taboos that are invisible to the outsider – Thai and *farang* alike. A Lahu village will sometimes erect a bamboo cross outside a house as a sign of illness or some particular ceremony or as a warning to visitors to keep away. In a Lisu house one should never stand in the doorway, as this hampers the passage of spirits. While such a belief may seem whimsical to the tourist, to the tribes-people spirit anger is enough to cause the entire village to move. There is the story of two exuberant Italian tourists who grabbed a colourfully attired Hmong woman coming out of a house and, despite her protests, made her pose between them for photographs. Her distress prompted inquiries which revealed that she had just emerged from a session mourning her dead child. Photographers are the worst, for the machine takes over, hunting down its prey like some exotic animal ready to be shot. When after twenty minutes and several rolls of film the tourists depart in a cloud of dust, all too often they take with them no knowledge of the tribal way of life, only memories of the villagers' indignity.

A more authentic way of seeing the tribes is by trekking, an increasingly popular way of spending up to a week in the hills. In 1987, 100,000 people took treks, mostly operating from Mae Hong Son, Chiang Mai, and Chiang Rai. Although the area around Mae Hong Son has less tribal diversity, being inhabited largely by Karen, it is the least spoilt of the trekking routes. Here the forests stand like great blocks of greenery, tunnelled by narrow trails which see little sun. The tracks are lined by teak, whose huge leaves are used as thatching, plates, wrappers or impromptu rainy-season hats, and huge conifers hung with Spanish moss, their lower trunks draped with lianas, their roots sprouting wispy ferns. The steep tracks, where the constant passage of mules has cut a series of long steps into the red earth, are punctuated by ramshackle wayside general stores that sell basic articles and the ubiquitous Pepsi-Cola. The border with Burma is virtually unmarked, except for perhaps a broken wooden fence or stile, but there are the occasional unofficial border guards, Shan teenagers wearing kepi-type caps and carrying an assortment of arms. And there is evidence of the smugglers' routes – favourite camp sites easily identifiable by the stains of old fires, rusty tin cans and the odd broken rubber sandal.

The most popular starting points to trek are Chiang Mai and Chiang Rai. The official umbrella group, the Jungle Tour Club, sponsored by the Tourist Authority of Thailand, has about fifty members, but there are probably as many unofficial companies, some operating fly-by-night operations from a street stall or the corner of a guest-house table. The average trek is around three or four nights, and is reasonably priced at about 500 *baht* a head. A truck takes you to the starting point, and the journey proceeds with no more than five hours' walking a day along well-established trails covering terrain that can be managed even by the least fit. Nights are spent in the ordinary houses of the hill-tribes, basic wooden and bamboo structures built on stilts to accommodate the steep hillsides, and thatched with straw. The space under the house serves both family and animals, and the typical hill-tribe village scene is one of tranquillity and simple routine, far from the notorious Golden Triangle image. Yet even the well-run treks are changing the very nature of the people trekkers come to see. Where it was an automatic tradition for Karen or Lahu people to invite any guest for a meal and to share their bamboo hut for the night, now the price is often fixed like a city hotel. 'The tribesmen are normally very honest, straightforward people,' says Supoj Klinpraneet, president of the Chiang Mai Professional Guides Association and the man who did most to open up the tribal trekking. 'Now they're learning to be devious. They're thinking only about commission.' Even with the best intentions, misunderstandings can occur. Visitors may wish to show their appreciation of tribal hospitality by eating a lot of the food offered, not realising that if they finish it, the wives and children waiting outside will go hungry.

Then there are the do-it-yourself trekkers, who take off on a motor-bike and head for the hills, with or without a maverick guide. Despite their intention to avoid the commercialisation of the over-visited places, these maverick trekkers do just as much harm in the long run. Virtually none of them speaks Thai, let alone the northern Thai the tribes understand, they are largely ignorant of tribal customs and they often spoil a village by inflating prices for all who come after them. These 'budget travellers' consider themselves at the very pinnacle of the itinerant hierarchy, and would shudder at the very mention of the word 'tourist', yet their desire for one-upmanship can lead to trouble. In the summer of 1987 a spate of jungle robberies in the hills north and east of Chiang Mai culminated in a young New Zealander being shot dead by a tribes-person demanding money. This unfortunate incident (not the first of its kind) at last galvanised the authorities to take control of a situation that had become out of hand. Police and tourist officials now co-operate in checking agencies, guides and routes, and police have set up posts at sensitive points to monitor the treks. Some of the romance may have gone, but so has some of the danger. In general, a trek should be organised by a registered company and undertaken with a registered guide who knows the language and customs of the area you are planning to visit. The further you are prepared to walk, the less spoilt will be your destination. A visit to the Tribal Research Centre on the campus of Chiang Mai University can also help in preparation for what can be one of the most enjoyable features of a stay in Thailand.

One result of the tourist boom is that Thai Airways, the domestic airline, is usually overbooked. It is always wise to buy tickets as far in advance as possible, especially on the Chiang Mai to Chiang Rai route, for only a certain number of seats are allocated to each tour operator, a system that demands much flexibility of larger tour groups. An alternative is to take the road via Fang as far north as Tha Thon, a small village near the Burmese border, over-looked by a giant white Buddha on the hillside. From here it is a five-hour boat journey along the River Kok to Chiang Rai. You can eat well in the largest restaurant on the riverbank, though the place has well and truly entered the travel business by being the only place in Thailand with the nerve to try and charge its *farang* customers for using the lavatory facilities. The picturesque river trip is in the 'long-tailed' boats that are found wherever there are navigable rivers in Thailand. Powered by a ten-foot propeller shaft, these sleek craft skim over the surface of the water with the noise of speedway bikes and the speed of sharks, spurting a plume of water out behind them and creating a violent wash. They are manned by a bunch of cowboys, well aware of their status as the undisputed kings of the river. The route passes several tribal villages, mainly Lahu, the largest of which, Mae Salak, is the starting point of many adventurous treks, especially to the Wawi area to the south. The river journey is usually accompanied by an armed guard, a legacy of the Golden Triangle days, though it has been safe for a number of years, and if the journey is after lunch, the chances are that your escort will spend most of the time asleep. I remember landing at Bangkok some time ago to lead a tour, and being told by our local agent that a tourist had been shot dead by a sniper a couple of weeks before. Seeing my face fall he reassured me in true Thai fashion: 'Oh don't worry! It was a mistake. The sniper was aiming for the armed guard, he just happened to miss!'

There is little to see in Chiang Rai, the gateway to the Golden Triangle, though the town has a couple of temples, Wat Phra Singh and Wat Phra Keo that have housed famous images in their time and are attractive structures. Wat Jet Yot and Wat Klang Muang are also worth visiting as examples of the graceful northern style of architecture, with low roofs sweeping to the ground and intricately decorated exteriors. There are many inexpensive hotels and two luxury ones, and of the several places that serve good food in the town the Clock Tower restaurant, with its attractive open-air garden section, is renowed for its excellent fish. Chiang Rai is enjoyable as a place that has not yet become a centre of tourism in itself, and it is possible to walk the back streets of King Mengrai's former capital without meeting other foreigners.

Further into the Thai part of the Golden Triangle lies Chiang Saen, a delightful town on the Mekong River. When le May visited it in the early years of this century, he had to cut his way through the jungle inside the city walls, and the District Officer told him that he had recently fired at a rhinoceros nosing around his office door. Today Chiang Saen is relatively tame, but as Mengrai's original city and the beginning of the Lanna kingdom, it still boasts a wealth of archaeological remains. Wat Pa Sak, which dates from 1295, is a mixture of Shrivijaya, Dvaravati and Sukhothai styles, and near Wat Chedi Luang there is an interesting small museum with a good collection of artefacts in its grounds. Many of these are Chiang Saen Buddhas, whose typically thick bodies and prominent 'mango stone' chins give them a very solid look. Chiang Saen's lovely setting, and the wildness of the surrounding area, gives it a romantic atmosphere. The view over the town from Wat Prathat Chom Kitti, an ancient site with a *chedi* once clad in bronze plaques in the style of the region, is superb.

The most scenic way back to Chiang Rai from Chiang Saen is the three-hour boat ride along the Mekong, but the availability of this depends on Thailand's relations with the new Pathet Lao government, which have recently been strained. It is a picturesque trip that skirts the mouth of the Kok River and continues past steep clad mountains and through deep gorges and eddies to Chiang Kong. Highway 1020 returns from here to Chiang Rai. As the crow flies, the road back to Chiang Mai that passes through Mae Suai and Wiang Pa Pau appears much shorter than Highway 1 via Phayao and Lampang, but the former is a long and arduous mountain road which, to judge by the spirit-houses that cluster its edge, has claimed many lives. Despite its breathtaking scenery, most people avoid it if they can. Highway 1 is beautiful enough as it winds alongside heavily forested mountains, particularly verdant after the rainy season. Phayao stands on a lakeside under blue-grey mountains, a jumble of roof lines slung between a white and orange temple at one end and the tall chimneys of rice- and saw-mills at the other. The main street curves along the lakeside and thrusts piers out into the water providing a favourite place for the locals to *pai-tio* in the evening after work. The lake has thick clumps of water hyacinth, but for once the lilac-coloured plant has a use, as the enterprising townspeople weave hats, baskets and bags out of its dried stems. Phayao is only just building its first hotel, and is still a simple agricultural community, making its living out of glutinous rice, tobacco and the lichees for which the area is famous. The two main temples – Wat Pa in a forest glade on the edge of the town, and Wat Analayo, overlooking it – are both thriving centres of Buddhist teaching. Many move to the area to be under the instruction of the abbot Achaan Phaibun, who is in charge of both places, and new buildings are springing up on the hillside to accommodate them. The abbot is a former government official and the son of a herbalist doctor in Lampang, and his temples are renowned centres of traditional herbal medicine. This type of treatment is enjoying something of a revival, partly prompted by the interest that Princess Chulaborn, the youngest daughter of the King and herself a scientist by training, has taken in the subject. At the beginning of each August there is a festival dedicated to natural healing that draws many visitors from all over the north.

Few visitors to this quiet place of boating, fishing and relaxation will take a detour to the village of Dok Kham Thai which lies a few miles east of Phayao. Those who do will doubtless be surprised at the large number of new buildings in a community that appears to have no particular reason for such conspicuous prosperity. The source of this hamlet's unlikely wealth lies in an equally unlikely combination: the droughts of recent years and the renowed beauty of the local girls. For in the last two decades, partly due to crop failure, Dok Kham Thai has become notorious as a supplier of girls to the 'service industry' of Bangkok. The scale of the village's involvement can be judged by the fact that in 1979, remittances worth over £1½ million passed through its tiny post office.

Thirty-five miles south of Phayao lies the junction of Highway 1 and Highway 103, which runs south-east for about forty miles until it in turn meets Highway 101. Following this for sixty miles through sparsely wooded hillsides, the adventurous traveller will come to one of the truly unspoilt parts of the north: the isolated valley of Nan. Up until recently this tract of land about sixty miles long and never more than fifteen wide, was, along with its surrounding mountains, so troubled by bandits and insurgents that visitors were discouraged from going there. Government attempts to build roads into the province were hampered by the local people, who spent each night removing work that had been done during the previous day. Bangkok still designates Nan as a 'remote province' and though its outlying areas may still be uncertain, anywhere that can comfortably be visited is now safe. Fertile and well-watered by the River Nan, the valley is a long thin rice-bowl, and was an independent kingdom until as late as 1931, when it came under Bangkok's rule. It is a place of very great beauty.

The town walls of the city of Nan, rebuilt in 1857 after a severe flood, are circular, thus betraying the influence of the Mons who established the settlement in the late fourteenth century. The centre of what was the old city is now marked by Wat Chang Kham, a *chedi* supported by elephant buttresses, which contains a superb Sukhothai walking Buddha in gold, dating from 1426, and there is Sri Lankan influence observable in the style of the Buddha images at Wat Phata Wat, to the west of the city outskirts. Several other venerable *wats* adorn the town. Wat Suan Tan, the only temple with a *prang* in the north, has a 500-year-old bronze Buddha, also in Sukhothai style, which was supposedly cast in 100 days on the orders of King Tilokaraja from Chiang Mai to celebrate his conquest of the city. Wat Phumin exemplifies a contrast that makes many northern temples pleasing: a simple exterior of white-washed walls, supporting a tiered shingled roof, shields an interior that is a blaze of muted gold. The centre-piece is formed by four Buddha images facing the cardinal points, and the interior walls are covered with murals. The lines of this cruciform building are elegant and clean, and uncompromised by bright, gilded ornamentation. About a mile south-east of the town centre, on a small hill reached by a *naga* flanked approach, sits Wat Phra That Chae Haeng, a walled temple dating from the eleventh century. This dignified building is the site of a boisterous firework festival in the fourth lunar month each year.

The route which completes the loop back to Chiang Mai passes through Lampang, a town in which the Burmese influence is very evident. Half the size of Chiang Mai and far less developed, Lampang was a favourite retiring place for the wealthy, and presents a clash of building styles that well illustrates the aesthetic gap between modern, secular buildings and tradi-tional, religious ones. The residential and commercial structures

here are typically urban Thai: concrete, flat and featureless, while
the temples are typically Burmese rural: wooden, carved and
sumptuously decorated. The chapel at Wat Phra Keo Don Thau
rises in flaming tendrils in imitation of the mountain at the centre
of the universe, and has an interior studded with chunks of
coloured glass that glow in the half-light like a Tiffany lamp.
Around these mock jewels flutter incongruous *putti*, for the
chapel was built in the eighteenth century to serve the community
brought from British Burma to work in the teak trade. The hard,
glittering surfaces of many Thai *wats* may offer little emotional
sustenance to the visitor who is not part of the Buddhist fold;
Lampang's wooden temples are by comparison homely, living
structures, warm and maternal. They breathe, look and smell
natural, and the highly polished teak floors, such as can be found
at Wat Shri Chum, spring responsively under the feet, giving a
marvellous sense of organic unity between human and building.
Nowhere is the obligatory Thai custom of removing shoes
indoors more rewarding. Burmese images too are often more
approachable than their Thai counterparts; small, with cat-like
faces they invite closeness not just respect. Buildings such as Wat
Shri Chum remind one yet again that the natural medium of
Thailand is wood, preferably in close proximity to water, and as
always in this country it is a relief to find places that have as yet
escaped the attentions of the ubiquitous Siam Cement Company.

The abbot of Wat Shrii Chum is a charming and elderly
Burmese, who speaks good English. He is the leader of the town's
Burmese community, which is augmented every so often by
young men who have walked for several days over the border to
escape from the Socialist Republic. The main hall of the temple,
which also serves as the abbot's sitting room, is hung with pictures
and photographs of the homeland. There are also fine red lacquer
murals depicting nineteenth-century life in Lampang, as well as
the obligatory temple status symbols of elephant tusks and
European clocks accumulated in the days when the *wat* was the
local timekeeper. The finest temple in Lampang, and one often
missed by tourists, is actually twelve miles south of the city. This
is Wat Phra That Lampang Luang, all that is left of a walled city

that flourished more than a millennium ago. Set on a small wooded hill, the *wat* was restored in the sixteenth century, and its main *vihan*, set in a sea of silver gravel, is beautifully carved and inlaid. The ancient trees, the atmosphere of learning and refined workmanship all combine to make this one of the loveliest *wats* in northern Thailand.

Each town in Thailand seems to have its unique form of public transport; Lampang's contribution is the horse-drawn carriage. Wearing bemused expressions under their bells and pom-poms, some of the horses may have seen better days, but this is more than compensated for by the roguish panache of their drivers, complete with cowboy hats and dark glasses. By no means unique to Lampang, but as well observable here as anywhere, is the Thai love of entertainment. Much of this focuses on hotels, some of which have their own massage parlours, and virtually all of it is a male preserve. The Tipchang Hotel is one of the two best in the town. Although not huge (it has about 170 rooms) it offers a concentration of music unheard of in a European equivalent. No less than four live bands – in the coffee shop, lobby bar and the two cocktail bars – play each night. Indeed the coffee shop music starts at eleven in the morning, and throughout the day a seemingly endless stream of girls drifts on to the stage, each one singing three or four numbers and then tailing off to make way for her successor. Many are extravagantly dressed in creations of their own design, and each town has a sizeable dressmaking industry at least partly sustained by the demand for these flamboyant outfits. There must be thousands of these girls in the country, travelling from place to place to find their fortune. Among the young, a singer enjoys a fair amount of status, and the job caters well for the Thai love of *than samaj*, being 'with it'. The songs are for the most part slow, sweet and wistful, and when Western music features it is all the nostalgic stuff of High School romance from the 1950s and 1960s – Connie Francis, Pat Boone and the Everly Brothers. Thai is arguably the most seductive of languages – a consequence both of its softness and its breathless falling tone – and even when bent to the hymns of teenage love, loses little of its charm. Many of the girls have good voices, for it can be no easy thing to sing a tonal language and hit the notes cleanly. Velvetine articulation is what the Thais look for in their nightclub singers, and the successful are rewarded with garlands of flowers strung with banknotes passed up from admirers. The audience is composed mainly of groups – large, male and very convivial.

Thais are generous people, and consider money is for spending, especially if one's status can be enhanced by a public demonstration of largesse. In any party, it is the inviter who pays; the idea of 'going Dutch' would strike the Thai as being very odd, especially among a group of people who will meet again and thus have the chance to repay hospitality. Natural reciprocity, rather than a stubborn individualism, is the rule. Of all the countries I know, only Thailand tempts me into night clubs, for they are so much part of the national scene as to be well-nigh irresistible.

IV

THE NORTH-EAST

11

Buddhas and Beliefs

The young man swaggering down the aisle of the Lampang to Phitsanulok train is a walking restaurant. Over his right arm swings a plastic bucket crammed with bottles nestling in ice – coke, orange juice, beer, whisky and various vitamin tonics, sugary pick-me-ups consumed in great quantities by the poorer Thais. His right hand brandishes a sheaf of kebabs – chicken, beef and dried fish – impaled on bamboo skewers a couple of feet long, the whole bunch wrapped up in cellophane like some gastronomic bouquet. From his left shoulder are slung skeins of matchboxes that rattle like talismans and two string-bags, one full of cigarettes, the other of yet more whisky. To make his nonchalant mastery of his art quite clear to anyone who might not have noticed, the lad holds in his free hand a vivid green lollipop which he sucks every so often in a loud and lascivious fashion. His patter is rapid, bawdy and, to judge by the reactions, very funny. This consummate juggler is but the first of a steady stream of vendors who patrol the train, carrying baskets, buckets and boxes, kettles for tea and coffee, cups, straws, bottle-openers, food and drink; a veritable culinary orchestra conducted by a maestro who makes his sweeping appearance every so often, dramatically bearing aloft a plate of rice topped with a cyclopean fried egg. They say an army marches on its stomach. Thais certainly travel on theirs.

But not all. Across the aisle from me sit two monks, wrapped in saffron solitude. As their rule decrees, they have eaten their last meal of the day before noon, some five hours ago, and must not eat again until tomorrow's sunrise. As members of the most respected group in the land, they are the only people in the crowded compartment to have a seat to themselves. Respect accords distance, especially from women, who should never touch a monk, or even hand him anything directly, and I notice all those sitting closest to the monks are men.

My immediate neighbours are a family. The mother is dark and with a nose that is so snubbed it only really protrudes from her face into a pair of magnificently flared nostrils that give her an expression of great *hauteur*. Compared to her I can see why *farangs* are referred to as 'long noses'. Her husband is good-looking in a rakish sort of way, with a lazy smile and a fancy *ikat* border to his silk shirt. He has come prepared for the journey with his own plastic bucket to serve as an ice container, and a large bottle of Mekong whisky. They have four children, the three youngest wriggling with excitement and running up and down the aisle, much indulged by all the adults. Students of child-rearing practices say that the sort of pampering the Thais lavish on their young tends to create a pleasant and easy-going character that lacks initiative or the desire for competition. Perhaps this is no bad thing in a society still governed by traditional roles, and one which will later expect unquestioning filial respect. 'Be subservient, be obedient, and your good deeds will protect you' runs an old village admonition to children. Yet on a Bangkok bus, adults give up their seats to children, the exact reverse of the situation in the West. The little boy opposite is fed continuously, balls of sticky rice, chicken, chewing gum. His elder sister, who must be about twelve, is the butt of many passing quips from the vendors; the poor girl takes these good-naturedly, no doubt as backhand compliments on her budding femininity.

Ten minutes out of Lampang we shudder to a halt with a shock that knocks over my neighbour's bucket and fills his wife's shoes with ice cubes. A few seconds later a rivulet appears between the little boy's feet, snaking across the floor to disappear down the grille beneath the washbasins that stand at the end of the compartment. He throws his mother a long-suffering look, and she laughingly changes his pants, spreading the wet ones out on the arm of her seat to dry. Such relaxed attitudes to children's natural functions are evident even in Thai homes. Your hostess will not bat an eyelid if your child starts absent-mindedly to defecate on her wooden or linoleum floor, yet she would be very offended if you had forgotten to remove your shoes before entering her house. As the train rattles on into the descending darkness, the occupants of the carriage settle down into replete and untidy heaps, snuggling into whatever human pillow is nearest. Only the monks remain watchful.

Lulled by the rhythm of the train and the pervasive smell of food, my mind drifts back to childhood journeys that perhaps implanted the seed of a wanderlust still unsatisfied. These trips were from London to Edinburgh, on the *Flying Scotsman*, when the driver would always make up for lost time on the stretch after Berwick, playing havoc with the waiters' attempts to administer the last serving for dinner. The food was different then: Oxtail soup without a hint of chilli or lemon grass, and no one, as I remember, was allowed to pee on the floor.

The town of Phitsanulok hugs the east bank of the River Nan; a meeting of buildings and water which softens some of the modernity of a town almost completely rebuilt after fire destroyed its wooden structures in 1969. The river is lined with houseboats – or rather, bamboo rafts supporting wooden shacks whose corrugated roofs bristle with television antennae – and its steep banks are chequered with allotments. Now, in August, there are still several yards of bright red earth and plants visible; by the end of the rainy season in October, these banks will be reduced to mere strips of green separating the swollen terracotta torrent from the road above. River, road and railway all run straight through Phitsanulok, a flat town surrounded by a flat plain that stretches far into the hazy distance.

Despite unprepossessing first appearances, Phitsanulok is a centre of attraction for Thais as it is the home of the kingdom's second most important Buddha image – the Phra Buddha Chinaraj at Wat Mahathat. The temple in its compound by the bridge somehow escaped the fire and remains a superb monument, its gilded *prang* soaring above the surrounding sea of red and orange temple roofs. The interior of the *bot* in which the Buddha holds court is more impressive than its exterior suggests. Exquisite mother-of-pearl doors open onto a long room, above which the roof sweeps down very low, supported on black and gold pillars, diminishing the wall space and accentuating the nave, to focus attention on the image at its end. Though this Buddha is considered less holy than the Emerald Buddha in Bangkok, it is certainly more accessible, being hardly elevated at all, and its massive gilded bronze body glows like molten gold. The elongated flame-like *ketumala* rises from a head covered in shell-like spiralled curls and surrounded by a flame-shaped nimbus – a very rare feature. Dramatically lit from below against a black backdrop decorated with gilded angels and flowers, the figure is very powerful, its fleshy face and aquiline nose conveying a grave, and almost fierce, serenity. Dating from the fourteenth century, the Phra Buddha Chinaraj perhaps gives a clue as to the origin of the Sukhothai style, of which it is a late but superlative example. Art historians have often claimed that Chinese influence played a part in the Sukhothai style, in line with the generally accepted notion of pervasive Chinese influence in matters of high culture.

Relations between the court of Sukhothai and China were cordial, and the annals record that the Sukhothai monarch Ramkamhaeng paid two visits to the emperor, the first in 1294 while Kubilai Khan was still alive, the second in 1300. On the latter occasion he was said to have married a Chinese princess and to have brought back with him the potters whose innovating role has been challenged by the evidence from Ban Koh Noi. But despite these good relations and the tribute Ramkamhaeng sent regularly until his death, there is no indication that he was ever influenced by the Chinese form of Buddhism or that he introduced any Chinese form of the Buddha image. That Sukhothai was a dramatic break with the realism of the preceding Khmer style cannot be doubted, but looking at the Phra Buddha Chinaraj, the link seems more likely to be with earlier Chiang Saen figures. There is here the solidity and fullness that distinguished that school, though tempered by an almost feminine softness in the true Sukhothai idiom.

The inside of the *bot* is filled with a desiccated rattling like the sound of a thousand cicadas. Each kneeling worshipper is busily shaking a bamboo tube containing 'fortune sticks' (*chensi*) – flat spills of bamboo not unlike giant matchsticks. Each is inscribed with a number, and the one that pops out ahead of all the rest is tallied with a numbered pigeon-hole containing a printed fortune. This Chinese form of automatic divination is very popular wherever there is a large Chinese community and can be observed in many temples throughout the country. I have never seen it more enthusiastically practised than here in Phitsanulok, perhaps because the acoustics of the low roof amplify both sound and fervour to extraordinary proportions.

Outside the *bot* another way to deal with the vagaries of fortune is much in evidence. Forming a continuous chain among the parked cars and trees and shrines receiving worship stand dozens of white booths selling tickets for the government lottery. Thais love to gamble. Every town has such booths in addition to numerous strolling ticket vendors, and each bus ticket carries a lottery number. Many of the presents piously offered to the monks in the *wat* will be followed by an ingenuous request for a couple of numbers, to be used in *huay*, an ingeniously simple numbers racket that rides on the back of the official lottery. The government draw has six figures; *huay* operates by betting on the last two or three of these, and pays whopping odds of 500:1 for correct guesses. Not only does this allow even the poorest to have an occasional flutter, but many migrants to the city become *huay* collectors to boost their earnings. The future of what must be the national sport seems assured, not only by its popularity but also by the high rank of its organisers and the cordial relations they enjoy with the police.

In one corner of the compound crowded with stalls selling food and souvenirs stands an elevated platform, a stage on which hired dancers perform the classical dance *lakhon nai* as thanks for a prayer answered or a vow redeemed. When not dancing, the girls sit around in their sparkling sequinned costumes gossiping, arguing or flicking through fashion magazines like any other teenagers, but when summoned to perform they are metamorphosed, assembling mutely to weave through the crowds to the sanctuary, gaze fixed in the middle distance and arms outstretched, bending and weaving in their stylised dance. I remember once seeing a similar troupe, wheeling like a flock of exotic birds around the entrance to one of Bangkok's main hospitals. They were accompanying a little girl who was being taken home by her parents after unexpectedly surviving a car accident.

The walk from the Wat Mahathat back into the centre of the town passes along the river bank, and it is very pleasant indeed. The bank is shaded by flowering trees, and a number of vendors have set up their stalls above the steep pathways that lead down to the floating restaurants below. Most numerous are those selling amulets, a veritable battery of weapons against possible misfortune – miniature Buddha figures, stones and roots, tiger's eye and onyx beads, snail shells inscribed in copper, tamarind seeds, animal teeth, coloured threads. The tiny Buddhas are the most common, some are encased in gold, and if especially potent, can become collectors' items, costing many thousands of *baht*. These bestowers of protection, self-confidence and well-being can be cast from metal, stamped in clay or moulded from compressed vegetable matter. The ingredients are crucial in determining an amulet's power; one anthropologist was recently dismayed to find that a common material is ash obtained from burning the most ancient sacred texts in the monastery. A Buddha amulet is considered more sacred if it has been made by a monk renowned for his holiness, and all talismans must be sanctified before they can be effective. Such ceremonies charge the object with not only the monk's power, but the energy of his spiritual lineage, and are held on days when the spirits are particularly strong, such as Tuesday or Saturday, or the fifth day of the fifth month. Amulets are big business; there are at least six magazines exclusively devoted to the collectors' market.

All of this is the visible part of an invisible but consistently structured world view. Amulets offer protection in the potentially dangerous realm of amoral power the Thais call *saksit*, an area of life governed by capricious spirits whose co-operation is won by offerings and gifts. It is a mechanical world of bargains struck and favours received, devoid of connotations of good and evil, amenable to manipulation by the technology of the sacred.

Saksit power is invested in temples, *chedis*, and Buddha images, and accounts for the personal quirks that many of the famous images have in addition to their miraculous powers. Thus the Phra Buddha Chinaraj likes offerings of pigs' heads, whereas the Emerald Buddha is rather partial to hard-boiled eggs. *Saksit* also inheres in ritual objects, holy water, chanting, spirits and spirit-houses, and strange natural occurrences such as white elephants or deformed babies. Its physical province is anywhere beyond the familiar, safe territory of home and *wat*, which are places invested with another power, *khuna*. *Khuna* is morally good, beneficent and protective, and is found chiefly in homely, emotionally sustaining things such as the mother, women in general, the monk and the teacher, and in physical nourishers such as water and rice, both of which are female in Thai mythology. The essential thing about *khuna* is that it gives its blessings spontaneously and unasked; there is no need for offerings or supplication. This generosity helps explain the tremendous sense of moral indebtedness to parents and authority figures that is a conspicuous aspect of the Thai psyche.

Journeys away from home involve a transition from the safe realm of *khuna* to the unpredictable realm of *saksit*, and many a Thai prepares for his up-country trip by adding several extra amulets to the chain around his neck. The vulnerability inherent in travel accounts for the taxi-drivers' gilt Buddha encased in a plastic dome on top of his dashboard, alongside the cassettes, cigarette packets and glossy brochures advertising the local massage parlour. It is noticeable that amulets are favoured more by men than women. This is because women are, by virtue of their sex or role as mother, naturally invested with *khuna*, and also because, in the traditional pattern of life, they ventured away from the safety of the home far less than the men. There is one class of amulet that is an entirely male talisman, the phallic emblem known as *phlad khik*. Traditionally given to small boys and believed to ward off snake- and dog-bites, they are today worn by men of all ages, and blessed by monks as is any other talisman. Indeed, they are almost as popular as Buddha images, but far less conspicuous, being either carried in the pocket or worn around the waist, never around the neck. Most Thais are happy to show off their amulets and explain the particular properties of each, but they should never be touched by anyone except the owner, and, like Buddha images, should be treated with respect by being kept as far as possible in a high position, and never be allowed to come in contact with sources of ritual pollution.

Beyond even the realm of *saksit* lies the realm of chaos – *decha* – where evil powers roam at will causing harm, loss, illness and death. Such random forces can be tamed only by the skills of the village spirit doctor, or the special class of magically gifted monks who act as white magicians or exorcists when the need arises. Indeed, it is the monk's pivotal position in this animistic world that makes him such an important figure. As a natural repository of the morally good *khuna*, the monk and the sacred places associated with him help propitiate the amoral powers of *saksit*, and act as the principal allies in the constant battle with the forces of *decha*.

All of this is not mere academic anthropology. An article in the newspaper informs me that the governor of Phitsanulok is considering slapping a ban on a proposed contest between a sixty-five-year-old fortune-teller called Lamon and an Alsatian, age unspecified, called Jumbo. Lamon, 'well-known in the area for his boasting and strange behaviour' claims to have magical powers that can withstand any dog-bites, and wants to stage the bout at the provincial stadium in aid of charity. There is even talk of a local politician sponsoring it. Kukrit Pramoj, the country's leading elder statesman and a man of sardonic wit, refers to the fight in his regular column in the *Siam Rath* newspaper as a bad omen for Phitsanulok, and opines that it is unbelievable that the people of such a religious and historical province should agree with this 'evil', and be willing to place bets worth millions of *baht* on its outcome. Kukrit continues by suggesting that an air force dog-trainer should referee the fight to ensure the man is not fatally bitten, and adds that a monk should be present at the ringside to prevent the man from kicking the dog to death.

Phitsanulok is normally viewed by tourists only as a stepping stone to the more historic sites further west – Sukhothai and Si Satchenalai – but the town is making efforts to attract tourism in its own right. The Tourist Authority of Thailand (TAT) office here, the most friendly and helpful I have encountered, has drawn up maps and walking tours of the town, and together with one of the big hotels runs a pedicab tour to take the evening air. The Edwardian rectitude of this outing is somewhat offset by the appearance of the drivers, a wild-looking crew in dark glasses and cowboy hats, willow-patterned with tattoos which include not only dragons, Buddha heads, magic diagrams and sacred syllables, but often a splendid phallus, complete with legs and tail.

Two places recommended by the TAT office and well worth the visitor's attention are both the brainchild of one of Phitsanulok's most celebrated citizens: Sergeant-Major Tawee Booranakate. After a military career, he retired to oversee his family business: a factory casting Buddha images. This is located to the east of the town attached to his large private house, in whose grounds perhaps forty people are employed at various stages of the moulding and casting process. The procedure followed is the standard 'lost wax' method, and all over the compound sit serried ranks of images big and small, like dolls on an assembly line – headless, armless, in different stages of completion. The smaller images, and those made of gold, are first shaped in wax that is an amalgam of paraffin resin and coconut oil, and then when the details are correct, dipped five times into a mixture of chalk and diluted cattle manure and allowed to dry each time. Coats of sand and clay are added which, when baked, will form the mould. The figure is then bound in iron rods to help it withstand the intense heat of the firing which melts the wax out and leaves the hardened mould ready to receive the liquid metal. Finally the fired figure is primed with coats of lacquer and covered with gold leaf. The images are in all sizes; scattered drunkenly around the yards are some huge ones, perhaps eight feet high and costing eventually nearly 8000 *baht*. The demand for Buddha images is considerable: three months ago, for the Visakha Puja in May, 10,000 were sold. Everyone seems to benefit from the way the factory is run. The conditions are spacious and the pay is good – a skilled craftsman commanding more than 100 *baht* a day.

Across the road from the Buddha foundry stand three adjacent
houses that together form the Folk Museum, a unique record of
one man's devotion to a way of life that is fast disappearing. Over
the past fifteen years the Sergeant-Major has been collecting a
wide array of items from a vanishing heritage of everyday life. The
collections of cooking and eating utensils, ceramics, material and
furniture is enthralling, but it is the agricultural implements that
really fascinate. In a country too often scarred by modernisation
without development, this collection is a revelation. Ploughs,
nets, birdscarers, tools – all are fashioned out of wood and
willowy, lissom bamboo, and all combine practicality with a purity
of line that is beautiful to behold. Especially ingenious are the
traps – for birds, snakes, fish, rats, mongooses. Intelligently
designed and delicately operated, they are evidence of a profound
harmony with the natural surroundings. This insight into an
authentic stratum of traditional life is heartening, and well
reflects the character of the man behind the museum. Dressed in
the simple blue garb of the farmer he has a great dignity, an
integrity rooted in the land and the strength of the two traditions
that have sustained Thailand over the generations: religion and
agriculture.

20 A husband and wife grind maize in a Lisu village on the banks of the Kok river near Chiang Rai, the gateway to the Golden Triangle

21 A Yao woman smoking her bamboo water-pipe, near Chiang Rai

22 Women of the Akha tribe, whose characteristic headdresses are fringed with silver rupee coins from the days of the British Raj, smuggled over the border from Burma

23 A typical Akha village near Chiang Rai. The thatched wood and bamboo huts are built on stilts to cling to the steep hillsides

12

People of the Far Province

'Goose morning, me washing you today?' inquires the smiling face popped round my door. The query comes not, it transpires, from a peripatetic massage girl, but from the laundry lady on her morning rounds.

'No, not today, I'm going to I-saan.'

'Ooooh, I-saan!' the black eyes roll expressively. 'Good luck to you!'

For a second I wonder whether there is a hidden omen in this, the most common of valedictions in English here, but dismiss my fears as the momentary twinge of nerves that assails even the most seasoned traveller on abandoning the familiar to launch out into the unknown. Itinerants' stage fright apart, there is an aura hanging over I-saan; a sense of mystery, almost foreboding, felt by Thais and *farangs* alike. Named after Ishana, the Hindu lord of death and the north-east, I-saan, the 'Far Province' of north-east Thailand juts out towards China like a pugnacious head, its face delineated by the Mekong and its chin resting on Kampuchea. The 'Far Province' holds a special place in the national consciousness; a special chapter in the country's myth. Comprising a third of the country and almost a third of the total population, it is in many ways the most distinctive region, clearly defined with its own astringent flavour. The people here are hardy and virile, more self-contained than the genial folk of the central plain, and darker than those with Chinese blood; their fine features betraying the influence of nearby Laos and the many Mongolian border tribes that have intermingled with the native Thais. The citizens of Bangkok may regard the I-saan people as country bumpkins and mock their dialect, which is virtually Lao, but they are a proud people, steeped in an ancient culture that unites them as much to Laos as to mainstream Thailand.

I-saan is held in awe in the popular imagination because life there is so hard. The area has always been the poor relation, with chronically infertile soil, lack of water, limited transport, low income. Traditionally, I-saan has remained isolated from the mainstream of Thai life, existing with virtually no assistance from the central authority. In the Ayutthaya period the Thais were too busy trying to control the invading Burmese to worry much about what was happening on this periphery of the kingdom; what interest they did show was directed only to the southern strip of the plateau, vulnerable to the sporadic influx of Khmers from Cambodia. Later, under the Bangkok dynasty, I-saan continued to remain isolated, relying on a circumscribed but self-sufficient economy, catering to its own security and survival rather than any demand from outside markets. The staple crop, then as now, was 'sticky rice', a variety of the grain with no export demand. This translucent, gritty mash, eaten from woven bamboo holders, is well suited to a marginal economy – it expands in the stomach and small amounts suffice. The gastronomically ignorant visitor soon learns to treat 'sticky rice' with respect. Too much, especially if washed down with beer or tea, turns the stomach into a leaden sack for hours afterwards.

'Our backs to the sky, our faces to the ground – forever' runs an I-saan saying and here, as elsewhere, the rainy months are a time of back-breaking work in the fields, planting out seeds, trans-planting the baby shoots, anxiously watching the skies to see what rains the gods will bring. But in I-saan the anxiety is heightened, for drought is the curse of the area, and no other region is as poignantly aware that water is life. The dry season is ferociously hot – averaging 98°F by day and night – and in summer the heat reduces the earth to dust and the marshlands to gaping fissures. Water becomes brackish, and the luxury of steamed catfish lying plump on a bed of rice flavoured with salt and sweet basil, can turn to a diet of frogs and mud crabs, red ants, lizards, roots or nothing but chillies. The rains come – if they come at all – in two waves. The first is in May. This monsoon, thwarted largely by the mountains that form the western and southern edges of the I-saan plateau, is nevertheless the excuse for wild displays of *sanuk*.

In Ban Phai, for example, some twenty miles south of Khon Kaen, there is a rocket festival, where fantastically decorated missiles twenty feet in length hurtle a couple of miles, often causing considerable damage as they spiral madly out of control or explode on take-off. But damage is better than nothing; the man whose rocket fails to take off is ignominiously rolled in the mud. Rockets of a more sophisticated sort are being developed in the battle for more rain. Two types that can be used alone or with planes to scatter rain-inducing chemicals in the atmosphere are soon to be submitted to their final tests by the rather quaintly named Royal Rain-Making Research and Development Institute.

The May rains, gratefully remembered during the dry time of June and early July, are only a prelude to the dark, heavy clouds that are beginning to rumble up from the South China Seas. These typhoon clouds, already partly spent, will eventually release their boon in August and September, hissing and steaming like the celestial dragons the Chinese myth-makers saw in them. This is the wettest time, when rivers overflow, villages are flooded, and the rain brings a shine to the skins of the water-buffalo, and a glow to the faces of their owners. But the people of I-saan, like the citizens of Troy with the Greeks, have come to mistrust these heavenly messengers even when they bear gifts. For the rains of August and September, though they account for half the annual rainfall, are volatile. They come in violent, torrential bursts, in thunderstorms and cyclones, and they are inconsistent and unpredictable. One part of the region will be left gasping from the ferocity of the rains, another from the lack of them. Four inches can fall in a night, then nothing for weeks. Drought can turn to flood and shrink back to drought with bewildering speed, and the sandy soil acts as a sieve, retaining nothing but memories of opportunities lost. Whatever benefits the rains may bring are soon evaporated by the advancing year. Many of the large freshwater lakes simply disappear in the dry season, and even if they stay, their use is minimal, for only one acre out of every twenty in I-saan is irrigated, the rest relies on rainfall. Wells dry up rapidly and the deeper underground water is shielded by layers of rock impenetrable to traditional tools. The soil is large silica, with rarely more than one part in a hundred of organic material, and hopelessly infertile. No wonder the people are hardy.

Despite its handicaps, I-saan continued to survive the hard life, buttressed by religious orthodoxy and a strict but caring village morality. Once the rice was planted safely in July the three-month period of Lent began, celebrated in memory of the period the Buddha spent preaching to his mother in the heavens. This is the time when many adult males will be temporarily ordained, swelling the numbers in the robe by 30 per cent. Processions, plays, music, fancy-dress shows, acrobatics and fire-dancing mark the celebrations as Lent begins, and in I-saan enormous candles, tall enough to burn right through the coming three months are made of beeswax and paraded around the village in a bullock cart, with a prize awarded to the best. The men return to the community at the end of Lent in October, and in November the cool dry winds from China begin to stir the villages, and the kapok trees burst into fluffy bloom.

With luck, the December harvest would yield enough rice to pay off debts, provide food for the rest of the year and seeds for the next. Throughout the year the stored grain was supplemented by hunting and gathering in the abundant forests, which provided vital additional food supplies, a fact soon to be overlooked with disastrous consequences. The hot and cold seasons, October to April, were devoted to repairing the house, 'making merit' by religious activities, and *sanuk* in the form of socialising, weddings and music making. Most importantly, this was the time to weave silk, which until recently was an important exchange commodity in a barter economy that placed very little reliance on hard cash. When the crop was poor, or failed, the tightly knit communities, which operated as extended families, would support each other, working together, sharing food and resources, making do as the poor always make do. Indeed, the generosity of the I-saan villagers is legendary, for those with little to lose make friends quickly. Despite the occasional disasters, such as the appalling drought of 1939, life continued, protected by its hermetic balance revolving around the axis of fish, rice and forest; its equilibrium undisturbed by contact with the outside world.

After the Second World War, I-saan began to be affected by the upheavals in neighbouring Indo-China. The one thing that infertile land does breed is discontent, and the insurgency of the late 1950s increasingly developed into the violence of the 1960s. The Thai government, aided by the Americans who were by now embroiled in Vietnam, turned its attention to the Far Province and instituted a development plan. Towns sprang up, electricity reached villages, medical facilities increased, experimental dams and agricultural stations were built. Eyes were opened to a totally alien way of life based on urban materialism, and a large new servant class was created to sustain the American presence – waiters, clerks, bartenders, auto- and air-conditioning mechanics, medical orderlies, bargirls and prostitutes.

One aspect of this sudden change was a new agricultural policy, controlled from the centre and designed to turn I-saan into an economy supplying cash crops for the world market. The brightest star on this distant horizon was seen to be cassava, a plant which thrives in poor soil, the root of which provides tapioca. To make room for cassava, enormous areas of forest were cleared. The big trees, mainly slow-growing teak, were felled for cash and shipped out along the newly built roads; the smaller support trees were cleared for space. An intimate ecological balance that had taken hundreds of years to evolve was destroyed at one blow and gone was the peasant farmer's safeguard against crop failure. An irreversible change had taken place; given the length of time it would take for the forests to grow back, the balance could never be recaptured.

Cassava is now Thailand's second biggest agricultural export after rice, much of it going to the European Economic Community as cattle feed. But exactly the same problems faced by the rice and tobacco farmers of the central plains are present in I-saan in a more dramatic form: world markets are subject to manipulation, political pressure, sudden price fluctuation and gluts, and the farmer is the victim of unscrupulous middlemen and uncertain government policies on prices and quotas. In a familiar Third World story, a widely based variety of crops relevant to local food needs has been sacrificed to a single cash crop. If that fails, or is not needed, the farmer has only the moneylender to fall back on. And money does not come cheap in I-saan. Local moneylenders are often preferred to banks, as they are flexible in the timing of their demands for repayment, take account of the borrower's circumstances, and usually require no collateral. The catch is that they charge a crippling 10 per cent a month.

The forests were an integral part of the life of the north-east. When they went, so did the rain. Many cash crops have since perished from the combined effects of rainy season drought and the unremitting heat during the rest of the year: tangerines, pineapples and mandarin oranges being three recent examples. Yet illegal logging is still rife over what wooded areas of the country remain, even on the relatively inaccessible hillsides. Powerful entrepreneurs often employ impoverished locals to do the felling for them, and any campaign against what the papers call 'influential people' requires the incorruptibility of officials at all levels. By a cruel irony, the capture of stolen wood also tends to put innocent workmen out of a job in the local saw mills. The first few months of 1987 saw a number of scandals break, with convoys of stolen wood being intercepted in various parts of the country, and it was revealed that the Minister of Agriculture had been offered no less than 40 million *baht* to turn a blind eye to illegal logging in Mae Hong Son.

With ancestral lands decimated by subdivision, families too large for available resources, and persistent lack of water there seems little to stem the haemorrhage to the cities. What little money there is may well go on the status symbols of radio, fridge and television, even though the latter costs up to six months' income for an I-saan farmer, and the electricity supply to the village may be sporadic. Children who leave I-saan rarely return. Though they may send money back when they can, or come to help at harvest time, family life is being whittled away, and while the boys are offered to the monastery, the girls may well end up in less salubrious establishments. For the young, the first pair of jeans is a passport to a new world, the harsh realities of which are never imagined. And all the time, another, more brutal form of change lurks across the border.

My plan is to travel from Phitsanulok to Loei and thence to Nong Khai, taking the road that borders the Mekong for what is by common agreement a particularly beautiful stretch of the river. My intended route passes through wooded mountains and a couple of national parks, and is remote enough to provide a sense of pioneering. The people in the Tourist Office share my enthusiasm about the journey, but are a little vague as to how it might best be accomplished. They explain that the office which deals with I-saan is actually in Korat, itself many hours' journey away, and that the people there would know about such things. I nod understandingly though I cannot quite follow the logic. Anyway, the first thing is to get to Loei, and this seems very straightforward. A bus leaves Phitsanulok at 12.30, which allows time for a last stroll around this pleasant town.

Returning to my room after breakfast I surprise three room maids sitting on the floor, enjoying a pile of shiny green guavas spread out on towels in front of them. My unexpected intrusion – or perhaps my surprised expression – sets off prolonged shrieks of laughter; to cause such merriment by a mere entrance does wonders for the ego.

My departure from the hotel is completed with the sort of good-natured unreality that is daily fare for the traveller in the remoter parts of the country and will be the pattern for the next few days. I ask the girl at the hotel desk how many minutes it takes to get to the bus station. 'Three,' she replies with such prompt certainty my suspicions are aroused. Her colleague intervenes, with equal confidence, 'Ten' and then, furrowing her ivory brow in a great show of thought, 'Fifteen'. The first girl nods in vigorous agreement. Suspecting that they are just trying out their knowledge of English numerals, I decide to allow a quarter of an hour to be safe. As it turns out, the station is four minutes away by pedicab! I ask for a ticket to Loei, to be met by stares of total incomprehension, followed by prolonged giggles. Much hysteria and many patient explanations later, feeling like a creature from another planet, I take a seat on a bench in the stifling air. Next to me sits an old girl, the traditional chequered *phaasin* tucked between her sturdy legs to form a pair of voluminous knickerbockers. Her hair is steely grey and cropped close; she wears no jewellery over her plain white blouse. A blind man and his female companion pass in front of us. Both look wretched, ragged and dusty, as if they have been on the road for days, and they move with uncertain lurches that betray a manic tiredness. The woman dumps a battered military kitbag on the ground and guides the man to it, where he sits, head bowed, eyes skewed to heaven, suspended in his inner world. The soles of his spatulate feet are split with cracks and fissures, like all the dried-out mud flats they have tramped across in their search for a living. This is the first time I have seen such destitution in Thailand.

As the bus pulls out, one of my fellow passengers fixes me with a lop-sided grin and takes the seat across the aisle. He is very drunk but, rather to my surprise, speaks good English. 'Worked in Udon for the American Army, man. Eight years and fourteen days. Medic. Quit in 1967. Eight years and fourteen days.' He is wearing a checked shirt and white jeans hastily tucked into ornate but very scuffed cowboy boots. 'I'm shit drunk man,' he admits, 'shit drunk.' We chat a little, his speech becoming more slurred the further he slides down into his seat. He was on his way to Udon a couple of days ago, but got waylaid by a lady of ill repute, so now he has to sober up before he goes home. 'Wife very serious.' He pulls a face. 'Very serious.' Then after a reflective pause he leans across the aisle and punches me lightly on the arm, 'I like you, man. I like you!'

After a few minutes, the bonhomie turns a little sour. There is an argument with the bus conductor, a young man with the fingernails of his left hand varnished scarlet. It is one of the very few arguments I've seen in Thailand; an unusual violation of the golden rule of *jai yen* ('cool heart') that so effectively stifles public expression of disharmony. Cowboy Boots' posture has degenerated into a sprawl half-way across the aisle. He addresses a few belligerent remarks to the people around, berating them for their lack of sociability, and is met with polite and general disregard. Then he turns to me, his glazed stare fixed unsteadily on a point a couple of inches beyond my right ear. 'Watch out for AIDS, man.' As if exhausted by the gravity of this apocalyptic piece of advice he slumps into sleep, loose-jointed as a discarded marionette.

My neighbour on the other side is a very different proposition. A man in his sixties with grizzled hair and a walnut skin stretched tight over fine bones, he sits cross-legged on the wooden seat, expressionless, silently proclaiming the nobility of a true peasant.

We wind our way through paddy fields diced with coconut palms and the odd plane tree. Soon the fields give way to hills covered in teak, banana, bamboo and the dark green pelleted leaves of mango. Forty minutes out of Phitsanulok we brake violently and swerve to miss a jeep that has pulled without warning into the middle of the road. Those still awake grin to each other at the near miss. It is indeed a beautiful road. We pass fields of maize shaded by the soft foliage of mimosa, huge clumps of pampas grass and many castor-oil plants, their leaves splayed out in a pudgy star. An archipelago of straw-thatched roofs peeps out above an emerald sea of paddy stretching into the far distance, with a cluster of monks in brilliant orange standing like Californian poppies against the green. Here and there a white egret picks its way fastidiously through the fields. Far below, the river is a glistening ribbon of caramel, while up above birds flock and wheel, flung like tea-leaves against the rimless bowl of sky.

Skirting the Thung Salaeng National Park, we turn off the Khon Kaen road and head north towards the border. Only after an hour's climb do the first bald patches appear: charred fields of stubble, blank swathes where trees once stood. The exposure seems doubly cruel at such a height, too near the sun. Yet there are still intermittent and brilliant fields of paddy. Some are fringed with papaya trees, whose heavy fruit hangs down like bunches of pendulous green breasts; others with tall bamboo, pluming feathery as fennel into a majestic curve over the surrounding foliage. After Nakhon Thai the road climbs over the rim of the plateau, whose edge crinkles into a series of wide folds, each crest sparsely forested, each trough with a velvet pelt of green. There are no animals to be seen. For half an hour the hills grow steeper, the intervening valleys cast into deeper and more precipitous shadows, and then, suddenly, we are over the crest, descending through a series of hairpin bends into a large flat plain. Below is spread the village of Dan Sai, and on the far side, beyond the Phu Pua National Park, lies Loei.

Everyone seems to wake up at once. As if to celebrate the fact we are on the home straight, music is switched on; not the romantic synthesised pop of Bangkok, but the local I-saan brew of *moran*, a driving and repetitive singing to the accompaniment of the bamboo *khaen* – an insistent energising sound characteristic of Lao culture and much favoured to summon the spirits in tribal dances. The music stirs my neighbour, who has remained virtually motionless all this while. He produces a polythene bag, clotted with a dark rust pulp, and like some terminal consumptive, disgorges several long jets of bright red spittle into it. I now realise that the impassive demeanour which so impressed me earlier was not the result of stoical temperament forged on the anvil of hard living, but of his mouth's being so wadded with betel that all facial movement was completely inhibited. Having spat out the last vivid dribble, he ties the bag neatly closed and tosses it out of the window.

Perhaps an hour later we reach a town. Cowboy Boots is still unconscious, so I turn to the betel chewer and ask, 'Loei?' In what is his most animated display for the previous four and a half hours he shakes his head vehemently, motioning me to stay in my seat. Something warns me not to trust his advice, and I ask another passenger who is getting off. He nods. I disembark, followed by the ruminant's unblinking stare.

Although Loei is almost thirty miles from the Mekong and Laos, it has the atmosphere of a border town, wild, open-ended and dusted with transience. It is one of the major distribution points for goods smuggled into Thailand, especially the marijuana grown by Lao farmers from seeds supplied by their government. But the most important type of contraband here is people, and finding illegal refugees a niche in their new country is a profitable business. In the summer of 1987, the Loei immigration police chief had a price on his head of 200,000 *baht* for launching a drive to uncover a fake ID card racket that involved several local officials as well as village headmen. There are also legal refugees in the province – Hmong tribes-people in government camps. One of these, Ban Vinai, made the news at the beginning of 1988 when it was announced that the inmates were to be banned from using post office and mobile telephones because so many were contacting relatives in the United States to send them money to bribe the local officials and get more of their relatives into the camp.

The whole border area here has been very sensitive in the last few years, and open conflict erupted at the end of 1987, culminating in the Laotian forces shooting down a Thai Air Force jet, and Thailand's appeal to the UN to settle the dispute. Behind the Lao army hover the 40,000 troops that Soviet-backed Vietnam has stationed in the country. Although the actual scene of fighting is a few barren hills, each with its impersonal identifying number, the possibility of full-scale escalation is always present. The situation must seem particularly absurd to the villagers living along the River Heung, which, although little more than twenty feet wide at some points, forms the border between two countries as defined by the Franco-Thai treaty of 1907. Such treaties have little meaning to families with the same surname living on opposite banks, or whole villages split down the middle by the water. Trading has always gone on between the two sides and many people now have their livelihood threatened by an international conflict and the presence of armed border police who, with hand grenades, blow fish out of the once peaceful river.

At the Phu Luang, the best hotel in town, two girls in their early twenties are at the desk.

'How much for a room?'

'A hundred and twenty *baht*, plus fan.'

I assume the last two words refer to the room rather than my payment. With a practised flourish I produce my letter of introduction from TAT, which is by now a little dog-eared. The senior-looking girl takes it and reads it aloud slowly and carefully, a process that takes about three minutes, and has everybody in the

lobby temporarily distracted from the television. I feel the weight
of a dozen curious gazes, an embarrassing position, as in talking
to Thais I have more than once got the impression that they
consider writing a book, especially about their country, an
incomprehensible and not altogether seemly undertaking. After
the oration is over she hands the letter back with a charming
smile.

'So, how much is a room?' I ask again, scenting victory.

'A hundred and twenty *baht,* plus fan,' comes the reply. This is
an irretrievable loss of face. Not only is it the first time my letter
has not secured me preferential treatment, but hotel prices in
Thailand are usually negotiable anyway, whoever you are. Too
tired to argue I head for my room along linoleumed corridors
lined with spitoons, sure signs of Chinese ownership. It is stifling.
The fan coughs into life to plough heavily round through the thick
air. After wheezing asthmatically for a few minutes it begins to
sound like a light aircraft in serious trouble, and I foresee another
sleepless night.

Back downstairs I ask about buses to Nong Khai. The same
girl who booked me in replies in Thai that she thinks my eyebrows
are beautiful. Such directness, whether about appearance, age or
salary, is one of the more disarming traits of Thai social
intercourse, but I am determined not to be deterred by such
flattery. Luckily there are three or four locals chatting at the desk,
one of whom speaks a little English. After lengthy pidgin
negotiations, we work out that my intended route is indeed
possible – 'but only with', he rolls his eyes here, 'the green bus.'
And how long does it take? He thinks for several long seconds.
'No idea!' he concludes with a triumphant grin. He and his
companions gently chide the girl behind the desk, who replies
that since she has never left Loei, how can she be expected to
know anything about buses out of town? I realise now that her
compliment was a way to avoid both disappointing me and
betraying her own ignorance. Much as I appreciate her ingenious
display of tact, I cannot help thinking of the enthusiastic plans to
turn I-saan into the latest tourist destination which I have heard
mooted in various TAT offices. I hope it never happens, but if it

does, some of the people who deal with the tourists might be taught a little English and supplied with the odd bus timetable.

The coffee-shop-cum-nightclub, as is often the case in Thailand, is so dark that you must read the menu by the light of the waitress's torch. This operation requires considerable patience on her part, as it runs to seven large pages. I pass up such local delicacies as Pig's Appendix Salad and Fish Bladder Roll, and settle for two renowned representatives of the pungent I-saan cuisine – *kai yang* (which the menu has 'Chicken leg cocked in I-saan style') and *somtam*, a fiery salad made from grated unripe papaya, fish sauce, garlic, lime juice and freshly ground pepper. Both are delicious, and should be part of everyone's experiments in Thai eating. A short stroll after dinner around the town reveals it to be a more peaceful place than I had imagined from its reputation, offering a regular grid of shophouses with a small night market, three or four Chinese hotels and quietness by half past ten.

At eleven o'clock the next morning the bus station is full of waiting passengers and the ticket office is closed. I explain to a conductor that I want to get to Nong Khai, and he bundles me enthusiastically on to his bus. Further inquiries reveal it is going to Udon Thani, the southern route I am having so much difficulty avoiding. Everyone seems to think my plan to go north is very strange. I enlist the help of a bicycle rickshaw to find someone whose English is better than my Thai, and set off on a tour of banks, which are all closed as apparently it is Saturday, and hotels, where everyone is watching TV and no one seems interested in my queries. A Tourist Office looms out of the haze. It too is closed. By now the heat, lack of sleep, and the frustration are beginning severely to tax my *jai yen*. As I have found before, after days of uninterrupted and smiling bonhomie, an irritation that has been building up unnoticed, suddenly surfaces, and for no good reason and in totally inappropriate circumstances, I commit the unpardonable offence of losing my patience. It is a shaming experience, and gets me absolutely nowhere, but it is something I seem powerless to prevent. I am consoled to see that even long-term residents appear prey to this syndrome. I know of several *farangs*, married to Thais, who still have to return home every so often to cool off for a few weeks.

Suddenly a woman appears who speaks a little English. It now transpires that there is after all no 'green bus' along the river road to Nong Khai, but it is possible to catch a series of *songthaews* involving at least three changes and an overnight stay. *Songthaews* are fine for short hauls, but the prospect of a succesion of long, hot, squashed journeys, with no real visibility, strung out over the next thirty-six hours defeats me. I decide to bend with the wind and go to Udon after all. It must be age. Not long ago the prospect of hardship and an indefinite time scale would have added allure to a trip, now I'm easily seduced by comfort and ease. As I ponder these changes, my rickshaw speeds past the bus station. I don't know where the driver was heading for so intently, but I redirect him. This whole affair is assuming farcical proportions – Jacques Tati in Thailand.

Half an hour later the bus is on its way, my equilibrium restored by several cups of Chinese tea – an invaluable psychic balm – and a portion of the local speciality *kai ping*, eggs skewered into a kebab and roasted in their shells. After several minutes of crawling around the town trawling for passengers, we join the main road east to Udon Thani. The few passengers are all clustered up at the front of the bus to watch the Bugs Bunny cartoon on the video. One little boy is uncertain whether the long-eared rabbit on the screen or the long-nosed *farang* in the back is the more interesting, but Hollywood wins in the end. Already it is a different world from yesterday. The road is more built up, the fields full of the spindly cassava; here and there girls are fishing in the paddy fields with long rods of bamboo, wicker baskets strapped round their slender waists. But there is again the incorrigible variety of green – a verdant backcloth rent every so often by the rich yellow and scarlet of canna lillies, or stippled with pink and orange lanatana. Water buffaloes are everywhere, both the ponderous charcoal variety and the less dignified albino, pink as pigs. Kids with gleaming smiles and wide-brimmed straw hats sit astride their broad backs. Now and then the bus cuts through a whirring cloud of dragon flies that hovers in the midday glare, while huge black and white butterflies flap languidly along the verges. At one stop a vendor gets on, brandishing an armful of lotus pods that look like green shower nozzles. At another a drunk sways into the seat beside me, and I begin to wonder whether the real purpose of my trip is to provide company for the country's itinerant alcoholics. The new arrival offers the conductor five *baht* and asks for the stop at which he boarded. No amount of persuasion can convince him of his mistake. He conducts a low monologue for about ten minutes, which I punctuate every so often with a polite 'krap, krap'. (This does not, as might appear, mean that I think he is talking rubbish, but is the word used for 'yes, good, fine' when spoken by a man.) Then, his tale told, he puts his head on my shoulder and falls asleep like a child.

Udon Thani is a tree-lined town and much of its shophouse architecture is surprisingly mellow. In its time the place served as one of the most important American bases, but apart from the obligatory disco, massage parlour and a couple of clubs, that wild era is just a memory here, evoked only by the burnt-out shells of the bars and clubs – The Cobra, The Wolverine, The Tigress – that line the road south to Khon Kaen. As a result, Udon has an unexpected provincial atmosphere, which I like.

The chief attraction of the area lies some thirty miles east of the town, in the village of Ban Chiang, a sleepy hamlet that is in the process of rewriting history. The story begins in July 1966 when Stephen Young, an anthropology student and son of a former American ambassador to Thailand, tripped over the roots of a kapok tree in the village. Picking himself up, he noticed that the surrounding area, perhaps fifty feet by fifteen, was full of pot rims sticking out of the earth. Intrigued, he collected a batch and sent them first to Bangkok, then to the University of Pennsylvania for analysis. Although the initial sherds gave what were later to prove widely inaccurate readings, it was soon established that Young had, literally, stumbled upon an archaeological site of major importance, for the pots were over 5000 years old.

It had been known for years that buff-coloured clay jars painted with red whorls and swirling designs existed in profusion in I-saan. Occasional examples would turn up in the antique shops of Bangkok without exciting much interest or fetching much of a price, and in I-saan, whenever they were found undamaged, the pots were put to domestic use. But Young's find, and the subsequent excavations, alerted the smugglers, and the village became the scene of a modern gold-rush. Wealthy dealers in Bangkok and abroad encouraged the traffic; middlemen appeared from nowhere, first in single cars, then in convoys. Farmers in the area left their fields to dig, often doing irreversible damage in the process. Some of the booty crossed the Mekong to be flown out in carriers belonging to Air America, the CIA airline. It wasn't until 1973 that, bureaucratic delays finally overcome, a leading Thai archaeologist, Pisit Charoenwongsa, and his colleague from Pennsylvania, Chester Gorman, finally arrived to dig. By then the site had been severely depleted; as Gorman said, 'The kind of excavation archaeologists only dream about was practically destroyed.' Yet a mere two years of digging yielded eighteen tons of material – tools, weapons, ornaments – all in a wide variety of materials, and 126 burial pits. Pots were found in seven distinct strata, ranging from sophisticated Thai celadons, Chinese blue and white and local earthenwares in the top layer (AD 1600) to simple black and grey decorated vessels in the bottom layer (3600 BC). Beautiful and valuable though these were, what really excited the archaeologists was the bronze. Not only was more uncovered in two years at Ban Chiang than in a century in the Middle East but the Thai material turned out to be the oldest ever found, going back to at least 3600 BC and possibly 3900 BC, and thus pre-dating the Middle Eastern finds by half a millennium. In one blow Ban Chiang shattered the received wisdom that bronze metallurgy developed in the valley between the Tigris and the Euphrates about 3000 BC and spread to South-East Asia 500 years before the beginning of the Christian era. In addition, the find caused historians and archaeologists to rethink their ideas about the ancient relationship of China and Thailand. The oldest known Chinese bronze goes back only to about 2000 BC, and given that tin and copper, the main components of bronze, are more widely available in Thailand, it may be that bronze technology went from there to China, rather than the reverse as has always been assumed. Whatever the final outcome, a major step in man's cultural history has had to be rethought.

Gorman's work over the previous twenty years well qualified him to be part of the Ban Chiang drama. One of his major discoveries was the important north-central site of Non Nok Tha, evidence from which suggested that rice cultivation could have been practised here even before India or China. Gorman died tragically young in 1981 and his death has considerably slowed the analysis of excavated material. Yet much has been accomplished in a joint operation which includes on the Thai side many volunteers from both the Ban Chiang area and the kingdom's various universities.

Apart from a few souvenir stalls, the village has now returned more or less to its former somnolence. There is no restaurant, no hotel, and no geodesic dome as envisaged by Buckminster Fuller, an early enthusiast, though all of these may yet come. At one end of the village is Wat Pho Si Nai, where two burial pits are displayed, their contents left *in situ*. The different layers and the way the funerary pots were used, either shattered over the body or buried alongside it, are well demonstrated. At the other end of the village is the small and beautifully laid out museum, which raises as many questions as it answers. Apart from the fact that they may have been the first to use bronze, we know little about the Ban Chiang people. Thailand's tropical climate has left no traces of their buildings, no vestiges of written material on palm leaf or bamboo. We do know the people hunted, fished, grew rice and probably believed in an afterlife. In the Middle East and elsewhere bronze arose in the context of a developed urban society; here in Ban Chiang it arose in the matrix of simple village life. Thus rather than military weapons or ritual objects, the Ban Chiang metalsmiths made tools for everyday use and jewellery for themselves and their children. We do not know where they mined the metals. Clay moulds have been found, but perhaps they also used the lost wax methods for their funerary bracelets and anklets and the everyday bangles that have been found in such profusion. The graceful pots were fashioned probably using the paddle and anvil technique, still common all over I-saan, for no trace of the wheel has been found. All the work displays a consummate aesthetic sense.

It is the children of Ban Chiang I find most intriguing. Many have been found buried in clay pots, most just a few weeks old, some still foetuses. Did they die of natural causes? Was there ritual infanticide for religious or economic reasons? Or were they worshipped in some way, by the ancestors of a society that still lavishes great attention on its children? Whatever the answers, their modern counterparts are out in force as I drive back to Udon in the late afternoon sun. School kids in neat white and blue uniforms cross the road in disciplined Indian files, each group led by a child bearing a long bamboo pole from which a red flag flutters. It is a charming scene. The women sit by the roadside, the day's work done, *phaasins* hitched up around their knees. They look like bandits, scarves wrapped across their faces under the tall crowns of sombreros. Clothes hang out to dry in the fields like rows of bunting, gilded in the dying light, while children stretch fishing nets over bamboo frames to snare the paddy frogs. At times like this, I-saan doesn't seem to have changed all that much since the time of Ban Chiang.

13

Borderlands

Khon Kaen, the provincial capital of I-saan, is a concrete town flavoured with garlic. Although it has only ten thousand more inhabitants than Udon Thani, it feels by comparison very much the big city, centred on an impersonal jumble of neon advertising, tangled wires and modern shophouses. There is an attractive university campus here and a very good branch of the National Museum, noted especially for its collection of Ban Chiang artefacts and many early stelae, which date back at least 1200 years to the Dvaravati period. Otherwise, apart from its position as a junction point almost exactly in the centre of the province, Khon Kaen, like all of urban I-saan, has little to attract the visitor. Even the nightlife here is relatively subdued, a legacy from the time of the Vietnam War when the city governor refused to allow the city to become a 'rest and relaxation' haven for American troops. South of the city, past leafy lanes and some substantial wooden houses, is a rainy-season lake. Around this are ranged a couple of temples in the attenuated style of the north-east – very tall and thin with elongated spires – and several small open-air restaurants, each one specialising in a few local dishes. This is by far the most enjoyable part of town to eat in, and the standard is high.

The road up to the border with Laos runs north-east of Khon Kaen to Nakhon Phanom on the banks of the Mekong, passing through Kalasin and then Sakhon Nakhon. Those who like their archaeological sites untamed would do well to turn off this road at Yang Talat, forty miles east of the capital, and head for Phong Tong, from where a track leads to the sleepy village of Ban Sema. Over a thousand years ago this was an important Dvaravati city, an oval delineated by two massive ramparts bordering a moat sixty feet wide. Many of the stelae in the museum were found here, and fifteen *chedis*, ranging from the seventh to the tenth centuries, have been rescued from the surrounding undergrowth. It is an atmospheric spot, and can be visited easily in a day trip from Khon Kaen.

It seems as if I am going to have as much difficulty getting to Nakhon Phanom as I had trying to reach Nong Khai. A series of inquiries at the desk of the Khon Kaen Hotel – a very friendly place and greatly preferable to the more touted Kosa – reveals that there is a bus which will take me to the border, but it leaves at 2 a.m. and will take 'about five hours'. In addition, I am advised it may be crowded, so I should get to the bus station early. The night of my departure, a warm wind that rustles the palm leaves like paper is the prelude to a spectacular electrical storm that lights up the sky for hours, reducing the huge full moon to a translucent circle amidst scudding clouds. The rain that follows floods the city in minutes, causing the *samlor* drivers, like drenched rats, to wade through the sodden streets wheeling rickshaws covered with flimsy arrangements of polythene sheeting barely secured to the threadbare hoods with string and rubber bands. By the time I get to the bus station, the rain has brought a soothing coolness, but also flushed out swarms of mosquitoes, most of which appear to find my pale skin a welcome change of diet. The bus eventually turns up at 3.30 a.m. It is full. There will be another one 'about five o'clock' so, *mai pen rai*, there is nothing to do but sit it out, dozing on the hard wooden seats or joining the *samlor* drivers in their interminable games of ludo played with beer-bottle tops. The bus arrives just before five, and I fight my way into the last free seat, at the very front. I slide into it with gratitude, and slip into sleep as the first food stalls are being set up on the pavements and the black night sky is cracking into a purple dawn.

An hour out of Khon Kaen, the entire bus wakes with a start at the scene of a hellish accident. Two tour buses have collided head on, and lie meshed together in an ugly crumpled embrace on the other side of the road. The cab of the oncoming bus is a crushed eggshell, its side ripped open like a tin can in a jagged wound from which chrome and plastic are splayed out at tortured angles. The glint of shattered glass is everywhere. Perhaps thirty people are scattered along the nearside verge, some sprawled motionless, others sitting or standing, stunned into isolation. The air is numb with shock. One man sits alone, his back to the road and his shirt so drenched in blood you can count his ribs. A lone policeman is walking up and down, and the worst casualties must have been removed already, but the crash can have happened only a few minutes ago. No one is allowed to leave our bus as the stewardess takes out a couple of lavatory rolls to help mop up the carnage. After a few helpless minutes we are on our way, with just enough room to squeeze past between the squashed buses and a couple of lifeless bodies on the verge opposite. As we draw away, the cause of the crash becomes clear – a water buffalo lies stiff-legged at the side of the road, its eyes the colour of milk. I wonder how many human lives the beast has taken with it. Buses in Thailand have a poor safety record, and more than one Thai has warned me against using them, especially at night or in the rainy season, when the roads can be unexpectedly slippery. Companies compete with each other on the basis of speed, and the drivers work long hours, often keeping themselves going with amphetamines bought under the counter at wayside garages. Despite the trappings of modernity, this is still Asia, where the fragility of life is rarely disguised.

For the next few miles we proceed with exaggerated caution, the driver hooting at the steady stream of dogs, ducks, chickens and vehicles that stray into the middle of the road seemingly unaware of our presence. I feel very vulnerable, shielded from the road only by a windscreen almost opaque with dirt that lies undisturbed by an ineffective pair of wipers. Little by little the laughter and chatter return, as we make a series of stops to let passengers off. I talk to the driver about the accident. He knew both drivers; one of them was a colleague from the same firm, who had left the depot at Korat only a few minutes before he did. I cannot discern the emotions behind his smile. Soon we are driving again at the usual speed, swerving to miss obstructions in the usual way as if nothing untoward had happened. We pass through Sakhon Nakhon, an orderly town set on the banks of the huge Nong Han lake, the only province in the north-east to enjoy plenty of water. At one stop a vendor patrols the windows with what looks like a bunch of peacock feathers – they turn out to be iridescent beetles skewered on bamboo sticks, shimmering kebabs of emerald and turquoise. Seven miles before Nakhon Phanom we pass the old American base, hidden behind grassy mounds, and enter the town through street markets where, in the mad days of the Vietnam War, you could buy fried bananas wrapped in discarded computer print-outs detailing the movements of traffic along the Ho Chi Minh Trail.

Nakhon Phanom is a ramshackle, placid town set on the banks of the Mekong. The riverside walk through the older part of the town is pleasant, and there are restaurants overlooking the river that serve tasty giant catfish. The river stretches flat, wide and muddy brown across to Laos, its far bank fringed by a line of deep green foliage, behind which limestone hills rise in a series of steep undulations, miniature versions of the Guilin hills reproduced in many a Chinese landscape painting. Mist drifts across the range in long wraiths, obscuring the peaks every so often, and the silence is stitched with drizzle. There's no traffic on the river, though the immigration office marks the spot where traders disembark twice a week with goods that are sold in the Chinese and Vietnamese riverside shops – heavy silk in geometric patterns and assorted basketry. A few boys are fishing, the *samlor* drivers doze in their cabs, and the clock-tower at the centre of the town is stuck at half past three. A number of newly painted *wats* glow vividly against the dripping green foliage; it is hard to imagine that this is still a high-security area.

The road south of Nakhon Phanom follows the river a little over thirty miles to That Phanom, another of half a dozen names easy to confuse in Thailand. A turning off this road leads to Renu Nakhon, a village famed for its weaving and, as one hears so often travelling around the north, its pretty girls. The speciality of the place is *ikat*, a technique of dyeing both the warp and weft of the heavy silk which gives it a shimmering richness. There is a modern temple here, brightly painted and intricately decorated in the confectioner's style popular locally. The north-east is traditionally a pious area, and even today there is no shortage of generous patrons for the many new temples that are being built or restored. In an ancient folk tale, a commoner tells the King that his subjects spend their money on four things: religion, parents, enjoyment and their wives – priorities that are probably the same today. The most famous temple in the locality is Wat That Phanom, containing a Laotian-style *chedi* that rises like a plump needle over the village of the same name, its proportions unlike any Thai style. Erected originally in the ninth century, the coloured spire underwent many restorations between the fifteenth and seventeenth centuries. Then, in 1975, after four days of torrential rain, it collapsed. Restored again in 1979, it now stands as the axis of a huge cloistered courtyard, surrounded by many Buddha images blistered with gold leaf. Lavishly endowed and believed to contain a rib of the Buddha, That Phanom has become the symbol of I-saan, and draws many pilgrims to its annual festival in mid-February. The short road that leads from the *chedi* down to the river passes through the old part of town, which has some attractively decrepit Chinese-French architecture, some good eating places and at least two eccentric hotels. It is at its fringes, here on the Mekong, that I-saan at last provides some interesting secular buildings, which together with parts of Bangkok are probably the nearest to a colonial genre in the whole country.

After delineating Thailand's border for well over six hundred miles, the stately Mekong finally veers eastwards, to cut across the south-east corner of Laos and plunge down through Cambodia, eventually to empty into the South China Sea just below Saigon, in a delta so wide it is known locally as the River of the Nine Dragons. As a parting gift she leaves Thailand her tributary, the river Moun, which flows for fifty miles due west before reaching the town of Ubon Ratchathani, 'Royal City of the Lotus'. Ubon is as important, if not as exotic, as its name implies, for it is the capital of the north-east's largest province and rises as a startlingly modern island above the timeless simplicity of the surrounding countryside. Yet, as so often in Thailand, the legacy of American attentions has not totally obscured a way of life formed over centuries by more than merely materialistic considerations, for

Ubon is still the site of numerous well-endowed temples, and host
to a number of important religious fairs. The most impressive of
these is the Candle Festival which celebrates the beginning of Lent
in late July. To the music, decorated floats and beauty contests that
accompany all sizeable festivals in Thailand is added a parade of
enormous beeswax candles, sculpted into a variety of fantastic
shapes – heroes, divine beings, mythological animals and birds.
The parade passes a number of *wats*, where the candles are
unloaded and ceremoniously lit to illuminate the coming months.
The festival is a high-spirited affair, lasting for five days, and is
especially profitable to the vendors of *kai yang*, a type of spicy roast
chicken that has established Ubon's gastronomic reputation all
over the country.

Half an hour's drive and over two thousand years away from the
city is Wat Ba Nanachat, a monastic retreat where the austere life of
the early Buddhist communities is practised. Located in a forest
clearing surrounded by paddy fields, the temple comprises a large
new reception hall, a few pavilions, an open-air kitchen and dining
area, and numerous individual huts scattered among the trees.
The whole clearing is very quiet, suffused with a silence that is not
just the absence of noise, but that lively stillness which is the fruit of
meditation. The monastery was established in the early 1970s
specifically for foreigners, under the guidance of a famous spiritual
teacher, Achaan Cha, a monk whose straightforward manner and
mischievous sense of humour cast him in the mould of the old Zen
masters. Since its founding, Wat Ba Nanachat has become
something of a showpiece of the reclusive life, and has inspired
forty associated retreat centres all over the world. The routine of
the forest mendicant is simple and austere – the monks make and
dye their own robes, eat one meal a day, go barefoot and have no
possessions – and provides a dramatic contrast to what is
observable in most other Thai *wats*. At present the community
numbers fifteen permanent members, drawn from different
countries, and a varying number of people who stay for retreats.

Today there are about forty lay members attending the
meditation session, almost all of them women. After an hour's
silent sitting, I accompany the monks to a pavilion where tea is

served along with frugal refreshment in the form of small dark green fruit dipped in a mixture of salt and sugar. They are so bitter I can stomach only half of one, despite its recommended virtues in 'cleansing the system'. Everyone seems relaxed and attentive; the talk is desultory, consisting of a few questions directed to the abbot who answers with a brief sentence or sometimes just a laugh from his elevated settle at the end of the room. My confession that I write books produces general mirth; presumably the collective opinion is that there are more than enough mental distractions in the world already without my adding to them. Though the insights of Buddhism are still opaque to most Westerners, the people here are no mere followers of an exotic fashion, and Wat Ba Nanachat is no haven for drop-outs. One look at the faces shows both the rewards and difficulties of trying to transcend the mental habits of a lifetime. As the monks filter out to go about their duties, I stay for a few minutes to chat to the abbot. He is a Canadian who arrived in I-saan fourteen years ago and has never returned, a congenial man in his late forties with a gaze as sharp as a bird's. Although the Thais are deserting their temples, there is he says a growing interest in the essential teachings of the faith, stripped of its institutional corruption. The latest government five-year plan called for a return to cultural values, and a lessening of the wholehearted pursuit of material development that has dominated the last quarter of a century. To the Buddhist, desire is never-ending, and satisfied only by self-knowledge; thus to the abbot it is perfectly logical that although the per capita income in Thailand has never been higher, her people are more in debt than ever before, and the stability of her society is increasingly precarious. The restraining of consumerism is not an argument fashionable in the late 1980s and seems doubly ironic in the context of I-saan. I am reminded afresh that the Buddha himself was born a prince, in a position to renounce the material consolations that most people spend most of their lives struggling to attain. The faith he founded teaches that material possessions alone can never bring lasting happiness, and though the cynic may reply that at least they allow one to be miserable in comfort, it may be that if there is a future for Buddhism, it lies more in the affluent West than in its relatively impoverished native habitats.

Each evening the community goes to pay its respects to its founder. I am invited to join, and accept with pleasure, having read some of Achaan Cha's talks and been impressed by their simple clarity. The women kneel demurely, heads bowed, hands raised, as the young monks file into a pick-up truck, and though I am sympathetic to their endeavour, I find it strange to see such respect paid to fellow Westerners whose life until comparatively recently was probably little different to mine. I take up the rear of the convoy, feeling somewhat incongruous in my large white Pontiac with red seats and a dashboard littered with Dolly Parton cassettes. The afternoon rain has cleared the air, and we emerge from the forest under a brilliant rainbow arcing over fields bathed in pellucid light.

At Achaan Cha's residence, a neat modern bungalow surrounded by jack fruit trees, we join the group of over a hundred seated in the garden. I had heard that the man was ill, but am not prepared for the shrunken figure hunched in a wheelchair on the veranda, attended by two monks with surgical masks over their faces and palm-leaf fans in their hands. A stroke has left him paralysed and speechless, but at the first note of the rich Pali chanting he splutters into a semblance of life, clearly aware at some level. After forty minutes of chanting, agonising to those not accustomed to sitting with legs tucked sideways in the Thai manner, the master is wheeled inside, and the meeting adjourns. The whole episode is a telling lesson in the Buddhist teaching of impermanence, a point no doubt appreciated by the members of Wat Ba Nanachat, who have dedicated their lives to observing the birth and death of each moment.

That part of I-saan which borders Cambodia is famous as a supplier of the gentle and patient beast that is one of Thailand's essential symbols: the elephant. Celebrated in myth and legend, caparisoned in battles and ceremonies, displayed as a symbol of wealth and status, employed as a beast of burden and working animal, the creature has its likeness rendered in thousands of temples, carvings and decorations. It is above all the beast of royalty. Narai the Great of Ayutthaya was the most enthusiastic and skilled royal elephant catcher, chasing after them to lasso the back legs. The future Rama 3 commanded an elephant battalion in battle against the Vietnamese as late as 1844, and it was only a few years later that his successor Rama 4 wrote to Abraham Lincoln offering the President some elephants to dignify his entourage, adding detailed instructions for their safe transport from Siam to America.

Most regal of all were the white elephants, outward signs of the monarch's greatness and treated as supernatural omens of divine favour, especially when discovered early in a reign. The importance of the white elephant goes back to the story of the Buddha's conception, when his mother dreamt that a white elephant entered her body bearing a lotus flower. The first Thai monarch to own one appears, fittingly enough, to have been the father of the nation, Ramkamhaeng of Sukhothai, and the cult spread rapidly to Burma, Cambodia and Ceylon. The discoverer of such an auspicious beast was suitably rewarded; according to a foreign report in the mid-nineteenth century, he 'underwent the painfully pleasant operation of having his mouth, ears and nostrils stuffed with gold'.

Some early European travellers were not very impressed when they finally saw the creature whose fame had spread far beyond the borders of Siam, but their disappointment was as much attributable to semantics as to the over-heated imaginations of the Siamese. The Thai adjective *pheuk*, usually translated 'white', is rendered more accurately 'tawny' – a fair description of what are essentially albino animals. In fact, a few bleached patches, along with several other physical characteristics including white eyes and toe-nails, seem enough to qualify an elephant for the appellation. In addition, according to the seventeeth-century *Book of Elephant Science* the beast should demonstrate its nobility by its fragrant smell and the fact that when asleep, it never snores but emits the pleasant tinkle of Thai classical instruments.

As befits its status, the white elephant must be treated royally, especially where its gargantuan stomach is concered. The *haute cuisine* of the pachyderm world can be a costly affair – amounting to the weight of five *mahouts* in grass, bananas and sugar cane each day – and from this comes our English phrase describing a useless and expensive encumbrance. In former times it was the custom of kings to present an excessively ambitious courtier with a white elephant, but not the land needed to support it. Such a gift could not be refused, but it was ruinous.

White elephants still enjoy a favoured position today, and any found must be offered to the King. There are at present a dozen gracing the royal stables at Chitralada Palace in Bangkok, ten of which have undergone the arcane Brahminical ceremonies establishing them as bona fide. Among their most frequent visitors is said to be Princess Sirindhorn, who, in conformity with a custom dating back to Ayutthayan times, has penned a number of soothing eulogies with which the wrinkled colossus is serenaded at the Ceremony of Naming the Auspiciously Significant Elephant.

The elephant catchers of I-saan are the Suay, a small, linguistically distinct tribe that lives along the deeply forested Thai/Cambodian border. The Suay are part of the animistic folklore of I-saan. On their hunts, armed only with buffalo-hide ropes and magic, they spoke a special language from which all personal names were omitted, in order to confuse malign spirits and protect themselves from insects and snakes. The success of the hunt also depended on the co-operation of their women and children in the village, who would refrain from cutting or combing their hair, wearing fancy clothes and having relatives to stay for the duration of their men's absence. At the beginning of the century there were 100,000 domesticated elephants in Thailand and the skills of the Suay were much in demand. Today, with perhaps 4000 working elephants and as many left in the wild, their livelihood is threatened, but each November they and their elephants assemble at Surin, a silk-producing town midway between Ubon and Korat, for the annual round-up. This two-day event is one of the most popular in I-saan, drawing 40,000 visitors, and gives the younger Suay a chance to practise skills that are in danger of becoming obsolete.

South-east I-saan is very rich in archaeological sites, and, given its proximity to Cambodia, it is not surprising that the majority of these are testaments to the days of the great Khmer empire which governed Cambodia from the eighth to the fifteenth century and dominated east and central Thailand for much of that time. Hub of the Khmer power was the jungle citadel of Angkor Wat, sacked by the Thais in 1431 and forgotten for four hundred years until the French naturalist Henri Mouhot stumbled across it in 1860. Angkor was the symbolic home of the gods and the mausoleum of its founder, the god-king Suryavarman 2, and many such Indian-derived ideas were to influence the growing Thai civilisation. Three principle groups of Khmer ruins are easily reached as one travels west along the bottom of I-saan back towards Bangkok. Thirty miles south of Buri Ram lies Muang Tham, one of the most attractive sites in the whole country. The eleventh-century complex is surrounded by a laterite wall that is pierced by four ornamental gateways, and undulates like the *naga* serpents the Khmers worshipped. Behind the wall lie two courtyards. The outer is spacious and symmetrical, containing four ponds overlooked by trees and crowned by the pink water-lilies, while the inner houses the remains of the actual sanctuaries. These are the five *prangs*: the solid, chunky spire of the Khmer, far less elongated than a purely Thai style would have demanded. Very dilapidated, these buildings are imbued with a sense of abandon that heightens the nostalgic atmosphere, and the low knolls are scattered with fallen sandstone lintels carved in high relief, lying alongside great unworked blocks of stone. Muang Tham is a place of great charm, and I hope it escapes the attentions of the restorers and the consequent volume of admirers.

If Muang Tham in its present form typifies the private, intimate aspect of Khmer building, Phanom Rung, five miles away as the crow flies, is the grandiose and public statement of a mighty and self-confident empire. Its setting could hardly be improved, set as it is on the crown of Rainbow Hill, an inactive volcano that dominates a wide, flat plain stretching away southwards to the smoky Dangrek Mountains, beyond which lies Cambodia. Nowhere is the identification of monarch and deity

more clearly articulated than Phanom Rung, known by the
Khmer word for temple, *prasat*, which means 'castle' or 'abode
of the king'. The temple is approached by a triumphal avenue
almost 200 yards long and ten yards wide along which sandstone
pillars form an impassive guard of honour. Various auxiliary
structures, such as the white elephant stables, line the route.
The monumental staircase is broken by a series of broad
platforms, and flanked by balustrades that terminate in the
five-headed *nagas*, rearing imperiously with open hoods. The
temple was dedicated to the Hindu god Shiva, for the Khmers
were catholic in their religious tastes, and dates from the twelfth
century, though much of it is earlier, as we know from the many
inscriptions in ancient Khmer and Sanskrit that have been
found in the area. Khmer sacred buildings ordered the universe,
and are characterised by a symmetry evident here in the square
central sanctuary that faces the rising sun and its antechambers
aligned to the four cardinal points. The reticulated carving is of
a very high quality, and some of the lintels are sculpted with
garlands such as still decorate the doors of bridal homes in I-
saan. The sandstone glows like honey, and adds a touch of
lightness to the powerful sense of mass that is always a hallmark
of Khmer buildings.

The last, and best known of these early sites is Pimai, thirty-
three miles north-east of Korat. Like Phanom Rung, this has
been well restored, though a feeling of precariousness lingers in
the haphazard arrangement of many of the heavy blocks of
stone. Pimai, also built in the twelfth century, marked the
western extent of the last of the great kings of Angkor, Jayavarman 7. A road ran 150 miles from his capital here to Pimai,
passing through the staging posts of Muang Tham and Phanom Rung. The high relief carving is lovely, and the flat, almost
negroid features of the Khmer kings, courtiers, musicians and
deities are very clear. Although the temple was dedicated to
Mahayana Buddhism, Hindu motifs are clearly discernible,
especially in the carvings displayed in the open-air museum that
lies on the other side of an ornamental pond from the temple
proper.

It is a heartbreaking lesson in the vagaries of history to see such vigorous statements of a potent and refined civilisation in the light of the wretched plight of the Cambodian people today. Only a few miles south of these proud temples lie nine refugee camps strung out along the border, barbed-wire limbos for a quarter of a million dispossessed souls. They have been there for nine years, ever since the Vietnamese invaded their country in 1979, and their story is a tragedy that the Western media, always ready to agonise over the Holocaust or South Africa, have largely ignored. No other country has suffered as much in modern times. The refugees of Cambodia have no fresh water, no possibility to grow food, no reason for hope. They are kept alive by the ten cups of rice and the tin of fish that the United Nations relief agency dishes out each week to each person. The men are, in general, forcibly recruited into one of the three resistance movements which run the camps – the Khmer Rouge, the Khmer Peoples' National Liberation Front and the followers of Prince Sihanouk – while the women and children just sit and wait, unable to work, to plan or even to dream. Each night they pack up their meagre belongings, in case the Vietnamese decide to shell them again. Even those who do manage to get beyond the gates run the risk of stepping on one of the thousands of land mines the Vietnamese have sown along the border. Pathetically, the most dynamic area of Camp 2, a city the size of Exeter squashed into five squalid miles, is the workshop making artificial limbs for the thousands of legless inmates.

This ravaged border is an ideological faultline, along which the tectonic plates of super-power politics grind with harsh and relentless indifference. The camps are denied official refugee status and Cambodia is refused any international aid because it is occupied by Soviet-backed aggressors. Western governments show a token concern by recognising a resistance coalition that includes the unlikely bedfellows of Prince Sihanouk and the Chinese-backed Khmer Rouge who deposed him and, who, as murderers of half the country's population, are loathed and feared by most of those Cambodians who remain alive. Thailand sends her Army Rangers to police the camps – where they are accused of rape and drunken brutality – but will not accept responsibility for what she terms 'displaced persons' deprived of refugee status. Already unwilling host to thousands of recognised refugees from Burma, Laoe and Vietnam, she is wary of burdening herself further and incurring the wrath of the Vietnamese troops already massed along her eastern borders. Pol Pot, whose crimes of genocide equal those of Hitler and Stalin, waits in the wings to seize power when the Vietnamese troops withdraw, and Prince Sihanouk, the mercurial repository of whatever hopes the Cambodians may still have, periodically threatens to abandon politics altogether and leave his compatriots to their fate. Meanwhile Richard Nixon, whose saturation bombing of neutral Cambodia was the original cause of the country's destabilisation, is lauded as an elder statesman in America, where a ticket to one of his talks costs the same as the UN spends on feeding a refugee for four years. No belief in the god-kings of Angkor was madder than this contemporary reality.

All of this will presumably change, eventually if not in the near future, though change may not bring improvement. In June 1988 the Vietnamese government, in line with the current Russian policy of appeasement, announced a planned withdrawal of a large part of its occupying army as a step towards resolution. Given the intractable and international complexities of the situation, it is hard to see how this or any other foreseeable solution will help a people who have already suffered so much, but at least it is a break in the current stalemate.

The domestic political scene in Thailand is a far less depressing affair, and provides a form of entertainment that is a rumbustious inversion of the customary polite veneer of Thai society. Both the elected House of Representatives and the Senate, appointed by the monarch, engage in debates which are always lively and frequently spiced with insults – 'snake' and 'dog' being two favourite epithets. Allegations of corruption, a human fraility the Thais tend to regard with a certain indulgence, are a regular feature. In a society which rewards government service with much status but little pay, and in which middlemen and speculation abound, it is perhaps no coincidence that the taking

24 A spirit house, such as can be seen all over the country, complete with offerings of flowers, food, scarves and incense

25 Wat Phra That Cheong Chum in the centre of Sakhon Nakhon is modern, but built in the traditional northern style with stepped roofs, ornate decoration and low, sweeping eaves

26 A street scene in Nakhon
    Si Thammarat, with
    bicycle rickshaws, mobile
    food stalls and much
    gossip

27 A policeman on duty in
    Nakhon Phanom
    exemplifies the Thais'
    renowned love of uniform

of bribes is referred to as 'eating'. One among many dramatic examples of the theatrical nature of Thai politics is the case of Samak Sundaravej, leader of one of the opposition parties. Early in 1987, Samak was convicted of criminal libel for declaring that a former deputy leader of the Democratic Party had been guilty of smuggling tin and trafficking in heroin and using the proceeds to buy votes. After the verdict of a suspended jail sentence was announced, the Minister of the Interior suggested that Samak's status as an MP should be reviewed in the light of his conviction. A member of Samak's party leapt to his leader's defence, announcing that unless the Minister recanted and apologised, he would kill himself. This public suicide was to be performed on the Sanam Luang, the park in front of the Grand Palace much favoured for such dramatic scenes. The ardent MP announced one precondition: 'I will shoot the Interior Minister first,' he declared. Newsworthy though it was, the story merited low billing for such political fervour, only a small inside-page article in the English-language dailies, while the headlines were taken up mainly with the results of a boxing match.

More interest was shown in another story that erupted at about the same time, involving two veteran actors on the political stage, the ex-premier and man of letters Kukrit Pramoj, and the Commander-in-Chief of the Army, a character of adamantine solidity called General Chavalit Yongchaiyudh. The General has proclaimed sympathy for the poor farmers and a desire that Thailand should become an agricultural, rather than an industrial power – a change of policy he describes with the inflammatory term 'revolution'. Pramoj, who likes nothing better than to toss vituperative spanners into the political works, referred to Chavalit as a 'communist' and questioned his loyalty to the King. The next day an enraged mob of 300 Army Rangers – an élite answerable to the General – besieged the elder statesman's Bangkok house. It was an ugly scene, but no violence took place, and the news reports paid a typically Thai tribute to Kukrit's calm by adding that he enjoyed a substantial meal of fried chicken and Thai noodles while the soldiers were protesting outside his door. I suspect he also enjoyed the fuss, for the story was headline news for days.

The third long-running member of the political drama is the appointed Prime Minister, Prem Tinsulananda. One of Kukrit's former protégés, Prem was recently spurned by his erstwhile mentor in a typically acerbic outburst: 'Prem, what is Prem? He was nothing until I created him, and then I got tired of him, and threw the puppet away.' Prem's critics would claim that in his seven years in office he has done little but provide the mouth-piece for the real power in the land, General Chavalit. Be that as it may, all the top posts belong to army or ex-army men, and there is little doubt that the army constitutes the most effective political party, albeit a relatively benign influence in recent years. Prem's genial face appeared even in Western newspapers in the spring of 1988 when his coalition government was dissolved, killing two controversial birds with one stone: an unpopular bill, drafted under US pressure, to stamp out copy-right infringements, and a motion of no confidence levelled against the Premier. Earlier in the week he had been publicly accused of being homosexual and called upon to resign 'in the British way' by the opposition leader Chalerm Yubamrung. Chalerm threatened to expose the Prime Minister's personal life by producing two young army officers to testify against him. Prem's aide immediately leapt to his defence by describing Chalerm as a 'toad'. As a Western diplomat in Bangkok re-marked wryly, 'Whenever things get out of hand here, it's always best to shut down.'

That the volatile feuds of politics are freely reported in a country often criticised for its lack of free speech is an interest-ing paradox, but there can be no doubt that the Thais regard politics as a spectator sport, and their politicians with a healthy cynicism. While nine out of ten say they would prefer an elected Premier, most would also agree with the old adage that 'no matter who you voted for, the Government got in'. In this they remind me most of the Italians, lurching from one political 'crisis' to another, while life goes on pretty much its own way. The barometer of political fortunes is Korat, for if it changes allegiance, so will the country. During the early months of 1987, while General Chavalit was getting headlines with his demands for a 'revolution' to bring democracy to the country, I happened to be in Korat, and discussed the situation with a friend.

'Are you worried about the prospect of another coup soon?' I asked him.

'Worried?' he laughed. 'Oh no. If there's another coup we'll just stay here and watch it on television!'

North-east of Korat lie the Weeping Prairies, an area of I-saan notorious for drought. A few years ago in recognition of successful irrigation schemes the Government launched a campaign to find a new name for the area, but none of the suggestions has stuck in the popular imagination. In April 1987, over 30,000 people left the Weeping Prairies for Bangkok in search of work, many returning unsuccessful to stand in the queues that stretched from dawn to midnight at village wells. While people were dying in Chiang Mai from the worst floods to hit the city for thirty years, the army was sending emergency trucks of water into I-saan. Some villagers were desperately resorting to a more atavistic remedy. In an ancient rain rite, a cat – a symbol of drought because of its aversion to water – is processed in a bamboo cage around the village, while people drench it with water and chant for rain.

But around Korat itself the land is more prosperous. The mahogany earth is too soft to support tractors, but enterprising farmers make good use of a diesel engine, designed for water-pumps and imported from Japan, that they hitch in turn to threshing machines, carts, buggies and electricity generators. Duck farms line the road, and I have seen the dead birds carried gleefully home for dinner after being struck by hailstones as big as golf balls, which provide a free gift of ice into the bargain. As Thailand's second most important city, Korat stands as a symbol of optimism for I-saan. For the visitor it has two attractions: a bustling market section and the most beautiful species of cat in the world. This is not the nervy, overbred yowler popular in the West, but the original Siamese cat, a tiny creature with the chocolate coat of a Burmese, large ears, a face as soft as a doe's, and eyes the colour of lilac.

It is not only as the home of my two favourite animals – the cat and the elephant – that I like I-saan. Though few Thais would recommend it to the visitor, the place engages the heart more than anywhere else in the country. It is not just the dramatic contrast of the countryside, lush and desiccated by turns, nor the fact that it is as yet relatively unscathed by tourism, and will probably remain so, at least for the foreseeable future. It is the people. At first acquaintance they appear less friendly than in other parts of the country, but this reserve is born of diffidence in the face of unaccustomed strangers rather than hostility or indifference, and it yields to a forthright and unsentimented warmth, a humanity ennobled rather than diminished by hardship. Isolated, traditional and resilient, there is in I-saan a quality that seems, to me at least, to be very near the elusive heart of Thailand, an integrity rooted deep, despite the shallowness of the surrounding soil.

V

THE SOUTH

14

The Eastern Gulf

On arrival at Don Muang airport many visitors to Thailand ignore Bangkok and the sights to the north and, instead, head south for the bright lights of Pattaya Beach. The best way to see the eastern shore of the Gulf of Thailand, however, is not to jump on to a tour-bus the moment you arrive, but to hire a car in Bangkok and drive down the Sukhumvit Highway (also known as Highway 3) that links the capital to the Kampuchean border 250 miles away. The pace of such a drive should be leisurely, not only to enjoy the scenery which, especially for the latter part of the journey, is spectacular, but because in the event of an accident, it is an unwritten law that the *farang* is always in the wrong. For this reason many foreign companies discourage their *farang* employees from driving here. The only dangerous time, in my experience, is after dark, when the verges are full of unpredictable hazards, such as unlit bicycles wobbling under the load of an entire family, absent-minded water buffaloes or children cavorting on their way home. Apart from this, even including the maelstrom of Bangkok traffic, driving in Thailand is no more hair-raising than anywhere else in Asia.

Not so long ago the squarish chunk of land that lies between the capital and Kampuchea enjoyed a wholesome reputation as the country's main supplier of fish and fruit, as well as a touch of notoriety as the result of communist insurgents who hid out in its thick forests. Nowadays, Chachoengsao is still the country's most abundant mango orchard, and Chon Buri one of its most prolific oyster beds, but many of the trees have gone, and the government and army, having temporarily subdued the communists, are more concerned with flushing out the illegal loggers who have reduced the once copious woodlands to what the newspapers have poignantly dubbed 'the last forest in the east'. It is the familiar

story of landless settlers, some of them from neighbouring
Kampuchea, being bribed or forced by 'influential people' to cut
down trees, incurring the wrath of the central authorities and
eventually losing their homes. But it is the coastal strip that has
seen the most dramatic changes in recent times. What was
formerly a fishing economy, supporting a largely Chinese
mercantile community, has been transformed into a booming,
brassy riviera. The travel brochures describe this coast as a
veritable paradise. It may not be so for all who visit, but such a
glowing description would doubtless be endorsed by the specu-
lators of Bangkok.

The first part of the journey south from the capital is relatively
built up. Palm trees are outnumbered by television aerials which,
in conformity with the Thai preference for elongation, rise twenty
feet or more high, swaying like the antennae of an alien army on
the march. Temples are less in evidence than automobile
factories – BMW, Toyota, Shimuzi and others all have assembly
plants lining the road. These supply a market consisting solely of
foreign cars; imported models are subject to 400 or 500 per cent
duty, a system which reinstates a Daimler or a Rolls-Royce to its
former status as the car of the very rich.

Forty miles south of Bangkok lies the thriving city of Chon Buri
(the common Thai suffix *buri*, meaning 'town', is cognate with the
English 'bury'), a centre of the local sugar cane and tapioca
industries and the place where much local produce is canned.
The oldest and most important temple in the area is Wat
Intharam, which has murals dating back to the late eighteenth
century, but the most interesting feature of temple architecture
along this coast is the influence of the maritime life. At Wat
Dhamma Nimitr in Chon Buri an extraordinary Buddha image,
120 ft high and covered in gold mosaic is seated in a boat and
further down the coast there is an entire monastery, Ruh Sam
Pao, shaped like a huge hull pointing out to sea. Each of the cells
that house the 300 members of the community is also shaped
like a miniature boat; the elderly Chinese residents believe that
when they die their soul will be carried across the sea back to their
native land. This quaint place is a foretaste of two themes which

will recur again throughout the south – the importance of the sea and the presence of the Chinese.

The tour buses will not stop at Ang Sila, a little town where the sound of stone chipping never ceases, as the inhabitants shape the local granite into the pestle and mortars found in kitchens all over the country, and, every so often, an imperial lion for a Chinese temple. The neighbouring town of Bang Saen is overlooked by a hill-top shrine that celebrates the unhappy demise of a local girl, Sam Muk, who sometime at the end of the eighteenth century, drowned herself as the result of a love affair thwarted by parental disapproval. History has elevated this oriental Juliet to the status of a goddess, and pilgrims, predominantly Chinese, offer coconuts and firecrackers at her shrine overlooked by corpulent Buddhas and fluttering glitter. Kites, too, are offered, inscribed with the donor's name in the hope that when they blow away they will take any bad luck with them. If Bang Saen's legendary past is remembered by Sam Muk's shrine, its leisurely future is anticipated by the latest addition to its mushrooming outskirts, the Happy World Entertainment complex. This was opened recently with a great fanfare by the deputy Prime Minister and, with the necessary components of a Chinese restaurant, coffee bar, nightclub and massage parlour, it is hoped to put Bang Saen firmly on the *sanuk* trail.

Si Ratcha, a little way down the coast, is famous as the home of *nam plik si rachaa*, a fiery red chilli sauce best sampled as an accompaniment to the excellent seafood obtainable at restaurants overlooking the water. At the north end of the town a colourful Chinese temple sits on a rock connected to the mainland by a long jetty, while further out to sea lies the hilly island of Koh Sichang. This is a quiet place with only one town, and worth a day's exploration. There are limestone caves for the adventurous, a monastic hermitage, a ruined summer palace once favoured by Rama 5, and, high on a hill overlooking the sea, a spectacular Chinese temple built on several levels with shrines in various grottoes, a great favourite at the Chinese New Year in February. There are also beaches for swimming and snorkelling, though the area is the habitat of sea urchins whose sharp spines can cause painful cuts on the feet. The local fishermen have a simple remedy: rather than try to extract the brittle spines they simply crush them into the foot in the hope that they will eventually work themselves out and then sterilise the wound by standing in a coconut shell full of fresh urine. Perhaps beach shoes are advisable for the visitor.

Another place that the tour buses will miss is Chittrapawan Buddhist College, an unlikely example of the entrepreneurial fervour which is gripping the Eastern Gulf. Located about five miles north of Pattaya, this former cemetery houses perhaps the most controversial monk in Thailand, Phra Kittivuttho, a stout, moon-faced man in his early fifties with the imperturbability that a set of robes lends to a solid frame. To his supporters Kittivuttho is an energetic crusader against poverty, corruption and communism; to his detractors, and there are many, he is a right-wing gun-runner, a bogus businessman and a religious misfit. Returning in a Mercedes-Benz to his *wat* after lecturing the local policemen on morals, the man himself seems unperturbed by his sensational reputation, and guffaws at my suggestion that he is the best-known monk in the country. His harbouring of suspected criminals, and the discovery of a cache of arms in temple vehicles on their way to the Thai-Kampuchean border embroiled him in controversy, but most publicised was his statement that 'It is not a sin to kill a communist.' He laughs again when I remind him of his indiscretion. 'Of course, I really meant it was all right to kill communism,' he replies, and steers me firmly towards a tour of the temple grounds. Here there is no contemplative quiet, but the recalcitrant whine of workshops repairing cars and buses, and the dull drone of rice-milling machines. Perhaps because of the noise the monks around the compound communicate by walkie-talkie. At this temple such traditional occupations as prayer and alms collecting have been eschewed in favour of hard work and involvement in business – preoccupations the abbot believes will inspire success in the ordinary people of the province. His reasoning is logical enough: 'If you are not in want you will never become a communist,' he says, as we view his latest project, the rice mills that he hopes to install in every temple in the country.

His plan is for local people to mill their grain at the temple and sell it themselves, thus cutting out the middlemen and wholesalers who are the scourge of the small farmer. It is a revolutionary idea, which, although it would place the temple squarely at the centre of the community, has alienated many in both the monastic and mercantile groups. Another scheme is less controversial: water buffalo are raised at various temples and then distributed to poor farmers. The farmers for their part must promise not to sell the animals, which must be well cared for and, as Phra Kittivuttho adds with a mischievous twinkle in his eye, 'on religious holidays they must be given the day off'.

An altogether more substantial reappraisal of Buddhism's role in modern Thailand is being vigorously undertaken by the Army of Truth, the missionary wing of the Dhammakaya Temple, a well-organised and highly successful organisation devoted to nothing less than the complete moral regeneration of the country. This programme begins with instruction and meditation, and extends to an energetic promotion campaign around the country, particularly in the institutions of higher education, that draws over a thousand participants to the two-month Mass Ordination Course each summer. The Dhammakaya Temple is unusual in that it appeals mainly to university-educated middle-class Thais; it also enjoys the active support of many leading politicians and no less a sympathiser than Princess Sirindhorn. Each Sunday up to 5000 flock to the immaculately landscaped grounds of the temple, less than an hour's drive from Bangkok, and the funds are rolling in. The place is clean, cool and tranquil, and there is more than a touch of the Mormons in the combination of proselytising zeal and freshly scrubbed idealism married to a solid grasp of corporate reality. The movement disseminates high-quality glossy literature, audio-visual material and cassettes in that packaging of 'spirituality' familiar to the West in recent years. Particularly striking in the temple programme are the mass rallies held at important Buddhist festivals, when thousands of white clad meditating figures radiate out in star-shaped patterns from the stark white centrepiece of the main chapel like the cast of a spectacle choreographed by a spiritually regenerate Busby Berkley. Compared to this organisation, Phra Kittivuttho with his rice milling and water buffaloes seems a lone maverick indeed.

Behind its well-co-ordinated modern façade, the Dhammakaya Temple harbours some stern old-fashioned ideas. The vice-abbot has said that the unemployed may well be suffering the consequences of failing to make enough merit in past lives, and women are especially advised to concentrate on making merit 'so that they can be reborn a man in the next life'. Sexual propriety is very high on the Dhammakaya agenda, and men are warned that if they err they will be reborn as women, whereas monks face the appalling prospect of no less than 500 incarnations as women if they compromise their vows of chastity. The triumphant progress of righteousness, however, has not been entirely smooth. In 1987 it was alleged that there was an arms dump at the temple. No weapons were found, but suspicions about the Dhammakaya's long-term objectives remain. Soon after the arms cache story villagers claimed to have been thrown off their land to make way for the temple's expansion, evicted under the pretext that the King wished to use the area to conduct a conservation project. A large group turned up at the Sanam Luang, threatening to set fire to themselves if the police did not intervene in the case.

Whatever the truth of such incidents, the Dhammakaya is one aspect of a fundamentalism that is emerging from deep within Thailand's booming economic success. The clearest political statement of this mood is the Palang Dharma (Forces of Spiritual Justice) party, led by the highly popular governor of Bangkok, Chamlong Srimuang, who is himself a devout Buddhist. He has imposed a heavy dose of morality on his members, including barring them from buying votes. The Dhammakaya Temple is at present more concerned with the spiritual side of things, uncompromising in its criticisms of ecclesiastical corruption. The New Morality is on the march in Thailand as elsewhere, and should there be a realignment of power in the future, I would not be surprised if the Dhammakaya Temple were somewhere in the background, orchestrating the direction of the new order.

*

'Ah, you'll miss this when you get home, you know! It's in their tradition you see, the women here know how to treat a man. They're still feminine, considerate, don't intrude too much. And they know how to do things properly, eh Noi?' Jack, a small pink man from Leeds in his late fifties, throws a knowing grin at the girl who sits cross-legged at the other end of his extended arm, her slender brown fingers manicuring a hand that has the waxy pinkness of a bunch of pudgy chipolattas. At his feet sits another girl, lovely looking and a third his age, massaging his blotchy pink legs while she stares absent-mindedly out to sea. 'They cost, of course, but what doesn't these days? Come here every October I do, and I'll retire here in a couple of years. I've had it with England. Thatcher or no Thatcher, England's full of shit these days. I've done my whack. Sod 'em, that's what I say, sod 'em all. I know what I like.' Relaxed by the sun and the mid-morning beer, he settles into his theme. 'I've got a few friends settled out here who know the ropes, they're keeping their eyes open for a place for me. You can get a nice bungalow out here for forty thousand dollars. That's a quarter of what I'd pay at home, and just look at it!' He waves an expansive arm over the scene before us: Jomtien Beach, south Pattaya. It is indeed a beautiful sight: a wide expanse of honey coloured sand, sheltered from the road by a line of palm trees and running into a turquoise sea that is frothed with wavelets and scintillates brilliantly. Overhead the sun is climbing into a sky of a crystalline and unremittent blue, puckered here and there with the smallest pinch of white, as if to emphasise its unruffled perfection. Between the trees and the sea stretches a ragged line of thatched parasols. Under many of them lie white bodies, each attended by its dark familiar. Jack fishes under his deckchair for his wallet. 'Hey Noi, be a good girl and get us more beer, eh? *More beer*,' he mouths, as if she were deaf or a simpleton, and after a moment, shouts after the retreating figure: 'And make sure it's cold . . . *cold*!' Jack sinks back into his deckchair with a deep sigh of contentment. 'Amazing isn't it? Get off that plane at Heathrow and they all start treating you like a pig . . .'

If it were not for Jomtien, and the unvisited bays further south along the road to Rayong, Pattaya could hardly lay claim to being a

seaside paradise, for the beach that fronts this jumbled fairground of a town is small and uninviting, and the sea is so jammed
with small craft that swimming is difficult and dangerous. Some
35,000 people live squashed into the elongated oval grid formed
by two roads, Beach Road and Back Road, that run parallel along
the sea front, linked by a number of small interconnecting *sois*. It
is a claustrophobic huddle of hotels, clubs, bars and shops, where
there is little respite from the frenetic atmosphere of a place
wholeheartedly dedicated to 'having fun'. Even my hotel, a
relatively staid establishment patronised by Scandinavians and
set well back from the sea-front bustle, starts its breakfast menu
with a complimentary aspirin and glass of water, followed by
Gamel Dansk or Fernet Branca, as a prelude to a 'Bloddy Mary'
pick-me-up. The Walkman and Marlboro brigade is spreading
south to Jomtien, a short *songtheow* ride from Pattaya itself, and
gigantic luxury blocks are springing up in what until very recently
were palm groves.

   Norman Lewis, that most perceptive of writers on South-East
Asia, refers to Thailand as a country which 'by the almost
miraculous cunning of its rulers escaped enslavement by the
West only to become through liberty and prosperity hardly more
than a fun-fair reflection of the USA'. Pattaya is indeed the
raucous climax to the foreplay of GI culture that titillates much of
Thailand. Its growth from a fishing village to the 'premier beach
resort in Asia' began with 'rest 'n' recreation' binges of the
American sailors from the deep-water port of Sattahip,
twenty-five miles down the coast, and the air base of U Tapao
nearby. With the coming of American troops, the bars and joints
spread through Pattaya with the rapidity of a syphilitic rash; but
today the sailors from Sattahip are Thai, and the American Navy
makes only the occasional stop to relieve the frustration of
temporary exile from their bases in the Philippines. The bulk of
visitors are unaccompanied men, often in the package tours that
are the main thrust of a thriving international sex industry. So
exciting is the good time promised by Pattaya that some German
factories offer holidays there as an incentive scheme, with
condoms and antibiotics methodically handed out on the flight.

As its contribution to the Visit Thailand Year of 1987, Pattaya made some feeble attempt to promote itself as a family resort, but no one could take the idea very seriously. The place is, irredeemably, Patpong-on-sea, the Costa del sex, with *bratwurst mit brot* instead of fish and chips and where the silly hats, as befits the oriental finesse in such matters, read 'Kiss me slow'.

Each day a fresh load of tourists descends on this pericarp of lotus land like a swarm of plump white aphides, ready to be milked by the local ants. There are about 4000 bar girls clustered in Pattaya at any one time. Their mores place them well beyond the pale of Thai society and into a cultural no-man's land inhabited only by transient *farangs* and Arabs, but their money buys them back a certain status. They live in cheap padlocked rooms off long corridors where each doorway is marked by a heap of discarded shoes and the flaking pastel walls are covered in chocolate-box art – sad-eyed kittens and waterfalls, mountains and flowers, alongside pin-ups, pop stars and posters of the Royal Family. High up on the wall might be a gilded shelf for the Buddha image bearing an untidy jumble of offerings – plastic flowers, a bunch of joss sticks, some coloured threads and perhaps an empty Mekong bottle. The girls of Pattaya sleep late, and it is not until after midday that the cycle of washing, ironing, dressing, eating and gossiping begins anew. By mid-afternoon the tape recorders are on again, and as the sun begins to set, these hostages to the night hop into the fleet of *songthaews* that trawls around the circuit of Pattaya's centre, and head for the neon lights of the seafront bars.

Loyalty here lasts as long as the money, but many of the girls keep in touch with their boyfriends overseas, trooping into the Post Office in the centre of town to make reverse-charge long-distance phone calls, or collecting the latest money order. An incongruously medieval touch in the midst of such electronic communication, are the scribes, those girls who make a living writing love letters in English and other languages. The text is standard – declarations of love and loneliness moving swiftly on to tales of ill relatives, unwanted pregnancies, accidents or school bills for younger relatives – anything that might justify the demand for extra cash. And if the money that arrives is considered too little, there will be communal discussions as to whether it is worth continuing to invest 50 *baht* in a regular two-page letter that elicits only a stingy response. Young and old, rich and poor, brown and white, thus is the algebra of need calculated in the bars of Pattaya Beach.

To be fair, there is more to Pattaya than horizontal recreation. The resort is a haven for lovers of watersports. Scuba diving, snorkelling, wind surfing, sail and ski boating, parasailing and deep-sea fishing all help to lure the million or so annual visitors. The tourists bring more than just money. The sea is becoming heavily polluted by litter; each of the several daily boats to the offshore island of Ko Larn jettisons crates of garbage and the custom has caught on with the islanders themselves, who, tired with having their rubbish collected only three times a week, now load it into boats and dump it offshore. Below the bobbing beer bottles and coke tins more serious damage is taking place. The Gulf of Thailand has been virtually fished out, much of the harvest being processed for animal feed, and the abundant coral reefs that once made the area a paradise of marine life are in danger of extinction within the next ten years. In waters where the shooting of bottles with automatic weapons has become a macho sport, dynamiting is a popular technique of fishing, practised both by canning companies and local restaurants. Those parts of the reef that are not damaged by dynamite are often poisoned by the cyanide that aquarium suppliers use to stun the more exotic species they hunt. And as elsewhere, while the voracious Crown of Thorns starfish is eating its way through the coral, its only natural predator in the area, a type of conch, is being decimated to supply a tourist market that likes the shells for souvenirs. Belatedly aware of the dangers, the Institute of Marine Science up the coast in Bang Saen has resorted to building artificial reefs out of rubber tyres donated by Goodyear, but there seems little effort to stop the damage at source.

The wildest part of Pattaya is its southern end, 'the village', where the streets dissolve into a jumble of stalls, bars, clubs and massage parlours. Some of the bars, like the

Grace or Marine, are vast open-air arenas, where hundreds of Thai girls and boys sit waiting, mottled by stroboscopic lights, while above bald heads reddened by too much sun or beer, enormous screens show blood-and-guts movies or pop videos. The noise level in this part of town is indescribable, as each bar, whether it's a ball-room or a kiosk with a few stools, has its own music thumping out, and the larger establishments each have several live bands, sometimes only yards from each other. The result is an electrified cacophony of hard metallic sound, and to walk through the area is like being trapped in some giant pinball machine that has gone berserk. The pandemonium is laced with the bizarre. Pattaya has always had a large gay population, and recently the village has become host to a colony of *kateoys* – transvestites – who work as prostitutes or in the 'lady-man' cabarets that are one of Pattaya's renowned attractions.

Outside one such club, a group of blind musicians plays the haunting, electrified music of Laos, while a mewling monkey with pink silk hot-pants and a plastic teat in its wizened mouth collects money in a battered straw hat.

Down the road at the Siren Bar, two young boys, part of the contingent of orphans who work as prostitutes in and out of such places, are going through their paces in the elevated boxing ring. These waifs seem particularly wretched. Deprived of even the protection of a madame or massage-parlour boss, they are often forced to surrender their meagre earnings to the police, who are safe in the knowledge that the kids have nowhere to turn for help. Further along the road another boxing ring rises above a clutter of tables. This time the contestants are two girls, perhaps fifteen years old, who, to judge from the white scars that pit their sturdy brown legs, come from one of the fishing communities further down the coast. They slug it out remorselessly, kicking and battering each other with desperate, brutal lunges, urged on by the feral baying of the crowd. Each heavy blow sends a spray of sweat onto the ringside tables, and skeins of blood-flecked snot across the ring. The girls are followed by a man with a mongoose in a glass cage, perhaps four feet square, into which, after much clowning, he introduces a snake. The mongoose stalks and leaps;

walks, jumps and walks again, while the reptile squirms and
arches up the glass walls, sliding hopelessly left and right, its body
lathered in sweat as the heat in the cage builds up. I leave before
the kill, the howls of the crowd that greet each lunge still ringing
in my ears.

The unspoken question on everybody's minds is AIDS. The
virus is much less widespread in Asia than in the West (so much
so that there was at one time optimistic talk of a genetic resistance
to it) but the pattern of infection must eventually be the same here
as elsewhere. Thailand's first response to AIDS was *mai pen rai*;
that a fatal disease could stem from such a natural and
pleasurable activity as sex seemed unthinkable. As the cold light
of reality began to dawn, the first line of defence was that 'it can't
happen here'. The press in Thailand did not begin to tackle the
subject of AIDS seriously until as late as the spring of 1987, by
which time the global implications of the epidemic had already
been well known for some time. The official story is that the
country is relatively free of the virus. By the end of 1988 some
100,000 tests (which included compulsory mass testing in Pattaya
and Bangkok) had yielded only slightly over a hundred HIV
positive results, half of whom were inmates of Bang Kwang, the
country's main prison in Bangkok. This figure compares curi-
ously with Britain, which, with roughly the same population as
Thailand, also has about sixty confirmed HIV positives in prisons.
But whereas the official number with the disease in Britain is over
a thousand, and the estimated number of carriers perhaps fifty
times as many, in Thailand only thirty-odd AIDS-related deaths
have been registered (some of whom were foreigners), and there
is no projected figure for HIV carriers. As a result, there has been
no co-ordinated debate, no widespread campaign instituted
against the spread of the disease.

Many people worry that the Thai government is massaging the
figures to protect its tourist industry, frightened by the example of
Kenya, where the tourist dollars fell dramatically as the indication
of HIV infection rose. When the virus was first reported in the
Thai media at the end of 1985, the then health minister issued a

warning that frequent and unnecessary publicity could do irreparable harm to tourism, by then already the country's main source of foreign money. His concern was echoed by the director-general of the ministry's communicable disease-control centre, and though the global epidemic has increased considerably since then, Thailand's official policy still seems to be to underplay the whole business as much as possible. Journalists' inquiries tend to meet resistance from the authorities; but this is not unusual in a country where power keeps its privacy well guarded, and officials working with the World Health Organisation say they are receiving good co-operation from their Thai colleagues in the battle against AIDS. Nevertheless, anyone with eyes to see must be aware that Thailand is a major potential dissemination point for the virus, and that a concentrated programme of HIV education is long overdue.

No one would be better qualified to spearhead such a programme than Mechai Viavaidya, the man responsible for halving the country's birthrate in a decade, and currently the government spokesman on tourism. Mechai's witty and candid approach to birth control achieved a success unparalleled in developing countries. Barefoot doctors, mobile clinics and mass vasectomies were promoted by a string of flamboyant campaigns: sloganned T-shirts, condom key-rings ('In case of emergency break the glass'), family-planning songs in classrooms and bonus schemes for taxi drivers who got free insurance for every fifty clients they persuaded to have a vasectomy, and a holiday in Singapore for every hundred. The ebullient figure of the man himself was to be seen at country fairs and festivals leading children in condom-blowing 'balloon' contests and setting up sideshows with ovulation charts as dartboards. This brilliant combination of science, *sanuk* and marketing flair is encouraging in that the country is now well educated in contraceptive devices. This may well help to slow the spread of the AIDS virus, as may the fact that the Thais, like other South-East Asians, traditionally smoke their heroin rather than inject it.

South of Pattaya, the life of the Eastern Gulf returns pretty much to normal, with its lush vegetation, its gem mining and its fruit.

Pattaya marks the limit of most people's weekend driving, thereafter the coast is quiet and the interior agricultural, with wooden houses dotting the rolling hills and tall leafy plane trees lining the road. Rayong is famous for *nam plaa* (the fermented fish sauce that is the commonest accompaniment to most Thai dishes) and sea cucumbers. The name conjures up an image of some innocuous vegetable; they are, as it happens, ugly black slugs that doze on the sea bottom. When dried, however, they lose some of their sliminess and make a popular soup, but like much of the authentic provincial Chinese cuisine, they are an acquired taste. Raw shark, dipped in a sauce of chillies, lemon juice, tomatoes and cucumbers, Horseshoe Crab eggs and Fire Jellyfish salad are other more palatable seafoods common in this part of the country, and every meal is well rounded off with the young coconuts that are a staple part of the southern diet. Driving through much of the south is a heady olfactory experience as you pass through wave after wave of drying fish. Ban Pae's contribution to this sensory assault is in the shape of shrimps, which cover its wharfs in a pungent tangerine swathe. The little fishing village is the jumping-off point for Koh Samet, one of the latest islands to be discovered by those in search of the paradise promised by the travel brochures. Here, opposite a coastline of palm trees and pine forests, the famous nineteenth-century poet Sunthorn Pu retired to write some of the finest romantic verse in Thai literature, and although the island is slowly being developed, it is still a place of simple beauty. Most of the accommodation is basic and the water supply is fitful, but crowds of Thais descend for the major cool season holidays, when people are reduced to sleeping on restaurant floors. For the rest of the year the visitors are limited to the north-east coast. The big lure of the place is its sand: white, fine as salt and much sought after by glassmakers; it squeaks under the foot like newly washed hair, and gave the island its original name as 'The place with sand like crushed crystal'.

The most beautifully set of the large towns of the south-east is Chantaburi, 'City of the Moon', perpetually green from its exposure to monsoon rains that sweep across from the other side of the gulf. The city itself has the raffish swagger of a gold-rush town, as befits the capital of Thailand's thriving gemstone industry, and the place buzzes with motorbikes and gem-polishing lathes. Bangkok's status as an international gem capital rests on the mines around Chantaburi, but it was the Shan Burmese who first developed the small local industry whose rubies had been commented on favourably by Chinese travellers as far back as the fifteenth century. The Shans are the most skilled miners of coloured stones in the world. From the middle of the nineteenth century they arrived here in great numbers, though the early waves of settlers were decimated by malaria. Then, Chinese and Indian shopkeepers came to serve the growing industry, and a ramshackle community of bejewelled dandies, opium houses and gambling dens grew up. British concessions in the area and the loss of the best sapphire mines to the Cambodians in a border dispute caused the fever to die down at the beginning of this century, but in the early 1960s Burma closed her doors to foreign trade and the world's major supply of rubies dried up. Thailand stepped into the gap; now she produces over 80 per cent of the high-quality rubies and is a major source of sapphires. Chantaburi still retains historical interest. A couple of miles south of the town cannons glower from a deserted fort which crowns the hill where Taksin regrouped his shattered forces after the fall of Ayutthaya in 1767, and it was here that he assembled the fleet of warships that was to sail back to recapture his devastated capital. There is also a French Catholic church in the town, the largest in Thailand, built about 1880, that serves the Vietnamese community, migrants here over the last two hundred years, many of whom make their living weaving the locally grown reeds.

Each July and December, the air around Chantaburi becomes heavy with a rich, fetid smell that has nothing to do with the drying fish laid out along the roadside. At first sniff, the visitor could be forgiven for thinking that there is something severely wrong with the local drains, but in fact he has just made his first acquaintance with the durian, king of Thai fruits, a belligerent green rugby ball bristling with sharp thorny spikes that emits so powerful a stench of organic decay that some hotels forbid their guests to bring it in. Inside the armadillo skin lie half a dozen creamy-yellow segments with the texture of an avocado pear and the taste of almond butter, laced with very ripe Camembert. This sexy, animal fruit is both an offence and an addiction. A British governor of nineteenth-century Singapore described it as 'carrion in custard', yet Rama 2 so loved the fruit he penned an ode to it while the royal barge cruised past the orchards on the banks of the Chao Phya, and today the 'golden pillow', choicest of the 200-odd varieties of the fruit, can fetch over 600 *baht* a piece. Durians like the sulphurous soil of the Chantaburi region, and the south-east produces most of Thailand's annual crop of up to 500 million tons, many of which are exported to Hong Kong inside specially sealed packages. I know of no fruit that is so *alive* as durian, or has such a pronounced personality. You may love it or loathe it, but no one's visit to Thailand is complete without at least an attempt to sample this extraordinary sensory experience.

15

Islands and Islam

The way south is long, straight and simple, a journey of flat, low horizons, empty salted vistas stitched together by tousled coconut palms. It is a land of space, where sinews are toughened by spray and storms, and the mind is lulled by the ceaseless rhythms of the sea. A thin, leggy peninsula straggles its way down from Bangkok to Malaysia, a snaking strip of land that is sometimes little more than a pause between oceans, a breathing space in a vast and watery expanse. Yet despite its abundance of water, and despite its tangled jungle, much of southern Thailand has for me the emotional feel of the desert, for it seems an empty landscape, discarding, as it goes, beaches and islands as hostages to the elements. Part of this peninsula is shared with Burma. The border is creased into giant folds by mountains that began as the sacred peaks of the Himalayas, and will finally disintegrate into the myriad islands of the Indonesian archipelago, scattered like crumbs from the table of the gods. But it is the sea that has created the life of the south, and the spirit of the south lies not in the Thai farmers who work the land nor the Chinese merchants who dominate the towns, but in the aquatic nomads – sailors, fishermen, pirates – who set their frail craft into the teeth of the oncoming waves and chance their lives with every tide.

As paddy gives way to rubber, so the sloping roofs of temples are replaced by the domes of mosques, for one out of every five southerners belongs to Islam. Many in the border provinces look to neighbouring Malaysia as their spiritual and cultural brother, and though formal cesession may never come, the tradition of independence from Bangkok, fostered by distance, religion and language, is an ancient one. The would-be autonomy of the *Thai pak tai*, as the southerners are known, is buttressed by the region's prosperity: heavy rainfall sustains thousands of acres of rubber and coconut, abundant seafood is both a dependable diet and a regular source of income, and tin is mined extensively throughout the peninsula. The south's separate identity is enshrined in its language, for the *Thai pak tai* speak a dialect similar to the tongues of Malaysia or Indonesia, so rapid and clipped that it can be incomprehensible to the northener. The people of I-saan may feel diffident about their rustic Lao language when faced with the urbane tones of Bangkok, but the robust southerner doesn't give a damn. He speaks as he likes, wears his sarong long, Malaysian style, worships the Prophet and has his women cover their heads. Historically his roots lie not with the upland paddy farmers or the Khmers of Cambodia, but the ancient and mysterious empire of Shrivijaya, about which little is known apart from the fact that it was based probably in Sumatra, worshipped the Buddha alongside the Hindu gods, fought long and hard with south India, and ruled much of maritime South-East Asia from the eighth to the thirteenth century. Many exquisite pieces of Shrivijayan art have been found in southern Thailand, but the cultural jigsaw is still tantalisingly incomplete, and will probably remain so. Bangkok has long distrusted the south, but superhighways now link the two; government officials sent to work there are at last being encouraged to learn the dialect and customs; and the Royal Family has recently taken the time to make itself visible in the more alienated provinces that border Malaysia, and has built a palace outside the important town of Narathiwat.

The long distances involved in negotiating the peninsula mean that most tourists by-pass the smaller towns and head straight for the islands and beaches near Surat Thani or Phuket, or for the bustling southern town of Haad Yai, gateway to Malaysia. All three are accessible by road, rail or aircraft. Those travelling on to Malaysia, an increasingly popular combination with southern Thailand, especially for backpackers or Australians returning home overland, can take the comfortable and efficient Butterworth Express. Travelling in a single first-class sleeper – clean, air-conditioned and with its own washing facilities – it takes sixteen hours from Bangkok to Haad Yai, at half the price of an air ticket. Fellow passengers are invariably friendly, and a buzz from your compartment to the restaurant car will bring you the choice of forty dishes.

For those with a little more time, there are a number of interesting stop-offs on the road south from Bangkok. Petchaburi, a hundred miles south of the capital, has half a dozen good *wats* that can be seen in a couple of hours' tour around the town: Wat Yai has well-preserved murals from the last century and a considerably older and elegantly designed library; Wat Kampahaeng Laeng shows strong Khmer influence in spires that rise like elongated artichokes; Wat Ko has early eighteenth-century murals and attractive quarters for the monks – long wooden buildings raised on stilts. Petchaburi is surrounded by the steep rounded limestone peaks that will accompany you for much of your journey south. One of these, Khao Wang, is dotted with temples and the buildings that comprise the palace built by Rama 4, the monarch of *The King and I* story. The hillside gives a fine view of the town below, skirted by the river and hugged by paddy fields, and the view of the mountainous Burmese border to the west is especially lovely at sunset. Twenty miles down the road, Cha-Am is a seaside haunt favoured by young Thais, particularly at weekends when its casuarina-lined beaches erupt into impromptu parties and barbecues.

Then comes Hua Hin, the most rewarding of the resorts within easy reach of the capital. Located directly across the Gulf from Pattaya, it is in every way its opposite, having long been known as a resort of leisured gentility, patronised by the court and the fashionable, an oriental Brighton with a touch of Bath. By 1932, a guidebook published by the Royal State Railway Company was able to describe Hua Hin as 'the famous seaside resort of Siam', for it was the opening of the southern line shortly after the First World War that made what had previously been a 125-mile journey by *klong* and bullock cart an easy trip for the people of Bangkok. One of the earliest recorded visitors was King Mongkut, Rama 4, who travelled here in summer 1868 to observe a total eclipse of the sun that he had correctly predicted. This observation marked the end of an era; never again would people gather with guns, rockets, gongs and drums to frighten away the

dragon they believed had swallowed the sun. The transition to the
modern world view was ushered in with appropriate ceremony,
for many Europeans, including the governor of Singapore, were
among the party housed in elaborate temporary palaces set up on
the beach. Any apprehensions they may have had about the
conditions of such an out-of-station gathering were soon dispel-
led when, in the words of one writer present, they discovered that
'the food was prepared by a French chef, the wines were served by
an Italian *maître d'hotel* and the champagne was cooled by an
abundance of ice, which was then the rarest of luxuries.' (Such
Westernisation continued unabated during Rama 5's reign;
Thailand, incredibly, had both the automobile and the telephone
before Japan.)

What really established Hua Hin was the opening of the
Railway Hotel in 1923; it was the nearest to a Raj hotel in
Thailand, an elegant structure set on the shore, complete with
ceiling fans, wickerwork chairs, polished teak verandas and
balconies that overlooked the topiary and lawns. It became the
latest in a number of staging posts along the coast, but that the
Railway was no ordinary hotel is attested by the fact that the place
was designed and run by minor members of the royal family,
many of whom came to build their bungalows along the beach.
Prince Naris, a son of Rama 5, built the first of the royal palaces
here, Saen Samran House, and it was one of his own sons that
built the Klai Kangwol Palace for Rama 7. The Thai name, 'Far
from worries', was to prove ironical, as it was here that the king
first learned that a revolution in Bangkok had ended the absolute
dominion of the lotus throne. The royal family still use the palace.
Every so often the red, white and blue flags – like a double Pepsi
logo – announce their presence in the town, but nowadays they
come to review the local projects, ranging from handicrafts to
pineapple plantations, rather than for relaxing promenades along
the seafront.

The Railway Hotel regained a moment of glory when it starred
as the Phnom Penh Hotel in the film *The Killing Fields* and began
a trend of using Thailand as a location for a rash of films
reappraising the Vietnam war – *Platoon, Hamburger Hill, Good*

Morning Vietnam. Since then it has been renovated and renamed the Sofitel Central. I must admit to liking my nostalgia slightly weathered, and my opinion of the new hotel was formed on a trip when the refurbishing was not yet complete. A few more years will doubtless take the gleam of newness off, and restore at least some of its previous homely atmosphere.

Hua Hin still has an old-fashioned charm, which begins when you arrive at the station to be greeted by a gem of a station building, perched on the platform like a miniature temple. Daytime pleasures are innocuous enough: pony rides along the sand, strolls to the piers to see opalescent fish being laid out to dry on bamboo racks next to fishermen mending their nets, massage and manicure under parasols by the lapping waves, or a bike ride to the southern end of the town, where Chopstick Hill rises studded with temples and pagodas. For the more energetic, there is the best golf course in Thailand, designed in 1926 by a Scottish engineer attached to the Royal Siamese Railway, and the view from the fifteenth hole out over the turquoise bay could hardly be bettered. The evening entertainment is equally wholesome: beer and excellent seafood on the beach, pidgin chats with friendly locals, an early bed with a literary or human companion. At night you fall asleep to the sound of the waves, while the horizon is dotted with fishing boats, their sterns illuminated to lure the giant squid, strung like a necklace of irridescent pearls across the Gulf of Thailand.

South from Hua Hin on Highway 4, clouds of dry-season dust mingle with acrid smoke from piles of burning rubbish by the road. The Thais are appalling litterbugs, each town throughout the country is announced and seen off by an extended rubbish tip, predominantly the pale pink, blue, green and yellow plastic bags that serve as food and drink containers. The way they chuck litter everywhere seems out of character with so fastidious a people. It is partly a hangover from the days when everything was wrapped and carried in biodegradable leaves, and partly the result of a line drawn firmly, if unconsciously, between the domestic and the public world. Thais are scrupulously clean about their bodies, clothes and homes but once they venture on to public property,

which is someone else's responsibility, slovenliness overtakes
them. If the Tourist Authority wants to do something to improve
the country's image, I suggest they institute an anti-litter
campaign. The smoke hangs in thick wreathes, six feet above the
ground, obscuring the base of limestone hillocks. The procession
of trundling lorries seems interminable, some loaded with the
milky gravel of tapioca chips, others with the long, knotted trunks
of sugarcane. On the narrow grass islands between the car-
riageways, cattle are grazed by farmers, vestiges from a less
mobile age, and the dark water buffalo who can become hostile at
the unfamiliar scent of a *farang*, view the passing traffic with a
heavy-lidded gaze of distant disdain.

Although the road does not hug the coast all the way, you are
never very far from seaside restaurants, simple collections of
tables under trees where the food is inexpensive and unpretenti-
ous. As you near Chumphon, though, a frequent addition to the
menu will be birds' nest soup, for one of the main sources of this
delicacy are the islands off the mouth of the Chumphon river.
The swallows mate from March to August, during which time the
collectors scale the steep limestone cliffs to dislodge the nests.
They are believed, like many dishes favoured by the Chinese, to
impart both longevity and virility, and it is a profitable business;
some of the traders employ squads of armed guards to protect
their concessions. At Chumphon, Highway 4 turns right, to
continue down the west side of the peninsula, while Highway 41
goes on down towards the provincial capital Surat Thani. A few
miles before Surat Thani you reach Chaiya, a simple town of
unpainted wooden houses that gives a monochrome glimpse of
what the original southern town was like. Chaiya is believed by
some to be the ancient capital, or at least one of them, of the
Shrivijaya empire. The *chedi* at Wat Mahathat is certainly ancient,
and built in the style of central Java, with brick and vegetable
mortar standing on a square platform with a wide porch ringed by
smaller *chedis*. There is a small but interesting museum here,
containing some of the many beautiful Shrivijayan artefacts that
have been found in the area. Several other *wats* in the town have
structures going back to Shrivijayan times.

At the age of four, Nui is earning more than a middle grade government official, for he is one of Surat Thani's most successful coconut collectors. In full swing he can pick up to a thousand a day, choosing only the ripe and undamaged ones, and, having spun them off the tree, will help load them into the trucks and carry back baskets of fertiliser and insecticide. Nui's training began when he was barely six months old, much of it in the coolness of the night when his concentration was higher, and looking at his hairy hands with their well-incised lines, his straight body and thin lips, the experts agree that he has a good five years left of working life. This is no tale of child exploitation, for Nui is the star of the monkey-training school in Surat Thani, the only official one of its kind. Farmers in the south had long trained monkeys to take most of the work out of coconut cultivation, but in 1985 the school was set up as a royally sponsored project to formalise the training of about a thousand creatures and provide a tourist attraction. Apart from this, Surat Thani, a busy port dealing in rubber, coconut and shipbuilding, has little of interest apart from a busy night market grouped around a couple of technicolour Chinese temples. Yet each year throngs of people pass through Surat Thani, for it is the jumping-off point for the place whose name is still spoken in terms of awe on the international travellers' grapevine – the island paradise of Koh Samui.

The shape of Spain, Koh Samui has beaches for just about every step of its 25-mile circumference, and a thriving economy based on tourists and coconuts. The bus from Surat Thani to the port of Ban Don is crammed with *farangs* looking pale and drained from their overnight train journey from Bangkok, their natural whiteness scored by stubble and dark circles under the eyes. Many have colds, one or two look distinctly ill. In general, they are an unattractive bunch, and compare badly with the bland smiling faces of the two or three Thais on board. At the pier a ferry boat waits, its deck already heaped with rucksacks of every nationality and its rails lined with passengers. As I clamber aboard and find a space, another bus turns up, disgorging a fresh cargo with their Walkmans, money bags, paperbacks, dark glasses and

sun-tan lotion. After many days among the sartorially fastidious
Thais, I am shocked at the greasy hair and unwashed bodies of my
fellow Westerners, as they shuffle and cough their way past the
sprucely uniformed ticket collector – 'You pay? You no pay?' –
onto the boat. Ten minutes later yet another minibus arrives, and
we finally set off with 500 people crammed on board, the boat
people of Koh Samui, refugees from a world of electronic
affluence headed for the simple life.

A long jetty sticks out into the sea from the island's main town
Na Thon, which snuggles prettily under a soft line of hills. The
pier is crammed with returning passengers, looking incomparably
healthier than the arriving ones. Na Thon has a cool bank where
an assembly line of clerks sits processing the flow of passports and
travellers' cheques, and souvenir shops, cafés and a prosperous
bustle. It reminds me of some of the more popular Greek islands
a decade or more ago. A long road loops the island, passing
for much of the way through coconut plantations whose
clearings have bungalows on stilts their occupation semaphored
by lines of T-shirts, towels and swimming gear. Taxis crawl for
custom through the narrow streets of the town, but many people
hire motor-bikes and make their own way round. Each beach has
its own character: Lammai is the wildest with many bungalows
and toytown shops and bars; Chaweng is the biggest; Bo Put the
quietest; and Choengmon probably the most pleasant mixture.
There is no sex tourism on Koh Samui. As is the case with the
majority of Thailand's islands, most accommodation cannot be
booked in advance, so it is a case of turning up and seeing what is
available, spending if necessary, the first night on a floor or rush
matting. The bungalows cater for all tastes from hippie to yuppie.
Clustered in groups with names like Big Buddha, Best Kiss,
Joyland and Munchies, they range from a basic room for a pound
a night to a luxury chalet of polished teak with its own swimming
pool for £40 a night. The typical pattern is of a group of
bungalows centred on a communal kitchen-cum-dining-cum-
socialising area, and so informal is the atmosphere that in many
places the guests keep a tally of their own bills and settle up with
the family that owns and runs the establishment when they leave.

The people of Koh Samui are very friendly, even by Thai standards, and have long considered themselves as distinct from the mainland. Until the tourists made some of them *baht* millionaires overnight, the most successful islander was probably the runner-up for the Miss Thailand competition in 1969. It is said that the tradition on Koh Samui was that the favoured sons inherited the coconut plantations set back from the sea, while the black sheep were given the useless land around the coast. Nowadays, as is the way of things, the black sheep are rubbing their hands over plots worth £50,000 an acre, (perhaps 500 years' salary for a typical islander) and the favoured sons twiddle their thumbs under the coconut palms. Coconuts, coconuts, coconuts, the place is full of them. The road is lined with great mounds of fluffy copra and the discarded green shells pile up like skulls in the killing fields. Even the seafood is dominated by coconut, its milk soothes the fiercer curries, its flesh makes a wide variety of *khanom* – Thai sweets – when combined with the local fruit, and is chopped into the salads that accompany such local delicacies as red squirrel fried in chillies. The magic mushroom that grows wild here is much in favour with the backpackers, especially in omelettes, but if Koh Samui is the Kathmandhu of the 1980s, the fun here seems less wasted and more wholesome, even if watching horror videos and listening to Bruce Springsteen tapes rather squanders the respite that such an island offers.

Koh Samui has an extraordinarily protective atmosphere, a tangible feeling of peace and safety. Off-season it is still something near paradise for a few pounds a night, but with the coming of an international airport its charm cannot last much longer. Those who wish to go should go soon, otherwise they will have to join the queues seeking out which of Thailand's many islands is to become the next 'undiscovered' paradise.

The first of these was Phuket, which ten years ago was probably much like Koh Samui. The island is accessible by road, but the best way to reach it is by air, for the flight in from Bangkok is utterly magical. For most of the way you pass over the chalky blue waters of the Gulf of Thailand, calmed by the endless expanse of sea, then, turning west, you cross the southern peninsula, flying over neatly chequered patchworks of complimentary shades of green, pleasingly regular. As the plane begins to lose height, the verdant fields begin to wrinkle and fold, nudged into hillocks of increasing size. The mainland slowly crumbles into shards, limestone islands sticking up out of the smoky blue-green water and mossed with trees growing in whorls so neatly aligned they resemble the curls on the head of a Buddha. Once you are over the end of the land, the water becomes a fathomless blue, with Phuket island lying below, a dark emerald lozenge girded by a strip of gold, like a washer protecting land from sea. The plane swoops out to sea in a long lazy curve over minuscule toy boats, then sweeps back to land at an airport ringed by palm trees and cooled by a warm salty breeze.

Much of Phuket is now a thriving tourist metropolis, with new developments springing up overnight, and the lapping of the waves all too often drowned out by the rumble of concrete-mixers. The island has always been prosperous, thanks to its extensive tin mines and its ability to breed rubber trees. These line the road from the airport to Phuket town at the other end of the island. Tall, spindly and foliate, with coconut cups tied to their scarred silver trunks they stand in regular avenues, forming a cathedral of deepening shade. Every so often a mosque dome pokes over coconut palms – much lighter than the northern variety – turquoise kingfishers straddle the telegraph wires slung over shoreline mangrove swamps, and many a house is surrounded by squares of latex hanging out to dry like dirty white doormats. Phuket was visited by the French, Portuguese and British from the seventeenth century on, and nearly became an outpost of the East India Company, but Penang was chosen instead. The town retains some vestiges of Sino-Portuguese architecture, for many of the tin-mining families were Chinese Malays, who looked more to Penang than Bangkok and sought to emulate the grand colonial buildings of the British colony. Houses set in spacious lawns and topped with roofs of Chinese tiles sprang up to announce the arrival of success, along with pilastered arches, doors, windows and capitals decorated in Chinese characters, colonnades, verandas and pastel façades. Government House,

28 Detail from the 11th-century Khmer-style temple at Muang Tham, showing the Hindu deity Shiva and his consort Parvati riding on the sacred bull Nandi

29 The 12th-century sanctuary of Pimai, once an outpost of the Khmer empire and linked by road to the capital, Angkor Wat, in Kampuchea

30 A fisherwoman on Ao Phra Nang beach, near Krabi, where limestone cliffs
drop sheer into the clear water

the Chartered Bank, the Court and the shophouses of Yaowarat Arcade and Talang Road yield the best examples left. Some of the island's smaller villages, such as Ban Don or Naithon, still have remnants of traditional Thai buildings too. These are not the stilted structures of the central plains – flooding was never a problem on Phuket – but single-storey buildings with woven bamboo walls. These have few windows because of heavy rainfall, and the loose weave of the bamboo provided adequate ventilation. In Kathu district, north-west of Phuket town, some Chinese houses remain, built by immigrants from Fujian over the last 300 years, that are made of mud mixed with rice husks, salt and sugar, topped off by an upper storey of wood and a tiled roof.

Phuket, like Koh Samui, has various beaches in different stages of development. On Patong, the most built-up, a Hard Rock Café has just opened amidst the tropical bierkellers and Veccio Mondo pasta bars. The road is churned by lorries loaded to the gunwales with crates of empty coke bottles, and the land is ripped and gashed in the frenetic rush to build, build, build. Everywhere you look plots of land are advertised for sale, and bars, clubs, hotels, bungalows and guest houses are jumbled on different levels, rubbing shoulders with offices offering car hire, laundry, real estate advice and travel agents, all advertised in fairy lights, or on posters, signboards or crudely scrawled pieces of card. Phuket has more motorbikes per square yard than anywhere in Thailand, and most of them seem to be around Patong – being bought, sold, repaired, hired or serviced. The air is full of their whine and fumes. The road that undulates over the hills from Phuket town to Patong is barely eight years old. Before it was built it was a question of carefully negotiating the journey by foot or on bike, now it is like a Grand Prix circuit, with bikes weaving in and out of the constant stream of minibuses that ferry guests to and from the hotels. Offshore two American warships bask like grey metallic sharks; the town is hung with banners 'Welcome to the US Marines', and the dark eyes of the girls glint in expectation. The official story is that the navy has chosen Phuket in preference to Pattaya because it is nearer its patrol routes in the Indian Ocean, but the buzz is that the lower incidence of drug use and

AIDS on the island is the real reason. Although many are doing very well out of Phuket's boom, not everyone is overjoyed. Many regular tourists are now seeking out the quieter beaches or deserting the island altogether, dismayed by the way it is becoming another Pattaya, while some of the locals are beginning to resent what is happening to their island. A couple of years ago a band of angry citizens burned down a Thai-American mineral refinery as a protest against pollution, and their leader was later elected a local MP. Then a judge was murdered, and a local Chinese godfather indicted but acquitted on 'lack of evidence'. A couple of days after my arrival, a lawyer is gunned down in a local restaurant. Phuket has become a gold rush island.

One way and another, the monarchy is much in the news. To begin with, everybody is talking about the fake royal honours scandal. Over a dozen people, including a former Education minister, several senior government officials and two prominent abbots have been arrested following the discovery of many forged decorations that are awarded to particularly generous donors to royal temples. Added to which, one of the abbots has been charged with having a stash of fake buddha images, allegedly blessed by a particularly revered monk, that would fetch no less than £10 million if sold to the faithful. One of the early suspects committed suicide in Government House, now monks are claiming to have visions of him in their meditation, demanding vengeance against those who wrongly accused him. An ex-MP turned monk arrives early one morning at Government House with Holy Water to banish the evil spirits he claims are the cause of all the trouble. It is a tremendous fuss, and although no members of the royal household are involved, it is headline news for days. To make matters worse, four southerners are arrested for distributing anti-monarchy leaflets. Locked in custody, they are refused all food from outside, in case someone tries to poison them. On top of all this, the Prince and Princess of Wales arrive in Bangkok to participate in the celebrations for King Bhumipol's sixtieth birthday. Everyone is much taken with Diana, the epitome of *than samaj* with her chic style and her blondeness. (To Thais, beautiful and fair skin is a sign of wealth and the soft life;

they find the *farang* habit of sunbathing a most peculiar aberration.) Much of the television news, which always contains lengthy bulletins about the Thai royal family, is taken up with the visit of the British couple, and as a compatriot I am often complimented on them.

For most of my stay in Phuket, I am cocooned in the seamless web of a Thai family. Three sisters and a brother-in-law, friends down from Surat Thani on a holiday, expand to become a shifting sea of smiling faces that ebbs and flows in waves of monosyllabic names – Deng, Dok, Soo, Ting, Gee, Toy, Lek. Friends of friends and children upon children form an entourage that swells, dwindles and swells again from day to day, as we drift from place to place from one smiling introduction to another until I feel my face is going to crack. Never knowing quite where we are going or what we are meant to be doing, I feel returned to childhood myself, cosseted in an amorphous group that provides warmth and comfort while denying independent volition. The only thing to do is to surrender to the collective consciousness and drift like a cork on the waves of sociability, though such a passive role sits ill with my temperament. One thing is sure, and that is the kindness that is lavished on me. It is a concern that is touching and very welcome after my recent solitary travelling, though at times I find it almost overwhelming. The apparently insignificant matter of breakfast acts as a focus for my growing irritation. Thais seem happy to wait for several hours after rising before they eat, and when the first meal of the day eventually arrives it is the same as all the others – meat, fish, rice, noodles, vegetables in various combinations. I, on the other hand, need sustenance first thing, and my metabolism demands a little food often. Much as I love Thai food, I cannot stomach it before noon, and menus that offer 'Four Things Soup', 'Assorted Ducks Feet', 'Stuffed Fishes' Stomach' or – the *pièce de résistance* – the aphrodisiac 'Steamed Bull's Penis' can reduce me to tears of frustration at breakfast time. There is nothing for it but to curb my impatience until we reach a restaurant where there is a chance of something edible, but it is a severe taxing of my *jai yen*, and much of each morning is consumed in fantasies of coffee and toast that grow more intense as my irritation mounts. As the pampered guest it is hardly my place to explode and demand Western food, and so we tiptoe round each others' feelings, doing everything to avoid offence, while who knows what is going on under the surface. It is in little things like this that one's distance from another country becomes glaringly clear, and whenever I think of Phuket, my stomach tightens with the memory.

Sixty miles around the coast from Phuket lies Phangnga Bay, a most spectacular spot. Here a jumble of limestone outcroppings tower sheer above the water in a series of fantastic gravity-defying shapes, like inverted mountains balancing on their peaks trailing wispy greenery, while at the waterline clusters of spiked stalactites curtain labyrinthine grottoes that disappear into darkness or tunnel right through a rock to emerge into daylight again on the other side. This weird landscape, charged with a primeval beauty, is easily visited by boats rented at Phangnga, a sleepy fishing village that has never quite recovered from being the location of some sequences from *The Man with the Golden Gun*, a recent James Bond film.

Many trips stop for lunch at the Muslim village of Koh Pannyi, an enormous and rickety pier housing a thousand souls grouped around an ugly new mosque, that clings like a nest of insects to a huge rock sticking precipitously out of the water. The friendliness here is very muted by Thai standards, for Koh Pannyi is chastened by that austerity which is the hallmark of Islam, and despite the tourists who come to eat and buy, there is an eery isolation in the atmosphere. In summer the heat and the stench from the littered grey sand that is exposed at each low tide must be intense. At four each afternoon the last boats leave, and the community puts up the shutters again, withdrawing into itself, like the last ramshackle outpost of humanity, a veiled city on the edge of the world, alone with its fishing, its children and its unimaged god.

Further down the road lies Krabi, a province the Tourist Authority is busy developing as the next holiday destination, widening roads and making beaches more accessible. Several islands nestle in the bay formed between Phuket and Krabi:

Koh Yao Yai, and Koh Yao Noi and Koh Phee Phee being the most important while a little further down lie Koh Lanta Yai, Koh Lanta Noi and Koh Klang – all relatively unfrequented so far, ideal for campers and lovers of solitude. Krabi town borders the river of the same name that empties into the Andaman Sea, and battered black junks from Penang dock here every so often. The *songthaews* ferrying tourists out to main beaches a dozen miles from town are full of travellers' talk: the appalling food in China, the tough Malaysian police, what 'presents' are most appreciated by the voraciously hungry officials in Burma. A woman from Mississippi counsels that if you take Johnnie Walker Red Label and Sony Walkmans into Rangoon, you can swap them for some 'nice little souvenirs'. I should hope so too. Squashed next to her is a man with a moustache who works in computers for the US Army in Germany, 'keeping the missiles out of Europe,' he explains, with a shade less than complete conviction. Mississippi nods encouragingly. 'You all get a good standard of living over there?'

At Aonang Beach they are moving the beds into the shell of a new hotel with sixty rooms. The road that skirts the beach is littered with dead coconut leaves, as dry as papyrus and eight feet long, like the spine of a primeval fish, its flesh long since devoured by the elements. At 6 a.m. I am the sole *farang* on the beach, accompanied by only two or three of the local fisherwomen in tall pointed bamboo hats who cast long whippy bamboo rods baited with octopus innards into water that stays shallow for fifty yards out. As the day lights up, wicked-looking chainsaws add their whine to the noise of bikes and pick-up trucks while the staff at my bungalow hotel are so busy drawing up plans and fiddling with pocket calculators that they barely have time to tell me I must spend another night on a breeze-block floor awaiting a vacant cabin. Even further along the coast, where the really adventurous hang out, you may have to wait a day or two for a tent, despite the rumours of scorpions and snakes eager to share the warmth of your rush matting. In the evening, the tourists sit singly or in pairs watching the sun dropping out of a blood-orange sky, while the locals crowd noisily round a TV set up on a table in the open air to watch a boxing match broadcast from Bangkok.

The people of Nakhon Si Thammarat have decided to do something about the unfavourable astrological influences which have plagued their town since ancient times. The remedy is to install a city pillar as a magical totem, for, as the Thais say, if you cannot get it by a prayer, use a spell. The pillar must be in the exact style of the good old days of the Shrivijayan empire, covered in Buddhist inscriptions and topped with a likeness of the founder of the empire, Jatukamramthep the Great. This might not be as easy as it sounds. To begin with, a complex ritual must be performed to charm the spirit of the deceased king into the body of a local medium, for it is only by questioning the deceased monarch that the historical accuracy of the style can be ascertained correctly. The spirit instructs the organising committee that only the wood of a certain rare type of teak will do for the pillar, and this necessitates a trip into the communist-infested jungle area of Ta Sala. Having survived ambush and felled one of these trees, the party then finds it is unable to shift the huge log, even though an elephant is used. Another ritual is called for, this one to inform the tree spirit what is going to happen to its erstwhile home. Happy with the intended use of the tree, the spirit releases it, and the log is brought back to Nakhon. On its arrival in the city a sacrificial ceremony is performed, after which the log is finally taken to the chief of police's home to be carved. People come from all over the province to donate money and gems to the pillar, and, when complete, it is processed around the town first in a ship, to recall the days when the area boasted a great navy, then on horses and elephants, under the sun-and-moon war banner of old Shrivijaya. Installed at the entrance to the city, the pillar will be officially inaugurated by the King later in the year.

Nakhon Si Thammarat is the cultural capital for the south, and the centre of many fairs and celebrations. As such, it is something of an island in an area which, due to its maritime history and the presence of Islam, is less endowed with the remnants of a high culture than most of the rest of the country. An attractive city with a long history, Nakhon once traded with China, Ceylon and southern India, and by the thirteenth century it was powerful enough to mount a campaign against the central Thai dynasty of

Lopburi and send a couple of military expeditions to Ceylon. But the city's fortunes declined as first Sukhothai and then Ayutthaya reduced it to a vassal, the latter sending a Japanese Samurai to be governor in the early seventeenth century. It was at this time that Nakhon produced some idiosyncratic Buddhas, examples of which are displayed at the excellent museum on the southern edge of town. Many are fashioned in the local ethnic style, with features that look Polynesian, squat and negroid, quite unlike the Aryan ideals of the high classical periods such as Sukhothai.

The cultural showpiece of the town is Wat Mahathat, a large and imposing complex with an Ayuthayan style *viharn* its high roof set on sloping pillars and topped out with the long protuberance known as a *chofa* ('bunch of the sky'), the last element to be fixed to a temple, before which it cannot be consecrated. In the Ayutthayan period the *chofa* becomes a particularly graceful, abstract curve, and it may owe its origin to the animal horn that sacralises the long houses of Indonesia, having entered the Thai architectural vocabulary through the south's connections with the archipelago. Towering above dozens of smaller structures the main *chedi* is pure Ceylonese in style and shaped like a huge bell, and commemorates the advent of Theravada Buddhism from that island in the twelfth century. The temple also houses many fine sculptures from the Dvaravati period; a favourite shrine with the locals is the one dedicated to Phra Puay, a spirit which has the power to grant children, many photographs of which stand at the foot of the image. Here at Wat Mahathat the bustle of building which characterises the south is again in evidence. New monks' quarters are being added to the complex, linking it to the large school next door. Novices aged no more than nine or ten study the plans seriously, looking old before their time. Some speak good English and we chat a little, my curiosity about the details of their monastic rule is more than matched by their eagerness to discuss the extraordinary current form of Liverpool football club.

After Phuket, it is a relief to wander through the streets and prolific bazaars of Nakhon and not see another *farang*. The local people pay me little heed, and there is a relaxed, disinterested atmosphere to the town. The good value for money continues here in the south. My hotel is clean, comfortable and friendly and costs me about £6 a night, with a laundry service that collects in mid-afternoon, delivers at eight the next morning, and washes two pairs of trousers and three or four shirts for less than a pound. But Nakhon really sticks in my mind as a place of exotic pets. One evening in the bar I am handed a baby black bear, perhaps three months old, whose body has a solid, compressed strength such as I have never felt before, so great is the feeling of potential power. It is not unusual for Thais to keep fully grown bears as pets, apparently they are easily domesticated as long as their nails are kept clipped. A couple of mornings later over breakfast at my hotel I get chatting to a girl who comes down every couple of weeks from Bangkok to buy nielloware, a type of *cloisonné*, in which a black alloy is inlaid into gold or silver, that is one of the specialities of the area. A man sits down at the next table and unwraps a bundle into his lap. It is a tiny gibbon, no more than a month old, with a soft furry body no bigger than a grapefruit, and limbs perhaps nine inches long ending in strong prehensile toes and spidery fingers. Its ears are the softest curlicues, like frilly brown fungi set into its tawny head. As it nuzzles into my stomach and sleeps, the girl leaves to catch her train, and I stay chatting to the owner, a drugs salesman also down from the capital.

He bought the pet a couple of days ago, and takes it everywhere with him on his rounds. The tiny creature whimpers in its sleep, no doubt missing its mother, and utters a series of high pitched squeaks as I try to unpluck it from my shirt. Trying to pay for my meal, I find that the girl has quietly settled my bill, an example of the impromptu hospitality that is not uncommon in Thailand. Only on the way back to my room do I notice a warm wet and utterly odourless patch on my shirt which announces that the little creature has also been the source of unasked for generosity.

The last major town of the south is Haad Yai. The name means 'Big Beach', but the town is well inland and has little to commend it aesthetically, though the public park, swimming pool and the attractive campus of the Prince of Songkhla University are places to relax in. Haad Yai's *raison d'être* is as a thriving commercial centre, a supplier of abundant consumer goods and nightlife. Both of these are eagerly patronised by Malays who hop over the border in huge numbers every weekend to escape the high prices and Muslim propriety of their own country. My own souvenir of the marketstalls that jam the town's central roads of Niphat-U-Thit 1, 2 and 3, is no electronic gadgetry but a humble set of keys. Somewhere along the line the keys to my case have gone missing. A few inquiries, 200 *baht* and half an hour's work have a set of Yamaha ignition keys filed down to fit my case exactly. The ready availability of such street ingenuity is a bonus for the traveller in Thailand, though it should also perhaps warn him to keep his hotel door locked at all times, even at night.

Despite its sybaritic reputation as the Bangkok of the south, Haad Yai seems to me relatively quiet, though the prices here are higher than anywhere else in the south and accommodation can be tricky to find. There are several traditional types of entertainment in the area; such as Nang Talung, a shadow puppet genre similar to those found in Malaysia and Indonesia, and the Manohra, a prolonged spirit dance. Haad Yai itself has two unusual attractions. One is the bullfighting that takes place a couple of times a month, which involves two hump-backed bulls, no humans and no killing, but enormous amounts of betting. The other is snake blood. There are perhaps fifteen shops in the town where for a couple of hundred *baht* you can choose a cobra (or for ten times the price a deadly hamadryad), watch it being strangled in front of your eyes and, after an apertif of the extracted venom, enjoy a cocktail of its blood mixed with a fiery local whisky. The whole thing is rounded off with the meat, flavoured with Chinese herbs, the gall bladder and sexual organs of the male being the most popular parts. The chief partakers of this grisly fare are Chinese from Malaysia and Singapore (some of whom come to Thailand just for this delicacy) who believe that such a diet is beneficial to blood, eyesight and virility. Indeed the Haad Yai folk seem a bloodthirsty lot. At the most important temple, Wat Haad Yai Nai, one can not only admire the third largest reclining Buddha in the world but even climb inside it, and make offerings at shrines next to the lurid depictions of the Master's lungs.

Milder pleasures await the visitor to Songkhla, the small village that serves as Haad Yai's nearest beach. If you are spending more than a night in the area, this is the best place to stay. It is only fifteen miles from Haad Yai, but the journey can seem much longer when you are crammed into a party taxi, with three passengers in the front seat and a driver who leans so far out of his window that he seems to be steering by remote control. Add to this the fact that the car has no brakes and the driver only one eye, and you will understand my relief when we finally arrive at the town which, with its cobbled streets and ramshackle harbour full of gaily painted little steamers bobbing up and down, has an almost Mediterranean air. Songkhla is famous for what is perhaps the major obsession of the far south – zebra doves. Almost every home and shop displays attractive bamboo cages, many topped with ivory or covered with a tasselled silk shade, in which the neat little black and white birds chirrup and coo. The Muslims are especially keen on these birds, which are believed to bring good luck, and one that has had a string of victories in cooing contests held around the country can go for up to £50,000. The beach at Songhkla is a long crescent, not as impressive as some of the island coastlines, but relaxing and peaceful, with numerous tables under brightly striped parasols where one can eat, laze and watch the long-prowed sleek fishing craft that glide past. Some of these are fantastically decorated with swirling coloured patterns, a local folk art reminiscent of the painted trucks of another Muslim border area – the North-West Frontier.

The south has its problems – Muslim separatists who tend to get mixed up with the Communist Party of Malaysia; hapless Vietnamese boat-people who still arrive by thousands often having fallen victim to rapacious gangs of Thai pirates; rackets involving smuggling light-skinned babies into 'adoption agencies' in Penang – but here at Songkhla, they all seem very far away.

Between Haad Yai and the Border lies a triangle of Muslim towns which can best be visited in an excursion by taxi from Haad Yai. The normal form of transport here is taxi, nearly always a comfortable old Mercedes, and on the road south is an almost continuous motorcade as you pass one after another, adding a

Teutonic stateliness to the ragged countryside, as they cruise along like a fleet of mechanised sofas. Nearest to Haad Yai is the coastal village of Pattani, a new town of concrete and Caltex petrol stations, with a busy harbour where boats unload the catch straight into baskets to be hosed down and slid along the ground to the wholesale market immediately behind the jetty. Pattani offers a Muslim not a Buddhist welcome; already there is a tinge of that boisterous curiosity bordering on aggression which is so much a part of the Muslim reaction to strangers. The positive side of this is the pleasant mosque, which offers a quiet respite from the blazing high noon. In true Muslim fashion it offers a midday dormitory, men lying sprawled in sleep along the cool corridors, whilst inside, hardy fishing folk with the faces of the poor swap tattered jeans for a faded chequered *sarong* from a pile by the door and prostrate themselves in prayer. In the market the women wear the floral *sarongs* typical of the area, and the men wrap *pakomas* into jaunty turbans, but the welcome is cool, and photographs are definitely disliked. This can be frustrating, for there is in many of the faces that Islamic sparseness which reveals a mind unagitated by images, features stamped with the dignity of omission. A dramatic contrast is provided by Pattani's street of polychrome Chinese temples, where the gilded dragons and phoenixes writhe along the roof tops with nothing short of frivolity.

Yala, twenty-five miles south-west of Pattani, is the capital of the most prosperous of the four Muslim provinces of the south, a centre of rubber with a healthy business sector and widespread education. The parks, boulevards and wide streets make this an orderly and pleasant place, and there are a number of restaurants overlooking water. Malay is commonly spoken here, and you feel you are inexorably slipping out of Thailand. This impression is confirmed at the last town of note, Narathiwat, a quiet seaside collection of old wooden houses, lovely and unfrequented beaches, Muslim fishing villages and Chinese shops. This peaceful place marks a fitting and tranquil end to a journey around the south. For those headed back to Bangkok, there is an airport; for those headed south into Malaysia, it provides a restful pause before launching out into another country, another reality, another dream.

I began my journey through the Lotus Kingdom by promising a Thai exiled in London that I would, if possible, 'write something nice' about her country. By and large, it has not been difficult to keep that promise. I trust the reader will have gathered from the preceding pages why that was so, and he may also have gathered what aspects of Thailand give me cause for alarm, for the strengths of a country, no less than those of a person, are its weaknesses when seen in a different light. As an island of 'freedom' in South-East Asia, surrounded by a sea of repression, Thailand has become the flag bearer of the Western way of life and is set to continue on this course. The energy of her urban centres is immediate proof of this, and the direction of the future may be gauged from the fact that nine of the world's top ten advertising agencies now have offices in Bangkok. What will happen to Thailand's cultural integrity as she proceeds along the path of mass consumerism remains to be seen, but in this she is no different from any other country, developed or developing. What is unique in her case is the question mark that hangs over the future relationship of the three Ms that have been her traditional bulwarks: the monarchy, the monks and the military. The Thais are blessed with a cheerful pragmatism. I hope that this will minimise the discomfort of any changes that may be coming.

Futurology aside, if there is one thing I would single out as the chief attraction of Thailand, it is her people. I am not talking here about the sophisticated tourist operation which has been mounted so successfully over the past few years and is now beginning to bear fruit, but that innocent *joie de vivre* that is an intrinsic part of the Thai character – the spontaneous kindnesses, the unforced smiles and irrepressible giggles that give the place so much sparkle. To a naturally sunny disposition has been added a refined and graceful sensibility nurtured by the gentle wisdom of Buddhism. Yet even here things may not be quite what they seem.

Niels Mulder is a sociologist who spent six years in northern Thailand, living among Thais and speaking the language.

Somewhere in his *Everyday Life in Thailand* he comes to the conclusion: 'I shall leave without having developed a single deep friendship.' I do not know how much his experience was conditioned by his role as outside observer, for the Thais tend to treat people according to the stereotypes expected of their particular position, but many *farangs* would probably agree with Mulder's rather sad conclusion. That this should be the case among such an apparently friendly people seems doubly cruel. It seems to me that Thais value respect rather than intimacy in human relations, and their penchant for living very much in the present, allied to a keen awareness of the inevitability of change, might perhaps mitigate against their forming deep attachments to those who are not recognisable equals or permanent fixtures of their environment. In Thailand the heart is a cool, mysterious one and certainly not worn on the sleeve, but though it may not be easy to get to know the people well, it can be enormous fun trying.

Appendix 1

The Principal Kings of Thailand

Sukhothai

Intradit (1238–70)
Ramkamhaeng (1279–*c.* 99)
Li Thai (Thammaraja) (1347–68)

Lanna

Mengrai (?–1317)
Tiloka (1442–88)

Ayutthaya

Naresuan (1590–1605)
Narai (1657–88)

Thonburi

Taksin (1767–82)

Bangkok (Chakri dynasty)

Rama 1 (1782–1809)
Rama 2 (1809–24)
Rama 3 (1824–51)
Rama 4 (Mongkut) (1851–68)
Rama 5 (Chulalongkorn)
   (1868–1910)

Rama 6 (1910–25)
Rama 7 (1925–35)
Rama 8 (Ananda) (1935–46)
Rama 9 (Bhumipol) (1946–)

Appendix 2

Major Periods of Thai History and Art

Prehistoric	Up to 1st century AD
Indianised (Hindu and Buddhist)	1st to 6th centuries
Dvaravati	6th to 11th centuries
Srivijaya	8th to 13th centuries
Lopburi	10th to 14th centuries
Sukhothai	13th to 15th centuries
Lanna (Chiangsen)	13th to 16th centuries
Ayutthaya	1350 to 1767
Thonburi	1767 to 1782
Bangkok (Ratanakosin)	1782 to present

Appendix 3

Selected Glossary

bot	The most sacred building of a temple complex, used for the congregation and ordination of monks.
chedi	Thai version of the Indian *stupa* – a hemispherical mound containing relics of the Buddha or a great Buddhist teacher, and surmounted by a tall, tapering spire.
farang	Caucasian foreigner.
jai yen	'Cool heart' – the equanimity considered desirable in all situations.
Jataka	Stories of the previous incarnations of the Buddha.
ketumela	Flame-like protuberance on top of the Buddha's head signifying enlightenment.
kinnara	Divine being, half-human, half-bird.
kreng jai	'Consideration for others' – a cardinal virtue in Thailand.
lak muang	The pillar-shrine that symbolically unites the community with the heavens.
mai pen rai	'It doesn't matter': the essence of the Thai *joie de vivre*.
naga	Celestial serpent or dragon, often adorning the roof or steps of a temple.

Pali	Ancient language of India, derived from Sanskrit, and the language of the Theravadin Buddhist scriptures.
pai tio	Holiday, time off, 'wandering around'.
sabai	'Feeling good', a sense of physical and psychological comfort very important to the Thai.
sala	Pavilion or reception hall.
sanuk	Fun, enjoyment; the essential ingredient of anything worth doing.
songthaew	Pick-up truck used as a party taxi all over the country.
thep	Divine being, angel, often depicted in temple murals.
Theravada	'Doctrine of the Elders': the original school of Buddhism which, in an animistic form, is the religion of 95 per cent of Thais.
vihan	The main chapel of a temple complex. Usually indistinguishable from a *bot*, it houses the principal images for public worship, and is used for sermons and lay gatherings.
wai	The traditional sign of respect. Hands are held together under the chin, and the head is bowed, slightly or deeply, depending on the status of the person greeted.
wat	A temple complex, which usually includes a monastery.
Wat Mahathat	Name of a temple believed to enshrine relics of the Buddha.

Appendix 4

Travelling Tips

Climate

Thailand has three seasons: Cool (November to February); Hot (March to June); Rainy (July to October).

In the South, the rainy season lasts longer, often until January, and the temperature is more even. Most of the country is humid, with the exception of the mountainous north. The rainy season is unpredictable, but generally it rains most in the central plains in August and September, whereas in Phuket the wettest months are May and October. Bangkok is often flooded in October.

From the point of view of the weather, the best time to visit Thailand is between November and February. December and January are best for the south, and February is a very pleasant spring month in the north.

Visas

Both Transit Visas (valid for 30 days) and Tourist Visas (valid for 60 days) are obtainable from the Thai Embassy in your country. No extension of the Transit Visa is possible, but the Tourist Visa may be extended at the discretion of the Thai Immigration Office, Soi Suan Phlu, Sathorn Tai Road, Bangkok. It is also possible to get a Non-Immigrant Visa (valid for 90 days), but this must be applied for in your own country.

Money

The Thai currency is the *baht*.
In August 1988, the rate was: £1 sterling = 42 *baht*
$1 US   = 25 *baht*

Tipping

This is not a normal practice in Thailand, although it is becoming customary in the expensive hotels and restaurants. Taxis are not tipped.

Bargaining

The Thais are always amenable to bargaining, and this applies even to those prices that might be fixed elsewhere, e.g. hotel rooms and department stores. Shops (apart from those selling tourist souvenirs or international goods), markets, taxis etc. will think you rather odd if you accept the first price.

Health

Thailand has no official innoculation requirements for visitors, but check if you are coming from an infected area. Malaria prophylaxis is recommended; consult your doctor before leaving. Water, ice, ice cream etc. is probably safer in Thailand than in many Asian countries, but apply your own rules. If you spend long up country, be prepared for an attack of traveller's diarrhoea. Generally speaking, street foodstalls are safe. Buy fruit you can peel.

Travel Agents

Virtually all hotels in Bangkok have Travel Agent desks that will fix your travel arrangements or book you into conducted tours. One of the largest and best established agents in Bangkok is:
Diethelm Travel
544 Ploenchit Road, Bangkok
Tel: 2524041–9

A good smaller company is:
Dee Jai Tours,
Warner Theatre Building, 2nd floor,
119 Mahesak Road, Bangkok 10500
Tel: 234–3701 ext 114/228 or 235–9896.

Do's and Don't's

The Thais are a courteous and discrete people. Equanimity (*jai yen*) is valued at all times; losing your cool or showing impatience is totally counter productive and should be avoided at all times.

Anything to do with the Buddhist religion or the Royal Family should be treated with the utmost respect. *Farangs* have been jailed for failing to observe this basic rule.

Dress with decorum when visiting temples, e.g. no shorts or revealing blouses.

A monk should not be touched, nor should women hand anything to him directly. Use an intermediary.

Buddha images, even new ones, should not be taken out of the country. This is not only an attempt to deter antique smugglers, but because the Thais are concerned that an image will not be treated with sufficient respect in a non-Buddhist environment.

Nude or topless sunbathing is *strongly* disapproved of. It is perhaps the *farang* custom Thais like least.

The head is the highest part of the body, both literally and ritually. Do not touch people on the head, and, should you wish to show respect to a person or an image, lower yours slightly.

The feet are the lowest part of the body. They should not be pointed towards a person or object (especially a Buddha image) that you respect, nor should they be used to indicate anything. One should not step over a sleeping or lying figure.

Try to speak softly to Thais, it is a sign of friendliness and harmony they appreciate.

A word about pronunciation. The 'ph' in Phuket is pronounced hard, like a 'p', though the Tourist Authority is considering changing the spelling to avoid *farangs* the embarrassment of mispronouncing it soft, like an 'f'. Such solicitude is touching, but will not help with the popular offshore attraction of the Phee Phee islands. Few visitors attempt to master the seductive cadences of a language that can caress the inner ear, but many have been amused that the most common rice dish is called a 'cow pat', a favourite beach resort Krabi and that Porn Hotels are common.

Appendix 5

Recommended Reading

Guidebooks

Insight Guide to Thailand, *Apa*. Hong Kong 1986. The best general guide. Beautiful photographs and an informative text.
Thailand – a travel survival kit, *Lonely Planet*. Australia 1987. The best guide for 'do-it-yourself' travellers.
Discovering Thailand, *Clarac and Smithies*. Siam Communications, Bangkok 1972. The best architectural guide.

Historical

Collis, Maurice, *Siamese White*. London, 1936.
Chakrabonse, Prince Chula, *Lords of Life*. Alvin Redman, London, 1960.
McCoy, Alfred, *The Politics of Heroin in South East Asia*. Harper and Row, New York, 1972.
Smith, Malcolm, *A Physician at the Court of Siam*. Oxford in Asia, Malaysia, 1982.
Smithies, Michael, *Old Bangkok*. Oxford in Asia, Kuala Lumpur, 1984.
Warren, William, *The Legendary American*. Houghton Mifflin, Boston.

Art and architecture

Boisellier, Jean, *Thai Painting*. Kodansha, Tokyo, 1976.
Le May, Reginald, *Buddhist Art in Siam*. London, 1940.
Van Beek, Steve, *The Arts of Thailand*. Travel Publishing Asia, Hong Kong, 1986.

Various authors, *Thai Culture (New Series) Pamphlets*. Department of Fine Arts, Bangkok.
Warren, William, *The House on the Klong*. Weatherhill, Tokyo.

Everyday life

Cooper, Robert and Nanthapa, *Culture Shock: Thailand*. Times Books, Singapore, 1982.
Hollinger, Carol, *Mai pen rai Means Never Mind*. Houghton Mifflin, Boston.
Klausner, William, *Conflict and Communication*. Bangkok.
Mulder, Niels, *Everyday Life in Thailand*. DK Books, Bangkok, 1979.
Segaller, Dennis, *Thai Ways*. Post Publishing, Bangkok, 1985.

Fiction

Pramoj, Kukrit, *Red Bamboo*. Progress Publishing, Bangkok, 1970.
Reynolds, Jack, *A Woman of Bangkok*. DK Books, Bangkok, 1985.
Shaw, John, *The Seal of Tammatari*. DK Books, Chiang Mai, 1985.
Sudham, Pira, *Siamese Drama*. Siam Media International, Bangkok, 1983.

Languages

Cummings, Joe, *Thailand Phrasebook*. Lonely Planet, Australia, 1984.
Robertson, Richard, *Practical English-Thai Dictionary*. Asia Books, Bangkok.

Index